Christian Thought in the Twenty-First Century

Christian Thought in the Twenty-First Century

Agenda for the Future

EDITED BY
Douglas H. Shantz and Tinu Ruparell

CASCADE *Books* · Eugene, Oregon

CHRISTIAN THOUGHT IN THE TWENTY-FIRST CENTURY
Agenda for the Future

Cascade Books
An Imprint of Wipf and Stock Publishers
199 W. 8th Ave., Suite 3
Eugene, OR 97401

www.wipfandstock.com

ISBN 13: 978-1-61097-575-9

Cataloging-in-Publication data:

Christian thought in the twenty-first century : agenda for the future / edited by Douglas H. Shantz and Tinu Ruparell.

xx + 212 p. ; 23 cm. —Includes bibliographical references and index.

isbn 13: 978-1-61097-575-9

1. Christianity—21st Century. 2. Christianity and Culture. 3. Christianity—Forecasting. I. Shantz, Douglas H. II. Ruparell, Tinu. III. Title.

BR 121.2 C40 2012

Manufactured in the U.S.A.

Dedicated to the memory of Peter C. Craigie (1938–1985)
and his vision for the Chair of Christian Thought in Calgary

Contents

PART 2: Philosophical and Theological Issues

PART 3: Encounters with Religious Pluralism and the Frontiers of Science

PART 4: The Academy and the City

PART 5: Approaches to English Literature and Film

Contributors

The Editors

Douglas H. Shantz has held the Chair of Christian Thought at the University of Calgary since 1999. It was his privilege to invite the contributors to this volume to come to Calgary as Christian Thought lecturers. Shantz's own research and writing are in the field of early modern German Protestantism, including radical renewal movements, spiritual autobiography, and apocalypticism. He has published three books and many articles and reviews in this field.

Tinu Ruparell has been Associate Professor of Religious Studies at the University of Calgary since January 2003. His research interests are in the comparative philosophy of religion, focusing on the Hindu and Christian traditions. Related interests include hermeneutics, religious pluralism and interreligious dialogue, Indian and Continental philosophy, and approaches to religious experience. His current work centers on idealism in Ramanuja and Leibniz as well as on science and religion.

Contributors

John B. Cobb, Jr. is Professor of Theology emeritus at the Claremont School of Theology and Claremont Graduate University. With David Griffin he founded the Center for Process Studies and with George Regas he started what has become Progressive Christians Uniting. His many theological writings include *Christ in a Pluralistic Age* (Philadelphia:

Westminster Press, 1975) and, most recently, *Spiritual Bankruptcy: A Prophetic Call to Action* (Nashville: Abingdon, 2010).

Peter C. Erb is Professor Emeritus at Wilfrid Laurier University, Waterloo, Ont., was Visiting Professor of Catholic Studies at the University of Prince Edward Island, Charlottetown, PEI (2005–2009), and continues as the Associate Director of Schwenkfelder Library and Heritage Center, Pennsburg, Pa. He is author of numerous books and articles on German Pietism and on nineteenth-century Anglicanism and Catholicism. He has recently published *The Correspondence of Henry Edward Manning and William Ewart Gladstone, 1833–1891*, 4 volumes (Oxford: Oxford University Press, 2011), *The Pietists*, edited by Emilie Griffin, with Foreword by Phyllis Tickle (San Francisco: Harper Collins, 2006), and "Gottfried Arnold" in Carter Lindberg (ed.), *The Pietist Theologians: An Introduction to Theology in the Seventeenth and Eighteenth Centuries* (Oxford: Blackwell, 2005), 175–91.

Craig A. Evans is the Payzant Distinguished Professor of New Testament at Acadia University and Acadia Divinity College in Nova Scotia, Canada. He has published more than fifty books, mainly on Jesus and the Gospels, including (with N. T. Wright) *Jesus, the Final Days* (Philadelphia: Westminster John Knox, 2009). Professor Evans has lectured in many universities and museums around the world and has appeared as an expert commentator on network television programs, such as *Dateline*, and in various documentaries on the BBC, the Discovery Channel, and the History Channel. He is married and has two grown daughters and a grandson.

Susan M. Felch is Professor of English at Calvin College and Director of the Center for Christian Scholarship. Her publications include articles on sixteenth-century British literature, Mikhail Bakhtin, contemporary novels, and Christian higher education. Two of her books, *Elizabeth Tyrwhit's Morning and Evening Prayers* (Aldershot: Ashgate, 2008) and the Norton Critical edition *Elizabeth I and Her Age* (2009), edited with Donald Stump, won, respectively, the 2009 Scholarly Edition Award and the 2010 Teaching Edition Award from the Society for the Study of Early Modern Women. Other books include *The Collected Works of Anne Vaughan Lock*, anthologies on the *Spiritual Biographies of the Seasons*, a textbook for teaching advanced English in China, and *The Emmaus Readers, Listening for God in Contemporary Fiction*, edited with Gary Schmidt.

Douglas John Hall is Emeritus Professor of Christian Theology, McGill University, Montreal, Quebec. He is the author of numerous books and the holder of ten honorary degrees and awards. His latest book, *The Messenger: Friendship, Faith and Finding One's Way* (Eugene: Wipf and Stock, 2011), is a study in mentorship, approached autobiographically.

Paul Knitter retired in 2002 from 28 years of teaching at Xavier University, Cincinnati, OH. In 2007 he assumed the Paul Tillich Chair in Theology, World Religions, and Culture at Union Theological Seminary in New York. Through the years the focus of his research and publications has been the promotion of a globally responsible interreligious dialogue (especially in *One Earth Many Religions*, Maryknoll: Orbis Books, 1995). Recently he has been engaged in a Christian conversation and collaboration with Buddhists and has published *Without Buddha I Could Not Be a Christian* (Oxford: Oneworld Publications, 2009).

Wesley A. Kort is Professor in the Department of Religion and the Graduate Faculty of Religion at Duke University. His books and essays relate religious and cultural/literary studies to one another. His most recent book is *Place and Space in Modern Fiction* (Gainesville: University Press of Florida, 2004), and his next book, *Textual Intimacy: Autobiography and Religious Identities*, will be published by the University of Virginia Press in May, 2012.

Dennis D. Martin studied history at Wheaton College (Illinois), the University of Waterloo (Ontario), and the universities of Marburg and Tübingen in Germany. His research focuses on medieval monasticism, particularly the austere and silent Carthusian Order. He has taught church history and historical theology at Associated Mennonite Biblical Seminaries (Indiana) and Loyola University in Chicago. His publications include *Carthusian Spirituality: The Writings of Hugh of Balma and Guigo de Ponte*, Translation and Introduction for the Classics of Western Spirituality series (New York: Paulist Press, 1997) and *Fifteenth-Century Carthusian Reform: The World of Nicholas Kempf*, Studies in the History of Christian Thought, 49 (Leiden: Brill, 1992).

Margaret R. Miles is Emerita Professor of Historical Theology at The Graduate Theological Union, Berkeley. Her recent books include *Augustine and the Fundamentalist's Daughter* (Eugene: Wipf and Stock Publishers, 2011), *A Complex Delight: The Secularization of the Breast, 1350–1750* (Berkeley: University of California Press, 2008), and *The Word Made Flesh: A History of Christian Thought* (Oxford: Blackwell, 2005).

Anne Moore is an Associate Professor with the Department of Religious Studies at the University of Calgary where she has taught courses on Religion and Film since 1995. She is a member of the Steering Committee for a Society of Biblical Literature Consultation Group on Bible and Film. Her other research interests focus on Christian Origins and Christianity in Late Antiquity with an emphasis on women during these periods. Her publications include "Search for the Common Judaic Understanding of God's Kingship," in Wayne McCready and Adele Reinhartz, ed., *Common Judaism Explored: Second Temple Judaism in Context* (Minneapolis: Fortress Press, 2008).

Charles Nienkirchen is Professor of Christian History and Spirituality at Ambrose University College in Calgary, Alberta. He is also Visiting Professor of Christian Spirituality at Tyndale Seminary in Toronto, Ontario and has been an Adjunct Professor at numerous seminaries and graduate schools across Canada and the United States. Additionally, he has been Scholar in Residence at both the University of Oxford, England and Tantur Ecumenical Institute in Jerusalem as well as Visiting Professor in Residence at Tamil Nadu Theological Seminary in Madurai, South India. He is the creator of the award-winning Down Ancient Paths Travel Study Program, which explores the spiritual heritage of the oldest Christian traditions in the world and the primary biblical landscapes of the Mediterranean and Middle Eastern regions.

James R. Payton, Jr. is Professor of History at Redeemer University College in Ancaster, Ontario. He is author of *Light from the Christian East: An Introduction to the Orthodox Tradition* (Downers Grove: IVP Academic, 2007), *Getting the Reformation Wrong: Correcting Some Misunderstandings* (Downers Grove: IVP Academic, 2010), and *Irenaeus on the Christian Faith: A Condensation of "Against Heresies"* (Eugene: Pickwick, 2011). From 2006–2011 he served as president of CAREE

(Christians Associated for Relationships with Eastern Europe), a UN-endorsed NGO which has worked in the region for more than fifty years in the pursuit of peace, justice, and reconciliation. From 2008–2011 he also served as Christian Co-Chair of the National Muslim/Christian Liaison Committee, affiliated with the Canadian Council of Churches.

Terence Penelhum is Professor Emeritus of Religious Studies at the University of Calgary, where has was formerly Head of the Philosophy Department, Dean of Arts and Science, and Director of the Calgary Institute for the Humanities. He studied at the Universities of Edinburgh and Oxford, and has held many visiting appointments at universities in Canada and the United States. His primary academic interests are in the philosophy of religion and the history of modern philosophy. His books include *God and Skepticism: A Study in Skepticism and Fideism* (Dordrecht: Reidel, 1983), *Butler* (London: Routledge & Kegan Paul, 1985), and *Themes in Hume: The Self, the Will, Religion* (New York: Oxford University Press, 2000).

Clark H. Pinnock (1937–2010) was a Christian theologian, apologist, and author. He taught at McMaster Divinity College from 1977 until his retirement in 2002. Pinnock authored many books including, *A Wideness in God's Mercy* (Grand Rapids: Zondervan, 1992), *The Openness of God* (Downers Grove: InterVarsity, 1994), and *Most Moved Mover: A Theology of God's Openness* (Grand Rapids: Baker, 2001). He wrote in the conviction that "unless the portrait of God is compelling, the credibility of belief in God is bound to decline."

John Polkinghorne is a Fellow of the Royal Society, a Fellow (and former President) of Queens' College, Cambridge, and an Anglican priest. He was awarded the Templeton Prize for Science and Religion in 2002 and in that year became the Founding President of the International Society for Science and Religion. He is internationally known as both a theoretical physicist and a theologian. He has published a series of books on the compatibility of religion and science, including *Belief in God in an Age of Science* (New Haven: Yale University Press, 1998), *Faith, Science & Understanding* (New Haven: Yale University Press, 2000), *Quantum Physics and Theology: an un-expected kinship* (New Haven: Yale University Press, 2007) and an autobiography, *From Physicist to Priest* (London: SPCK, 2007). Thomas J.

Oord has edited *The Polkinghorne Reader: Science, Faith and the Search for Meaning* (London: SCM, 2010).

Denis Renevey is Professor of Medieval English language and literature at the University of Lausanne, Switzerland. He specializes in late medieval English vernacular theologies. His recent publications include co-editions of *The Doctrine of the Heart: A Critical Edition with Introduction and Commentary* and *A Companion to the Doctrine of the Heart: The Middle English Translation and its Latin and European Contexts* (Exeter: University of Exeter Press, 2010).

Lamin Sanneh is the D. Willis James Professor of Missions & World Christianity and Professor of History at Yale University. His PhD is in Islamic history at the University of London. He taught at University of Aberdeen and Harvard University before assuming the Chair in Missions and World Christianity at Yale University. He has written over a hundred articles and numerous books including, *Piety and Power: Muslims and Christians in West Africa* (1996), *Abolitionists Abroad: American Blacks and the Making of Modern West Africa* (Cambridge: Harvard University Press, 2000), and *The Changing Face of Christianity: Africa, the West, and the World*, co-edited with Joel A. Carpenter (Oxford: Oxford University Press, 2005). He is editor at large for *Christian Century*, an ecumenical weekly.

Alan P. F. Sell is a philosopher-theologian and ecumenist who is employed full-time in research, writing, and lecturing at home and abroad. He has held posts in England, Switzerland, Canada and Wales; from January 1988 to December 1992 he held the Chair of Christian Thought at the University of Calgary and subsequently held the Chair of Christian Doctrine and Philosophy of Religion at the United Theological College, Aberystwyth, within the Aberystwyth and Lampeter School of Theology of the University of Wales. His latest book is *Four Philosophical Anglicans: W. G. De Burgh, W. R. Matthews, O. C. Quick, H. A. Hodges* (Aldershot: Ashgate2010). His books, *Convinced, Concise and Christian: The Thought of Huw Parri Owen*, and *The Person of Christ in Nonconformist Thought and Ecclesial Experience* are forthcoming.

Douglas H. Shantz is Professor of Christian Thought at the University of Calgary where he has served since 1999. His research and writing focus on radical movements in early modern German Protestantism. His recent books are *Between Sardis and Philadelphia: the Life and World of Pietist Court Preacher Conrad Bröske* (Leiden: Brill, 2008) and *A New Introduction to German Pietism: Protestant Renewal at the Dawn of Modern Europe* (Baltimore: Johns Hopkins University Press, 2012).

Margaret Somerville is Samuel Gale Professor of Law, Professor in the Faculty of Medicine, and Founding Director of the Centre for Medicine, Ethics, and Law at McGill University, Montreal. She has an extensive national and international publishing and speaking record and frequently comments in all forms of media. Her books include *The Ethical Canary: Science, Society and the Human Spirit* (New York: Penguin, 2000); and *The Ethical Imagination: Journeys of the Human Spirit* (Toronto: Anansi 2006; CBC 2006 Massey Lectures). She is a Fellow of the Royal Society of Canada and among her many other honors and awards are the Order of Australia, seven honorary doctorates, and the UNESCO Avicenna Prize for Ethics in Science.

Lynn R. Szabo is Professor of English at Trinity Western University and a scholar of the poet, mystic, and peace activist Thomas Merton, an emerging, significant figure in twentieth century literary studies. She has authored numerous articles on his poetics and is the editor of *In the Dark Before Dawn: New Selected Poems of Thomas Merton* (New York: New Directions, 2005). She has also recently co-edited *Through a Glass Darkly: Suffering, The Sacred and The Sublime in Literature and Theory* (Waterloo: Wilfrid Laurier University Press, 2010).

Bonnie Bowman Thurston is a founding member of the International Thomas Merton Society and served as its third president. After twenty-seven years she resigned as William F. Orr Professor of New Testament at Pittsburgh Theological Seminary to live in solitude in Wheeling, West Virginia. She is author or editor of fifteen theological books on scripture and spirituality, two volumes of poetry, and over one hundred articles, twenty of which are on Thomas Merton. Most recently she edited the collection *Thomas Merton and Buddhism* (Louisville: Fons Vitae Press, 2007) and authored *Belonging to Borders*, a collection of Celtic poems (Collegeville: Liturgical Press, 2011).

Marguerite Van Die held a joint appointment in the History Dept. of Queen's University and at Queen's Theological College from 1985–2009. Van Die's research interests have been primarily in nineteenth-century religion, gender, and class. Her most recent publication, *Religion, Family and Community in Victorian Canada: The Colbys of Carrollcroft* (Montreal/Kingston: McGill-Queen's University Press 2005) examines the interaction between nineteenth-century society and a Methodist family in Stanstead, Quebec. Her other, overlapping, interest is in the area of religion and public life in Canada, about which she has organized several conferences and has edited a collection of essays: *Religion and Public Life in Canada: Comparative and Historical Perspectives* (Toronto: University of Toronto Press, 2001).

Keith Ward is a Fellow of the British Academy and Professorial Research Fellow at Heythrop College, London. He has been Professor of the History and Philosophy of Religion at King's College, London and Regius Professor of Divinity at Oxford. He is a priest of the Church of England. He is author of many books, including a multi-volume work in comparative theology of which *Religion and Human Fulfilment* (Norwich, UK: SCM, 2008) is the fifth and final volume.

Arlette Zinck is Associate Professor of English Literature at The King's University College in Edmonton, Alberta. Her research and writing focus on seventeenth century literature and especially on John Bunyan's fictions and prose works. Recent publications include a coauthored article with Maxine Hancock entitled "Baxter, Bunyan, and a Puritan Reframing of Ageing," *Bunyan Studies: A Journal of Reformation and Nonconformist Culture*, Number 14 (2010), pp. 56–75 and "Dating the Spiritual Warfare Broadsheet," in Ken Simpson, ed., *Texting Bunyan: Essays on Attribution, Influence, and Appropriation from* The Recorder, 1999–2008 (Open Latch Publications, 2010).

Preface

VIRGINIA TUMASZ,
Chair, Department of Religious Studies, University of Calgary

ESTABLISHED IN 1986, THE Chair of Christian Thought was from its very beginning a bridge-building venture. The several years of fundraising that preceded its establishment saw people come together from various Christian denominations to work towards the common goal of endowing a Chair at the University devoted to the study of Christian Thought. The ecumenical effort that began the Chair continues to inform its work, as this volume testifies by the variety of Christian perspectives and interests represented among its contributions.

The Chair, in effect, bridges time as well in the sense that the endowment raised through that ecumenical effort ensures that Christian Studies will be included among the scholarly activities that take place at the University of Calgary far into the future. As long as the University continues, there is the guarantee that the intellectual traditions of Christianity will be the subject of study and discussion within its walls. Reflections on the rich history of Christian Thought, such as those included in the contributions to this volume, will continue here in Calgary in perpetuity thanks to the Chair of Christian Thought Endowment.

The final and most important act of bridging is of course carried out in fulfilling the explicit mandate of the Chair, i. e., to bridge the academy and Christian faith communities. The "ivory tower" of the university and the division between "town and gown" are stock phrases that draw our attention to the uneasy, distant, or even divisive relationship that has often characterized the interaction between the academy and its surrounding communities. The Chair of Christian Thought at the University of

Calgary was established as a deliberate attempt to nullify that division and to bring about a fruitful interaction between the University of Calgary and local Christian churches, between the study of Christian thought in the Department of Religious Studies and the life of the Christian communities that call Calgary their home. It is my hope that the chapters in this volume, written by scholars invited to Calgary by the Chair of Christian Thought, will serve to connect Christians with current scholarship about historical figures and movements from their own and other traditions and to acquaint them with current issues and debates that demand the attention of churches today.

The important role of scholars and scholarship in Christian life has ancient roots. The Chair of Christian Thought can be viewed as standing within the revered tradition that prizes critical scrutiny and informed judgment in the enterprise of understanding the intellectual dimensions and traditions of Christian faith. Scholarship should not be socked away in a tower, ivory or otherwise. It belongs on the streets, in churches and marketplaces; it belongs where people live their lives. The Chair of Christian Thought, so ably filled by its current holder, Douglas Shantz, does a remarkable job of bridging the gap, of placing current scholarship where it has an effect on life, where it makes a difference.

Introduction

DOUGLAS H. SHANTZ AND TINU RUPARELL

THE OCCASION FOR THIS book is the celebration of the twenty-fifth anniversary of the founding of the Chair of Christian Thought at the University of Calgary in Canada. The Chair was created through the initiative of Professors Harold Coward and Peter Craigie in the Religious Studies Department at the University, in cooperation with leaders from Calgary's faith communities. The Chair's mandate is to serve as a bridge between the academic study of religion and Calgary's churches. The Chairholder is responsible for organizing and hosting a program of four endowed public lecture events each year. The lectures are designed to expose people of faith in Calgary to the fruits of the latest Christian scholarship and to do so in an interesting and accessible way.

One of this book's editors, Douglas H. Shantz, assumed the Chair of Christian Thought in summer of 1999. He has brought to Calgary some of the outstanding Christian scholars of our day, inviting them to address issues such as the expansion of world Christianity and its future prospects, the need for both religious and scientific responses to the world, the search for ethical guidelines for science and medicine in a pluralist society, recent research into the historical Jesus, and trends in inter-religious dialogue. Several of the lecturers, such as John Polkinghorne of Cambridge University in England, Margaret A. Somerville at the Centre for Medicine, Ethics and Law, McGill University, Keith Ward of Oxford University, Lamin Sanneh of Yale University Divinity School, and Craig Evans of Acadia Divinity School are regularly consulted by the news media for their insights into the pressing issues of our day. Just a week after his lecture in Calgary in January 2002, John Polkinghorne was awarded the Templeton Prize, which honors a living person who has made an exceptional contribution to affirming life's spiritual dimension through insight, discovery, or practical work. Many of the Christian Thought lectures of the past ten years are available at the Chair's website: http://www.ucalgary.ca/christchair/

The editors invited past Christian Thought lecturers to reflect on how their mind has changed and how their academic field has changed over the course of their career, especially in the last twenty-five years. They were also invited to reflect on the pressing issues in their field of study that will need to be addressed in the twenty-first century. The intention of the book is to offer readers the mature reflections of these Christian thinkers rather than original scholarly research. Our invitation was met with an overwhelmingly positive response, with some twenty-five individuals agreeing to contribute to the book. The volume is international in scope, including scholars from the United Kingdom, Canada, the United States, and Switzerland. Our only regret is the delay in publication due to problems in finding a suitable publisher; the volume now commemorates the twenty-fifth anniversary of the Chair instead of the twentieth, as originally planned. As a result, the volume's contributions do not necessarily take into account scholarship from the last five years.

A key feature of the book is the many disciplinary perspectives it brings to bear on the question of Christian Thought in the twenty-first century. The contributors represent a wide variety of backgrounds, from Biblical studies, theology, and religious studies to history, English literature, philosophy, law, and ethics. As editors we settled on a fivefold division of the book's twenty-five chapters: those offering a Historical Perspective, chapters that address Philosophical and Theological Issues, chapters on encounters with Religious Pluralism and the frontiers of Science, chapters on the Academy and the City, and chapters in the disciplines of English Literature and Film.

A good number of contributions offer a historical perspective on the Christian tradition. Craig Evans speaks of a revolution in the study of the Jesus of history within the last twenty-five years, including new ways of understanding the Gospels. He suggests that the single most important development in study of the historical Jesus has been the rediscovery of his Jewish life and setting. Researchers now view Jesus and his Galilean family and disciples in the context of Torah-observant Jewish faith rather than in terms of Hellenizing ideology.

Dennis Martin issues a call for a return to the search for truth in medieval studies, a search long abandoned thanks to the prevailing influence of postmodernism in humanities faculties in both public universities and in many Christian colleges and universities as well. Members of the academy are in danger of becoming "knowledge workers" in the business of producing publications to gain self-recognition. The university markets itself in utilitarian terms as credentialing for careers; students become customers rather than disciples needing and desiring formation in truth or wisdom. As a scholar of medieval English mystical literature, Denis Renevey observes that the field has changed to an almost unrecognizable extent in the last twenty-five years, much of this the result of feminist scholarship. Traditional male church historians and theologians will have to tackle issues that their scholarly training and practice have not equipped them to address. For example, an interdisciplinary approach is clearly required to examine properly the impact of the liturgy in shaping the consciousness of medieval devotional and mystical writers.

The work of the current Chairholder, Douglas Shantz, focuses on the history of early modern German Protestantism, from 1500 to 1780. German Radicals introduced a new paradigm to Protestant Christianity, reconceiving traditional Reformation Protestantism in terms of personal renewal and new birth, conventicle gatherings for Bible study and mutual encouragement, social activism, and post-millennialism. The new forms of community and belief that arose in this period reflect the tumult of the times and laid the foundations for our modern world.

Margaret Miles considers the challenge of preparing students to enter a social and intellectual world in which Christianity cannot be considered as a unified and isolated phenomenon. Rather, it must be seen as a cultural product that exists alongside other religions in religiously plural Western societies. The well-trained historical theologian of the future will need both historical and theological skills and sensibilities. This will demand faculty who recognize the value of committed interdisciplinarity.

James Payton examines the histories of traditions often seen at opposite ends of the Christian spectrum: Orthodoxy and Evangelicalism. Payton considers new developments in Eastern Orthodoxy, particularly after the fall of communism. The Orthodox renaissance entails new freedoms as well as new challenges, not least from its first true engagement with modernity. Three key issues now face Orthodoxy: development of a consistent approach to the social and cultural issues now facing the

Orthodox faithful; finding a way to leverage the return to patristic theology so as to reinvigorate Orthodox theology as well as to create a bridge to western Christianity; and finally to integrate the increasing numbers of Western Christians now attracted to Orthodoxy.

Lamin Sanneh writes about the premature pronouncements of the death of religion. Christianity and the other religions, he shows, are far from moribund. He notes the rise in numbers of religious adherents worldwide. While secularism seemed to be on a triumphant march from Europe to the rest of the world, religion has proven to be an abiding presence, something Sanneh suggests should be neither feared nor regretted.

From a philosophical perspective, Terence Penelhum highlights the role and promise of analytic philosophy in Christian thought over the last decades. Unimpressed by both sides of the philosophical debate—those who practice a snide form of skepticism towards religious statements as well as those who fashioned disingenuous non-realist responses—Penelhum promotes a form of philosophical reflection on the claims of Christianity which illuminates how rational people of good will could justifiably take contrary positions on the truth and meaningfulness of Christian claims. Noting the importance of Swinburne, Plantinga, and Alston, Penelhum highlights three questions facing Christian philosophers today: the question of the religious ambiguity of the universe, the consequent issues which arise from religious pluralism, and finally, the still relevant challenge of evolutionary biology. The towering history of the Christian traditions, suggests Penelhum, should empower Christian philosophers to rise to these significant questions.

Clark Pinnock notes that his mind has changed over the last twenty-five years in part due to changes in ecclesial demographics. Thanks to the activities of evangelical parachurch organizations and the goading of Mark Noll's book, *The Scandal of the Evangelical Mind*, many younger and not-so-young scholars have taken up the challenge of developing a critical and rigorous body of evangelical theological reflection. Much of evangelical theology is infused with a self-identity of pilgrimage which, for Pinnock, often leads to a surprising openness. Such openness will be crucial for grappling with the challenges of natural science as well as the critiques of anthropocentrism.

In the last twenty to forty years process theology has undergone a reversal of fortune, according to John Cobb Jr., one of its preeminent spokesmen. It was once considered to be at the extreme of liberal

Christian thought, associated as it was with the appearance of the Death of God theology and the development of liberation theology. Now, however, process theology is considered quite conservative because of its recontextualization and association with traditions such as evangelicalism. Evangelicals and process theologians now find significant overlap in their concerns, chiefly due to the seriousness with which both camps approach the biblical witness. Evangelicals and process theologians have much to gain from each other through their new-found commonality.

Douglas John Hall suggests that in the last few decades scholars have been reacting to the tumultuous history of the first sixty years of the twentieth century. He calls for a strong dose of humility in facing the pressing issues of today. Hall suggests that Christians reflect on the historical orthodoxies/orthopraxies of their tradition in order to reinvigorate them; there is also need for a humble and authentic response to the issues of the environment, religious pluralism, and the place of Christian thought in civil society.

The issues of religious pluralism and dialogue have been at the center of Paul Knitter's long and productive career. He emphasizes the dialogical nature of both the Christian tradition—in its genesis and development, encounter and dialogue with the other have been a hallmark of the tradition—and the nature of faith itself. Only by returning to an open, honest, and risky dialogue will Christians rediscover their real mode of being. Knitter suggests that a new way of being a Christian is to return to its roots in dialogue. In recent years this openness to others has receded in the face of fears of global geo-politics.

Keith Ward has been a pioneer of comparative theology in the English-speaking world, focusing his attention on the study of theology in a global context. In our shrinking world, theology must be comparative in the tradition of writers such as Wilfred Cantwell Smith, John Hick, Raimundo Panikkar, Paul Griffiths, Francis Clooney, and Julius Lipner. These thinkers have brought the practice of "comparative religion" into the postmodern context—seeking to be sensitive to traditional Christian claims yet open to other traditions as sources of authentic truth and insights.

A different form of dialogue, that between science and religion, has been the focus of recent work by Cambridge scholar John Polkinghorne. Polkinghorne has had two illustrious careers: first as a particle physicist and then as an Anglican priest and theologian. From his unique vantage point,

Polkinghorne sees modern physics as opening up the possibility of divine providence in a world of intrinsically unpredictable physical states. Thanks to modern physics, theology finds itself called upon to set the agenda rather than defensively responding to the latest scientific discovery.

One of the most fruitful areas of the interface between science and religion is the area of bioethics. McGill ethicist Margaret Somerville, a leading voice in bioethics research, highlights the way in which developments in medicine and biological science have raised previously unimagined questions about the nature of human beings and human flourishing. Such questions, for Somerville, must inevitably overlap with religious concerns. A trans-disciplinary approach, that considers the wisdom found in theological and religious traditions, holds promise of a fuller and richer discussion of these issues in the public square.

Several contributions fall under the heading, the Academy and the City. The place of religion in the academy and broader society is the subject of reflection for a number of scholars. As a historian of Christianity at Queen's University in Canada, Marguerite Van Die has seen changes in the way religious history is taught in Canadian universities. The traditional religious history of institutions and dogma has been superceded by the new "lived religions" perspective on Christian history. This new approach to the history of Canadian Christianity has invigorated the field and excited young students. It offers access to new vistas where the faith of practitioners is understood to be sensitive to context and accident.

Charles Nienkirchen reflects on his many years of engaging with students' existential questions and struggles with their Christian identity. Nienkirchen argues that spirituality—by which he means a focus on the lived experience of Christian belief and practice—needs to be injected into the curriculum of Christian thought. This practical and existential turn may well reinvigorate the idea of the university itself and help it to return to its raison d'être, *universitas*. Inclusion of spirituality as an integral part of Christian thought will meet young people where they are, encouraging them to turn to more traditional forms of Christian community.

Peter Erb reflects on the varying trends and debates among religious studies scholars in the last twenty-five years, especially the exile of theology from the field. Erb considers, with some irony, the many theological themes that pervade recent popular literature. He highlights works by P. D. James, Umberto Eco, and John Grisham. These writers represent an important expression of theological thinking in our society, a vibrant alternative to the increasingly fruitless conflicts between Religious Studies and Theology.

A previous chair-holder, Alan Sell, reflects on the unique nature of the Chair of Christian Thought and the task of bridging the academy and the church—facing towards both Athens and Jerusalem. In the time he was in Calgary, and subsequently, historical theology has gained a more general acceptance in the academy, notwithstanding certain troubling issues concerning its accommodation by the study of religion.

The seemingly inexorable rise of urbanization and its complicated history with Christian thought is the subject of Wesley Kort's reflections. Although much current thought about space has relegated the city to the level of the profane, Kort argues that a more positive and nuanced understanding of cities is possible. The role of churches in shaping the space of urban centers is by no means slight. Kort suggests that the material space of cities can be read much as Christians read scripture.

Susan Felch and Arlette Zinck address issues facing Christian literary scholars in the age of theory. Felch argues that a religiously inflected literary critic may be in a better position to write about literature than the unbeliever since Christianity looms so large in the history of western literature. In a post-postmodern literary landscape, the contextualization afforded by Christianity allows the literary theorist and critic to produce criticism that is at once suspicious and rigorous yet open to the possibility of meaning which transcends the merely particular. Literary critics, Felch suggests, might fruitfully consider the creed as a touchstone for critical openness.

Arlette Zinck raises a pressing question for teachers of literature: "For those who make a living in university lecture halls, particularly those who proclaim a Christian worldview, the question is this: how do we teach literature in the age of theory and interdisciplinarity so the text regains its power to move us?" Some notable scholars outside the literary field have pointed to the power of literature to move readers and prepare them for life. Literary narratives connect us with our own deepest values and help us to notice when our actions are inconsistent with them.

The life and work of Thomas Merton are the focus of contributions by Bonnie Thurston and Lynn R. Szabo. Thurston describes Merton as a man deeply marked by the crises and issues of the twentieth century, a man whose life, rootlessness, privilege and conversion, provide a metaphor for his century. Yet he was also prophetic in addressing an agenda for the future. Merton's writings address some of the most important religious issues of the last half of the twentieth century: ecumenism and inter-religious dialogue, social justice, and spiritualities. For Szabo, Merton demonstrates a way of being authentic in a pluralistic and secular world. He affirmed the incarnational power of language and literature and their transcendent possibilities, both in his personal experience and in his literary legacy. In the decade before his death, Merton reached beyond his own monastic spirituality to deepen his commitment to oneness with humanity and God, reflected in his engagement with issues of war and racism and with eastern religions.

Anne Moore sees film as a way to interrogate the notion of religion in our day. She sees film, and films with religious themes in particular, as more than visual homilies, but as religion itself. Following Tarkovsky, Moore suggests that films create a narrative world aimed at preparation for death, a world in which joy and suffering, *eros* and *thanatos*, all play an implicit role. To watch a film is to engage with the filmmaker's reconstruction or re-descriptions of our world, a fundamentally religious act. To watch a movie is to engage in inter-religious dialogue. These dialogues require an open-minded attempt to understand the other through interrogating both the film as well as oneself. Film has become a quintessentially contemporary form of religion.

Our contributors point to some exciting new directions in Christian scholarship in the twenty-first century. Some of the more noteworthy include the field of Biblical studies. Craig Evans suggests that the large number of texts discovered in the last century and ongoing discoveries in archaeology will impact future research into the life and teaching of Jesus. Fragments of the sayings of Jesus and other documents telling us important things about first-century Palestine may yet come to light.

In the field of medieval English literature, Denis Renevey anticipates the production of an electronic corpus of devotional works in the major vernacular languages of the Middle Ages. This venture will require the involvement and financial support of an international team of scholars. Rather than producing the best critical editions, the goal will be to produce digitized medieval texts from good manuscript exemplars. Douglas Shantz highlighted a new development in the field of early modern Protestant Christianity: recognition of the Protestant contribution to the age of Enlightenment reason. There is need to investigate the many "ego documents" produced in this period, works destined to become the special genre of modernity.

The theological realm holds exciting developments in the dialogue between science and religion. Both Clark Pinnock and John Polkinghorne point to this, from different sides of the disciplinary divide. "A stunning world has been opened up in the big bang cosmology and in evolutionary biology." A new model for God will be explored in terms of "a trinitarian panentheism" which sees God and world exist in close inter-relationships and interactions. In this picture, God is "other" than creatures but also interior to them. Transcendence and immanence are not polar opposites but are somehow connected.

Terry Penelhum foresees some new challenges and directions confronting Christian philosophers. We live in a world marked by religious ambiguity, a world in which it is rational both to adopt a religious interpretation and to adopt a wholly naturalistic one. Our scientific culture, says Penelhum, has generated a situation in which reflective persons cannot be faulted for facing it with bewilderment and indecision.

Paul Knitter foresees a scholarly agenda that includes confronting the tensions and contradictions between traditional Christology, that sees Jesus as the one and only savior and as the bearer of God's full, definitive revelation, and the new ecclesiology, that sees dialogue as the new way of being church. There is need for an understanding of Jesus the Christ that preserves his distinctive message without subordinating the distinctive identities and message of other religious figures. Similarly, Keith Ward sees a key agenda item being the factor of globalization and the way it has opened Christian thinking to many different strands of thought. Globalization confronts us with the huge diversity of religious beliefs on our planet, with none of them able to establish itself with the theoretical certainty the natural sciences have. The challenge will be for people of faith to understand and learn from others, while following their own distinctive insights in a non-aggressive and non-defensive way.

This book offers a uniquely personal glimpse of Christian scholars in a self-reflective mode, capturing their honest reflections on the changing state of the academy and on changes in their own mind and outlook. The breadth and depth of insight afforded by these contributions provide rich soil for a reader's own reflections and an agenda that will occupy Christian thinkers well into the twenty-first century.

PART 1

Historical Perspectives on the Christian Tradition

1

Jesus and the Gospels

CRAIG A. EVANS

THE LAST TWENTY-FIVE YEARS have seen a revolution in the study
of the Jesus of history and new ways of understanding the Gospels.
Most of the developments have been positive, but there have also been
some unfortunate ones as well. What lies ahead will probably include
more of the same. My own thinking has evolved, resulting in changes
with respect to specific historical and critical issues and with respect to
theological and religious implications.

Last Twenty-Five Years

Perhaps the single most important development in study of the historical
Jesus has been the rediscovery of his Jewish life and setting. For too long
Christian interpreters have lifted Jesus out of his Jewish world and, in
effect, made him into a "Christian," and often a champion of whatever
theological and ecclesiastical emphases happened to be in vogue. The
Gospels are now seen as capable of yielding significant information about
Jesus, his teaching, and activities. The Gospels also reveal the factors that
led to his execution and why his followers continued to regard him as
Israel's Messiah and Savior.

In the mid-1980s it became clear to New Testament scholars that
a new phase of Jesus research had dawned. As the "New Quest" of the

1950s and 1960s faded from view, its theological preoccupations seemed strangely dated and irrelevant. The skepticism of German form criticism and redaction criticism, along with its preference for an almost non-Jewish Jesus, was subjected to much deserved criticism and loss of its position at the center of the discussion. The newer phase of Jesus research eventually came to be dubbed the "Third Quest."

Among a host of insightful studies are hefty tombs by John Meier (a Roman Catholic), E. P. Sanders (a liberal Protestant), N. T. Wright (former Bishop of Durham and an evangelical Anglican), and Dale Allison Jr. (moderate evangelical). These are among the best and most influential works of Jesus scholarship and demonstrate the ecumenical reality of this field of research. This new phase of Jesus research is not just a Protestant concern, or some conservative reaction; it is broadly ecumenical and remarkably interdisciplinary, including scholars not only in biblical studies and history, as one might expect, but in cognate fields of study. In my view, this is one of the most refreshing aspects of current study of the historical Jesus.

The fruits of these studies are seen in several important areas of Jesus research. One concerns Jesus' aims and mission. His appointment of the twelve, his healings and exorcisms, and his proclamation of God's rule (or, in literal but often misunderstood language, "the kingdom of God") point unmistakably to the redemption and restoration of Israel, God's covenant people. Jesus' mission spoke directly to the hopes of his Jewish contemporaries.

A second important area of critical advance is the new appreciation of Jesus' self-understanding. He almost certainly understood himself in messianic terms (though not in terms of the messianism of later rabbinic eschatology or later Christian Christology). Jesus understood himself as the "son of man," a human figure described in Daniel 7, to whom power, authority, and kingdom were given. In heaven Jesus received from God this authority, which on earth Jesus began to exercise: "That you may know that the son of man has authority on earth [to forgive sins]" (Mark 2:10).

As *the* "son of man," invested by God with authority *on earth* to proclaim God's rule, to forgive sin, and to make pronouncements relating to what can be done on the Sabbath (Mark 2:27–28) and what is clean (Mark 7:1–23), Jesus naturally thought of himself as a prophet, speaking forth the word of God. The strongest evidence for this is seen in a passage that cannot easily be explained as a Christian invention: "A prophet is not without honor, except in his own country, and among his own kin, and in his own house" (Mark 6:4). Because the saying is set in a context of rejection and opposition to his ministry, it is almost certainly not the product of Christian apologetic or piety but derives from Jesus himself. Evidently the public too thought of Jesus as a prophet (cf. Mark 8:27–28). When Jesus was arrested and mocked, he was asked to prophesy (cf. Mark 14:65), in all probability alluding to his reputation as a prophet. In context, this insult does not advance or reflect Christian beliefs about Jesus. For Christians, Jesus is the Messiah and Son of God, not a mere prophet.

Today scholars are more open to thinking that the Christian opinion, following the resurrection, that Jesus was the Messiah was due to what Jesus himself taught and encouraged his disciples to believe. There is evidence for this in Jesus' appeal to Isaiah 61:1–2 ("the Spirit of the Lord is upon me, because he has anointed me to preach . . ."), explicitly in his Nazareth sermon (Luke 4:16–30) and implicitly in his reply to the imprisoned and discouraged John the Baptist (Matt 11:2–5 // Luke 7:18–22). The messianic import of these allusions to words and phrases from Isaiah 61 and other passages in Isaiah has been clarified and confirmed by a fragmentary text found among the Dead Sea Scrolls. According to 4Q521, when God's Messiah appears, the sick will be healed, the dead will be raised, and the poor will have good news preached to them. According to 11QMelchizedek, the herald of Isaiah 61 was expected to proclaim the eschatological jubilee, which also appears to agree with Jesus' declarations that sinners (or debtors) are forgiven (e.g., Mark 2:5–10; Luke 7:47–49).

There is now among scholars a greater openness to the idea that Jesus in all probability anticipated his own death and attached significance to it. In my opinion it is almost a certainty that at some point in his ministry Jesus anticipated his death, either shortly before entering Jerusalem (as in the Synoptic Gospels) or perhaps shortly after entering Jerusalem in the final Passover week. The death of John the Baptist would have pressed itself on Jesus' thinking (cf. Mark 9:9–13), and, because Jesus was a realist, he would have known that the ruling priests were set on destroying him. The clearest evidence that Jesus anticipated his death is seen in his prayers in Gethsemane (Mark 14:32–40). The portrait of the frightened, grieving Jesus is hardly the stuff of pious imagination. One should compare the Johannine portrait of the composed, serene Jesus, who calmly discusses the glory that he and his heavenly Father share (John 17). The Synoptic portrait of the frightened Jesus who falls on his face and begs God to remove from him the cup of suffering (Mark 14:36) is surely historical.

If Jesus did indeed anticipate suffering and death, it is likely that he sought to find meaning in it. After all, the deaths of the righteous, especially in the time of the Antiochid persecution and the Maccabean revolt, were understood to be of benefit to the nation of Israel. Would Jesus think any less of his own death? I think it most probable that Jesus pondered the meaning of his death and sought to explain it to his frightened, discouraged disciples. Jesus saw the shedding of his own blood as a Passover-like sacrifice that would benefit Israel. At the same time Jesus remained confident that God would raise him up and that someday he would drink the Passover cup in the kingdom of God (Mark 14:25).

The words of institution, "This is my blood of the covenant, which is poured out for many" (Mark 14:25), appear to be a conflation of Old Testament texts that speak of the blood of sacrifice, covenant, and renewal (Exod 24:8; Jer 31:31; Zech 9:11). The tradition is ancient (1 Cor 11:23–25) and thoroughly Jewish (cf. 1 Cor 5:7 "Christ, our paschal lamb, has been sacrificed"). To the end, Jesus remains as Jewish as ever. Even the meaning of his death is seen in Jewish terms.

A third area of advance is a better understanding of the political factors involved in Jesus' death. Collaboration between local authorities and their Roman overlords was standard administrative procedure in the Roman Empire. In Judea in the time of Jesus' ministry, this meant collaboration between the high priest Caiaphas and his priestly colleagues, on the one hand, and Pontius Pilate and his retainers, on the other. The evidence indicates that the Jewish high priest and the Roman governor were able to work together. Caiaphas was appointed about one year before Pilate took office and the latter allowed the former to remain as high priest the duration of his administration (in contrast to Gratus his predecessor, who appointed a new high priest almost annually). Indeed, the nearly simultaneous removal, from office, of the high priest and the governor in early AD 37 suggests that they were implicated together in the violent Samaritan affair, an affair into which Caiaphas may well have dragged Pilate (Josephus, *Ant.* 18.4.2–3 §88–95). In any event, the evidence that we have—and it is rich thanks to the New Testament evangelists and Josephus, all of whom wrote within one generation of Pilate's administration—documents how Jewish and Roman authorities shared the responsibilities of government and allows us now to understand better the role each played in Jesus' death.

The Next Twenty-Five Years

It is difficult to forecast what lies ahead in this ever-changing field of study. It is certain that ongoing study of the large numbers of texts discovered in the last century and ongoing discoveries in archaeology will impact research into the life and teaching of Jesus. The Dead Sea Scrolls, especially those published in 1991 and in the years following, have not been fully digested. Some of these scrolls, such as 1QSa, 1QSb, 4Q246, 4Q521, and 4Q525, have already made major contributions to our understanding of the teachings and activities of the historical Jesus. Ongoing study of these scrolls may lead to further insights.

Not all of the papyri, especially the vast quantities excavated from the sands of Oxyrhynchus, Egypt, have been published. Nor have all the documents that make up the vast collection of retired books and documents discovered in the genizah of the old Cairo synagogue. It was in this collection that the first Dead Sea Scroll—the Damascus Covenant—was discovered. What else from Israel in the New Testament period might yet be found? Fragments of the sayings of Jesus and other documents telling us important things about first-century Palestine may come to light.

Archaeology of the land of Israel has uncovered much, but most sites remain unearthed. What more light will be shed on the world of Jesus and his contemporaries? Ongoing excavations, especially at Sepphoris, a city only four miles from Jesus' hometown of Nazareth, have had dramatic implications for understanding Galilean life. Excavations in recent years prompted some scholars to think of Jesus in urban, maybe philosophical terms. Ongoing excavations have revealed how firmly committed to the Jewish way of life the inhabitants of Sepphoris were in the time of Jesus. Many other sites in Galilee have revealed the high degree of commitment to Jewish customs on the part of the inhabitants. Discoveries such as these have encouraged researchers to view Jesus and his Galilean family and associates in the light of Torah-observant Jewish faith and not so much in terms of Hellenizing ideology.

Ongoing critical work in Josephus, Philo, and the numerous writings that fall loosely under the heading of Old Testament Pseudepigrapha will no doubt make important contributions. One such document—the

Testament of Moses—provides a significant parallel to Jesus' concept of the collapse of the kingdom of Satan in the face of the in-breaking rule of God. Exorcistic and medicinal traditions such as in the *Testament of Solomon* and various amulets help us contextualize with much nuance how Jesus' contemporaries would have viewed his ministry of exorcism and healing.

It is work such as this—comparative work in the fields of religious literature, history, and social science—that will continue to advance research on the historical Jesus. Of course, Jesus will remain elusive and to some degree mysterious, but careful critical and comparative research will continue to clarify and add greater precision to our understanding of this significant person.

2

The Dwarfs Are for the Dwarfs

Medieval Church History Today

DENNIS D. MARTIN

A T THE DAWN OF the third Christian millennium, faculty members specializing in medieval studies at a large Catholic university offered an interdisciplinary medieval studies graduate seminar. To launch the course faculty members from the core fields of history, English literature, philosophy, theology, and fine arts explained to graduate students from these fields how their disciplines participated in medieval studies. The historians and English literature specialists insisted that their fields of study originated with the nineteenth century. Even when challenged, the historians reaffirmed that scholarly study of history did not exist before modern methods had been applied to the story of a nation's origins, development, and rise to power. As exhibit A, students were pointed to great series of published texts: the *Monumenta Germaniae Historica* and the Rolls Series, both of which had been conceived in the service of nationalism. Likewise, not until the universities countenanced the study of modern languages as worthy of scholarly attention, did the scholarly study of literature begin, also in the service of English or French, German or Italian national pride and self-awareness.

But what of the Benedictine Maurists and Jesuit Bollandists and their tireless work of collecting texts from dusty monastic libraries and publishing them in the 1600s and 1700s? They pioneered the study of history, paleography, and diplomatics. Why was that *not* the scholarly study of history? No, the historians insisted, such earlier history-studying and history-telling was invested in a mythology dedicated to telling the story of a Christian culture, a study of history captive to religion and unworthy of the label "*wissenschaftlich*."

We now see plainly the subservience of nineteenth-century historians who proclaimed that they offered history "as it actually happened" but in fact were doing propaganda for the German or English national ideology. We contemporary scholars will never fall into that trap again. No one can really know what the Middle Ages were like and anyone who claims to know is manipulating his readers, simplifying the truly complex, ultimately unknowable, *real* Middle Ages in the service of whatever agenda he lives for and from.

As the dwarfs in C. S. Lewis's *The Last Battle* proclaimed: "the dwarfs are for the dwarfs"[1]—this after realizing they had been taken in by the demagoguing half-truths promulgated by the Ape named Shift. A proper scholar today will avoid being taken in by mythmakers and propagandists. The dwarfs refused to fight against the Lie because all those fighting against it had an agenda (the boy-king Tirian, whose throne has been usurped; the children from England, Jill and Eustace; the faithful unicorn Jewel; and a handful of other creatures who have not been taken in by the usurping rulers of Narnia). As Griffle, the Dwarf-leader put it: "'You keep a civil tongue in your head, Mister . . . I don't think we want any more Kings—if you *are* Tirian, which you don't look like him—no more than we want any Aslans. We're going to look after ourselves from now on and touch our caps to nobody. See?' 'That's right,' said the other Dwarfs. 'We're on our own now. No more Aslans, no more kings, no more silly stories about other worlds. The Dwarfs are for the Dwarfs.'"[2]

Next in the graduate seminar's self-presentations came the literature scholars. The study of (Latin) literature, going on for thousands of years, closely intertwined with philosophy and theology, was not scholarly because it too was bound up with the church and traditional religion. Only when freed from that could the study of literature become scholarly and only now, having seen how earlier scholars were taken

1. The dialogue is found in Lewis's *The Last Battle*, chapter 7, titled, "Mainly about Dwarfs."

2. Which did not, however, prevent the Dwarfs from fighting on behalf of the Ape's armies when it appeared that Tirian's forces were winning. So much for neutrality and objectivity.

in by nineteenth-century nationalism, can we begin to dig deeply into the reality of language and literature. Instead of creating the artifice of a critical edition that represents no text that ever actually existed, aided by hypertext, we will try to hold all the versions of a classic text up for study simultaneously. *El Cid*, the *Song of Roland*, and the story of *Perceval* exist *really* only in clusters of variations, each of which was very real to those who told and sang it, most of which are lost to us in their concrete existence.

Then came the turn of philosophy and theology. The philosopher, a religious agnostic, looked up in amazement and said, I scarcely recognize what you are describing. For me, the study of philosophy has always been about a search for truth. This matters to me personally and I do believe that the truth can be sought and found. That's what animates me as a scholar. Thus the 1600s and 1700s or the 1100s and 1200s are not pre-scholarly but very much on equal footing with more recent and contemporary study of philosophy. The theologian likewise insisted that, while the study of Christian theology employs data and methods from history, literary criticism, philology, sociology, psychology, anthropology and so forth, what distinguishes theology from the other disciplines is theology's truth claims. Only someone who believes in divine revelation can study theology, since by definition theology is analysis seeking deeper understanding of the data of faith. If one does not believe the Truth is discoverable, then one will be doing historical or literary or sociological study of religious believers and beliefs, which is a fine and honorable discipline (religious studies), but not the same as theology. And like classic philosophy, the discipline of theology sees a great continuum between the students of theology in the ancient and medieval and early modern worlds, on the one hand, and theologians today, on the other hand. The scholarly discipline of theology goes back for centuries. It was scholarly back then and remains so today. It did not first find itself in the eighteenth or nineteenth century with the new methods of *Religionsgeschichte*. Its practitioners are dwarfs standing on the shoulders of giants.[3]

3. In the famous words attributed to Bernard of Chartres by John of Salisbury in his *Metalogicon*, bk. III, chapter 4. See also Southern, *Scholastic Humanism*, for the claim that eleventh- and twelfth-century scholars in western Europe self-consciously set about to recover as much as they could of the knowledge lost with the expulsion of paradise. The first step to that goal was recovering by means of careful reading and commentary as much of the ancient heritage of human knowledge as possible. In my view, this could have served as the basis for a different kind of scientific-modern worldview—one that

The historians and literature scholars replied: if this definition of theology holds, theology has no rightful place in the university because university scholarship must be seeking real truth and truth-seeking today cannot be other than consistent debunking. That's what birthed the modern university—the banishment of all sorts of naïveté from what counts as true scholarship. The Enlightenment opened people's eyes to the pervasiveness of blindness, to the prejudices of one's tradition, and *we* now see the Enlightenment's blind spots. We are centrist, moderate debunkers, not nihilist deconstructionist debunkers. Yes, some of us actually draw from Marxist or gay studies or feminist frameworks, but we do so selectively. We remain in charge, we do not over-commit to any of these but choose on our terms the valuable elements they offer. We simply describe as best we can what we see in medieval people's lives and literature, recognizing constantly that our descriptions themselves represent some degree of our own moderately distorted "appropriation" of what "truly" happened back then. We cannot do otherwise, and we do not claim to describe *the* Middle Ages, only a set of glimpses of it.

All doing of history or study of literature involves *appropriation*—taking hold of something from the past and necessarily distorting it as one passes it under one's own lens, one's own standpoint, one's own modern context. The scholar's challenge is to minimize the appropriation, not eliminate it. If one appropriates cautiously, one can get a better and better glimpse of the past or of a body of literature, even if it is not *the* Text or *the* Past, even if it is distorted, filtered through my own present standpoint. Thus did chastened, centrist, moderately postmodern scholars of the Middle Ages explain to neophyte medievalists how things stand in their field.

And how do things stand in my field? What is my field? Trained as a historian, having taught theologians and seminarians for twenty-five years, specializing as a researcher in medieval church history but credentialed in late medieval and Reformation era "intellectual history" in a secular public university, my field is as interdisciplinary and

retained its Christian basis—had medieval scholars been able to turn the corner and incorporate advances in empirical "scientific" knowledge into their theoretical framework. The attempt, in Southern's view, failed, in the thirteenth century. Galileo and modern science employed a quite different understanding of the epistemological power of scientific explanatory models, which then led to the common modern perception of warfare between religion and empirical science. On the epistemological implications of Galileo's re-envisioning, see Hodgson, "Galileo."

"transgressive" of boundaries as anyone's is. I came to the study of history seeking truth about the past. My field did not begin with the nineteenth century university but reaches back to embrace Christians whose faith sought understanding since the first century. And because my faith seeks understanding, it has no place in my own Catholic university because it represents not a moderate mythmaking appropriation of the past but an extremist mythology, one that actually believes that the purpose of *Wissenschaft* is the seeking and finding of Truth, incompletely yes (this side of Heaven), but for all that no less really and truly. What I seek is deeper understanding of the Christian mysteries, and mysteries are infinitely comprehensible. Truly comprehensible yet infinitely so. Pursuing such comprehension, I learn to my discomfiture, is unscholarly.

How did things come to this pass? It would serve no purpose to rehearse here the Kantian debunking of access to the noumenal and the Nietzschean debunking of Kant's confidence nonetheless in practical reason and deontological moral principles, or, for that matter, to rehearse the collapse of Whig-liberal historical confidence in the face of hegemonic Marxist analysis (euphemistically called "social history) that reigned when I was in graduate school in the 1970s. Lurking outside the as-yet-unacknowledged hollow shell of Marxism, the disaffected and cynical dwarfs of the revolution of the 1960s were awaiting their cue: "enough already, no more ideologies, the dwarfs are for the dwarfs." Twenty years later, by 1990, they occupied center stage. Having unmasked the pretentious claims of those who think they know these things, for us process reigns supreme over content, and the "value-free" values and methodologies of the social sciences have taken the baton from ancient and Enlightenment humanities disciplines. We want none of that simplistic black-and-white thinking that gives rise to the world's wars of religion or nationalism or economic class. We have seen through that, we know that "it's all more complex than that." The scholars are for the scholars.[4]

No more master narratives of *the* Middle Ages, please, one might summarize medievalists' pleas over the last thirty years. The old

4. The shift was complete by 1990, as the *The American Historical Review* and the journal of record for interdisciplinary medieval studies, the Mediaeval Academy of America's *Speculum*, made clear in special issues on "the linguistic turn" in 1989 and 1990: *AHR* 94.3 (June 1989) and *Speculum* 65.1 (January 1990). For a fine summary with references to a wide range of related approaches to history, see Ghazzal, "Twentieth-Century Approaches to History" at http://zouhairghazzal.com/courses/Hist400Spring95.htm.

meta-histories of the Middle Ages must go. First to go were the Middle Ages understood as the Teutonic birthplace of North Atlantic free and democratic society. This was the WASP narrative of the nineteenth- and early, twentieth-century Ivy League historians who founded the Mediaeval Academy of America and ran most of the graduate programs in medieval history. Second was the Middle Ages as the greatest of all ages, the period in which a beautiful European Catholic civilization flourished only to be submerged by the chaos of late medieval nominalism, Protestant heresy, and modern secularism. This was the standard Catholic narrative found almost exclusively in Catholic universities which were not admitted to polite university society until the 1970s, though this meta-narrative began to peek out from under the anti-Catholic iron curtain through the work of Étienne Gilson and others at the Pontifical Institute of Mediaeval Studies in the 1940s. Third was the meta-narrative of the medieval renaissance before the Italian Renaissance that began to gain general visibility in the 1940s and 1950s.[5] Fourth was the soft Marxist social history meta-narrative of a two-tier society, elite and popular, oppressor and oppressed, highly educated and utterly ignorant and superstitious that characterized the 1960s and 1970s. All these collapsed under the pressure of the new micro-history and detailed local studies[6] which followed the rise and *krisis* of the "total history" of the Annales School.[7] Only if one studied local phenomena, only if one burrowed to the roots and concreteness of daily life and material life, would the raw material be generated for the sweeping global syntheses of Fernand Braudel and others. The Annales' "thick

5. The "revolt of the medievalists" against the claims that all that was good stemmed from *the* Renaissance of the fourteenth through the sixteenth centuries began in part with Haskins, *Renaissance of the Twelfth Century*; cf. the celebratory updating edited by Benson and others, *Renaissance and Renewal*. It represented a variation on the old WASP meta-narrative that located the origins of what we value most in contemporary society in the Middle Ages. Outsiders to the American Ivy League WASP establishment offered alternatives: Paul Oskar Kristeller, as a Jewish refugee Renaissance scholar further developed the medieval roots of the Italian Renaissance and Gerhart Ladner as a Catholic anti-Nazi refugee from Vienna brought to North America the symbolist *Geistesgeschichte* of Percy Schramm, Ernst Kantorowicz and others. Cantor, *Inventing the Middle Ages*, offers helpful vignettes on some of the leading medievalists, although at points he descends into mere gossip and badly distorts particularly the life and work of David Knowles.

6 Haigh, *English Reformations*; cf. Duffy, *Voices of Morebath*.

7. Ghazzal, in the course syllabus mentioned in note 4 above, notes an editorial in the December 1989 issue of *Annales: Economies, Sociétés, Civilisations* that describes the malaise among historians who had held out so much hope for "total history."

description" approach[8] borrowed heavily from sociologists and cultural anthropologists, including Clifford Geertz.[9] As study after study revealed the exceptions to generalizations and the complexity of life on the micro-scale, the larger narratives could no longer be defended.

Ironically, the final meta-narrative proposed for medieval church history was one that inspired the implosion of all meta-narrative. Created by both secular and active Catholic social church historians (Jean Claude Schmitt, Jean Delumeau, Gabriel Le Bras), it explained patiently that Europe was not really Christian during the Middle Ages. Instead, an elite Christian veneer disguised a still pagan world that yielded to Christianization only under the impact of regimented bureaucratic Protestant and Catholic catechetical apparatuses of the early modern state churches. In response, John Van Engen suggested that to have been christened, baptized, made into Christians, in a Europe in which nearly everyone was a christened-one, surely did not count for nothing.[10] This was a society that was obviously not still pagan. But neither did the very real Christianizing mean what Catholic apologists were perceived to have claimed for it: that most people were knowledgeable and committed to the doctrines and moral teachings. Some were and some were not, but all were Christians, understood themselves to be and could not have imagined otherwise. Within this basic commonality, immense diversity of behavior and belief coexisted.

In a recent survey of the last twenty years of medieval church history writing, Van Engen offers four books of the 1980s that epitomize the new trends.[11] All of them arose from the interest in "popular religion" broadly conceived and the turn away from study of formal doctrinal or institutional church history.[12] R. I. Moore had a sort of meta-narrative:

8. See Burke, *French Historical Revolution* and Braudel's studies: *Mediterranean*; *Civilization and Capitalism*; *On History*.

9. Regarding the application of sociological methods to church history, see O'Malley, *Trent and All That*, with its summary of the work of H. Outram Evennett, John Bossy, Delio Cantimori, Paolo Prodi, Giuseppe de Luca, Gabriele de Rosa, Paolo Simoncelli, Étienne Delaruelle, Gabriel Le Bras and others.

10. Van Engen, "The Christian Middle Ages," with references to the leading works by Schmitt and others.

11. Van Engen, "The Future." The four books are: Stock, *Implications of Literacy*; Walker Bynum, *Holy Feast and Holy Fast*; Moore, *The Formation of a Persecuting Society*; and Rubin, *Corpus Christi*.

12. In the United States this was most visible with regard to Reformation era-church

the church as an "all-encompassing disciplinary society, with clerics as self-interested manipulators of a state-like power" (p. 500). Brian Stock produced something of an overarching theory about the role of "textual communities" in medieval culture, replacing the traditional categories of monasteries and schools and bishops. These books illustrate the move toward recasting medieval Christianity "as culture and comparative religion" rather than as doctrinal or church history. The cultural anthropologist Arnold Angenendt recognized the medieval world as the period most deeply *saturated* by religion (though the early modern era of confessional conflict and polemics was more deeply *marked* by religion). Angenendt closed his work with quotations from the philosopher of culture and sociology, Leszek Kolakowski, and from Clifford Geertz, the "thick description" cultural anthropologist.[13]

A way of studying and understanding medieval (Christian) culture emerged that did not depend on intricate knowledge of Catholic monastic or scholastic teachings about God, the Trinity, the sacraments, the Church. These would now be left to the handful of specialists in philosophy and theology who might still be interested. But neither Moore, Stock, Bynum, nor Rubin thought that the doctrines of Christian faith were irrelevant. Their interest was in the fruits of these doctrines as they were filtered through whatever groups within medieval Christendom one chose to study. The sharp divide between elite and popular culture began to be elided. That formal doctrines filtered down to the common people, no one would deny[14] but in the process they were modified, transformed,

---

history as taught by Lewis Spitz at Stanford, Harold Grimm at Ohio State, and Robert Kingdon at the University of Wisconsin, with whom the teaching of church history spread from the Protestant divinity school where it had been housed into university history departments during the 1950s and 1960s, where, for a brief period they were welcome, only to be overwhelmed by the social history, popular history, and general revolutionary chaos of the 1960s and 1970s. Medieval church history was of interest mainly to Catholics in the United States and hence precluded from the prestigious universities. The WASP medieval establishment's disinterest in church history and theology is evident in the *Dictionary of the Middle Ages*, edited by Strayer, which had embarrassingly little coverage of theology or even of church history. Theology and church history did retain a place in British and Continental universities, which included theological faculties. Examples included Richard Southern and David Knowles in England.

13. Angenendt, *Geschichte der Religiösität*. Van Engen points out that Angenendt cites Leszek Kolakowski and Clifford Geertz. Van Engen, "The Future," 502n13.

14. Peter Brown offered a spirited challenge to the commonly held "two-tier," popular/elite religion thinking that dominated the soft marxist sociological histories of the

pluralized, even subverted or perverted, and all of this was now the object of historical study.

Given this colorful complexity that defies systematization, overarching explanations and narratives are, for the foreseeable future, premature. Any explanatory power arising from Christian belief taken straightforwardly as a living reality remains out of bounds. The power of beliefs after they have been run through a cultural anthropology or psychology methodological grid is within bounds. We can study processes of belief as distant objects but not as engaging, living, personal realities. Van Engen's call to begin to give attention to content (pp. 520–21) rather than mere process is not really being heard. Indeed, I think, it *cannot* be heard because the underlying problem is the university world itself. Higher education as a thirst for truth, for figuring things out—even simply figuring out what it truly means to be formed as a man or a woman, a husband or wife, a servant of God—such education as formation is largely gone.[15]

Once upon a time the conflict and conversation between Christians and *philosophes* was about rival visions of formation, about what it meant to be an intelligent, well-shaped, scholarly humane person. The goal of education was formation into knowledgeable, integrated, *honesti*, honorable, decent human beings. Christianity is a lived truth, a way of thinking, living, acting in accord with rock-hard truth, not merely thinking about what truth might or might not be. A long history of Christian philosophy, history, literature, and art has been dedicated not to process as an end but to process, arts, skills, ways of thinking, as means to the end of living more fully the Truth of the Universe.

How has my mind changed? Despite misgivings, I flirted with the language of moderate postmodernism in the early 1990s, believing it might permit a place at the scholarly table for Christians who candidly integrated their traditional Christian faith with their work, as I did in my first book.[16] It has not developed that way. But it could. Our challenge for the future is to open our eyes to the scholarly possibility of truly believing ancient visions of Truth, to take the risk of returning the University

---

1960s and 1970s in *Cult of the Saints*.

15. See Quay, *Mystery Hidden*, 396–403 for some stimulating reflections on the replacement of formation by mere learning in the later Middle Ages and the Reformation era. See also the studies of this issue by Griffiths, *Religious Reading* and *Intellectual Appetite*.

16. Martin, *Fifteenth-Century Reform*, especially the epilogue.

itself (not merely a handful of "Christian universities") to being a place for human moral, religious, social, and personal formation, among which Christian formation has its legitimate and honorable place.

Bibliography

Angenendt, Arnold. *Geschichte der Religiösität im Mittelalter*, 2nd edition. Darmstadt: Primus, 2000.

Benson, Robert L., et al., eds. *Renaissance and Renewal in the Twelfth Century*. Cambridge, MA: Harvard University Press, 1982.

Braudel, Fernand. *The Mediterranean and the Mediterranean World in the Age of Philip II*. Translated by Siân Reynolds. New York: Harper and Row, 1972.

———. *Civilization and Capitalism, 15th–18th Century*, 3 vols. Translated by Siân Reynolds. New York: Harper and Row, 1972–1984.

———. *On History*. Translated by Sarah Matthews. Chicago: University of Chicago Press, 1980.

Brown, Peter R. L. *The Cult of the Saints: Its Rise and Function in Latin Christianity*. Chicago: University of Chicago Press, 1981.

Burke, Peter. *The French Historical Revolution: The Annales School, 1929–1989*. Stanford: Stanford University Press, 1990.

Bynum, Caroline Walker. *Holy Feast and Holy Fast. The Religious Significance of Food to Medieval Women*. Berkeley: University of California Press, 1987.

Cantor, Norman F. *Inventing the Middle Ages: The Lives, Works, and Ideas of the Great Medievalists of the Twentieth Century*. New York: Morrow, 1991.

Duffy, Eamon. *The Voices of Morebath: Reformation and Rebellion in an English Village*. New Haven: Yale University Press, 2001.

Griffiths, Paul J. *Intellectual Appetite: A Theological Grammar*. Washington, DC: Catholic University of America Press, 2009.

———. *Religious Reading: The Place of Reading in the Practice of Religion*. New York: Oxford University Press, 1999.

Haigh, Christopher. *English Reformations: Religion, Politics, and Society under the Tudors*. Oxford: Clarendon, 1993.

Haskins, Charles Homer. *The Renaissance of the Twelfth Century*. Cambridge MA: Harvard University Press, 1927.

Hodgson, Peter. "Galileo the Scientist," *Logos* 6 (2003) 13–40.

John of Salisbury. *Metalogicon*. Edited by C. J. Webb. English translation by Daniel D. McGarry. Oxford: Clarendon, 1929.

———. *The Metalogicon: A Twelfth-Century Defense of the Verbal and Logical Arts of the Trivium*. Berkeley: University of California Press, 1955, 1962.

Lewis, Clive Staples. *The Last Battle. The Chronicles of Narnia*. New York: Collier Books, 1970.

Martin, Dennis D. *Fifteenth-Century Carthusian Reform: The World of Nicholas Kempf*. Studies in the History of Christian Thought 49. Leiden: Brill, 1992.

Moore, R. I. *The Formation of a Persecuting Society*. Oxford: Blackwell, 1987.

O'Malley, John W. *Trent and All That: Renaming Catholicism in the Early Modern Era*. Cambridge: Harvard University Press, 2000.

Quay, Paul M. *The Mystery Hidden for Ages in God*. New York: Peter Lang, 1995.

Rubin, Miri. *Corpus Christi: The Eucharist in Late Medieval Culture.* Cambridge: Cambridge University Press, 1991.

Southern, Richard W. *Scholastic Humanism and the Unification of Europe.* 2 vols. Vol 1: *Foundations.* Oxford: Blackwell, 1995.

Stock, Brian. *The Implications of Literacy.* Princeton: Princeton University Press, 1983.

Strayer, Joseph R., ed. *Dictionary of the Middle Ages.* New York: Simon and Schuster, 1982–1989.

Van Engen, John H. "The Christian Middle Ages as an Historiographical Problem." *AHR* 91 (1986) 519–52.

———. "The Future of Medieval Church History." *CH* 71 (2002) 492–522.

3

Reflections on Medieval English Religious Literature

DENIS RENEVEY

Eleven April 2006. Genolier, Switzerland. I sit at my desk in my rather spacious and cosy study in the attic, overlooking in the distance Lake Geneva, with Mont Blanc just appearing very faintly in the mist. As I prepare this contribution for the twenty-fifth Anniversary Volume for the Chair of Christian Thought, my two children play downstairs and I hear laughter or, occasionally, very brief weeping, followed by even more joyous banter. The rain has stopped since yesterday and the day is a most promising one. Next to my computer are a few books which I think should help me shape this contribution: *The Cambridge History of Medieval English Literature*; *God and the Goddesses*; *Anchorites, Wombs and Tombs*; *Fragmentation and Redemption*; *Holiness and Masculinity in the Middle Ages*; *Medieval Virginities*, and *Medieval Blood*. Looking at my bookshelf to my right, more books seem to call for attention, and many more which, if not physically present, loom in my mind more or less distinctly.

11 April 1989. Oxford, a rainy day, as usual, and as I have got used to now since my arrival in October in 1988. But the weather does not preoccupy me very much at the moment, and there are no children yet to take my attention away from my reading task. The beauty and the special atmosphere of the Radcliffe Camera matters much more than the weather outside, and they certainly have an impact on my perception of

Bernard of Clairvaux's Sermons on the Song of Songs. I am discovering the medieval mystical tradition and the experience of this discovery is mind-boggling (perhaps I should say soul-boggling). Next I should read William of St. Thierry, the Victorines (more especially Richard of St. Victor), and then move on to the Middle English mystics, to pause much longer on Richard Rolle. The path is smooth, and my vision and intentions very clear. Followed by further reading in the Upper Reading Room of the Bodleian Library, the thesis will happily come out as the result of this intense and life-enhancing reading.

I find myself caught somewhat by surprise with this request for a contribution to offer an assessment of my field. Although aware the term "junior" did not apply to my academic person any longer, I had not realized I had almost spent twenty-five years investigating the field. But the books mentioned above could not have crossed my eye then, and they (with many more, not to mention exceptional contributions in the forms of articles that would deserve reference as well) testify to the advance the field has made in the last twenty-five years or so. It is to general directions pointed at in those publications I would like to pay attention in this chapter, looking at how they have complicated our approach to medieval English religious literature.

There was a time when the field of medieval English religious literature was almost exclusively limited to mystical writers. Knowles' 1961 contribution, *The English Mystical Tradition*, placed in the foreground the so-called Middle English mystics: Richard Rolle, *The Cloud of Unknowing*, Walter Hilton, Julian of Norwich and Margery Kempe (there is also a chapter on the post-medieval Augustine Baker). His study assesses those writers in the way they contribute to Catholic theology and his interest lies therefore in extracting their mystical theology and placing it within the larger framework of the Christian mystical tradition. More than thirty years later, the impact of Knowles can still be felt in the contribution offered, for instance, by Marion Glasscoe. Her *English Medieval Mystics: Games of Faith*, with the obvious exception of Baker, takes up the same group of writers and offers for each a chapter that puts emphasis on both their literary and mystical achievements. Although I am not questioning Glasscoe's significant contribution, her book is somewhat misleading as to advances made in the field of medieval religious literature from the 1980s onwards. True, the book is part of a series that aims at introducing major literary and cultural topics in English literature and it attests therefore to the vitality of mystical writings as an object of investigation to be made visible to students of English literature and general readers. The book, and several others on the mystical tradition or on specific mystical writers, makes a foray into new canonical literary texts. Extracts of Julian of Norwich's *A Revelation of Love* and *The Book of Margery Kempe* have appeared in the Norton Anthology, and the mystics make a chapter in the recent *Cambridge History of English Literature*. I shall come back to this contribution by Nicholas Watson later on in my chapter, but suffice to say at this point that the gap between advance in scholarship and the slow acceptance of the Middle English mystics as part of the literary canon has never appeared as colossal as today.

First, thanks in part to the impact of feminist studies, there has been a healthy shaking up of the hierarchical order within this neatly compact group of writers. Julian of Norwich and Margery Kempe definitely seem to be gaining the upper hand in the classroom and in anthologies, against Rolle, Hilton and *The Cloud* author. More importantly, feminist scholarship has allowed for a different perspective on those female contributions, linking them for instance to other female contributions from the continent, assessing their specific feminine qualities, and investigating them thematically as groups of text written by or for women. More theoretical contributions, like those of Caroline Walker Bynum, Barbara Newman, Amy Hollywood, but also Jocelyn Wogan-Browne, to mention just a few, participate importantly in the rehabilitation of female mysticism and in the marking of its male mystical practice. In short, gender is now taken most seriously as shaping the mystical experience and its textual representation, with a difference.

Feminist critics have looked outside the Middle English mystics group for their investigation in the feminine. Also, and *pace* Knowles, mystical aspects have made room for other issues, like the importance played by the (female) body in the mystical experience, the representation of Christ as female, food consumption, anorexia and the feminization of the self. A vast array of texts were used for such investigation and, with regard to those new interests, the mystical qualities of the material under consideration were not necessarily the primary criterion for selection. The texts that raised interest often offered a wealth of information about author-audience relationship, or dealt with female religious behavior in particular, or were written by women themselves, or translated by women. Engagement with such issues relegated mystical aspects into the background, so that so-called theologically sophisticated mystical texts had to live in much larger and eclectic company. Whether one contributes to feminist criticism or not, and even if some excessively theoretical feminist contributions to the field sometimes lose touch with the primary material, one cannot but applaud the immense contribution which such an approach has brought to the field, with the (re-)discovery of female-authored texts and an even greater number of them addressing a female audience in the first place. It may very well be that no other field in the vast domain of English literature owes as much to the "second sex" as the field of religious medieval literature.

The article by Nicholas Watson on "The Middle English Mystics" in *The Cambridge History of Medieval English Literature* deserves special attention here as a piece reflecting, but also inviting, a fresh look at the field of medieval English religious literature. While the chapter offers a discussion of mystical texts, it works at deconstructing this neatly invented heterogeneous category and invites a much broader corpus of religious texts, to be discussed vis-à-vis or within a broader scholarly context. The line of argument followed by Watson relies upon some of his previous contributions, most importantly perhaps an article which, in the light of the impact of Arundel's Constitutions of 1407, proposes "vernacular theology" as a more inclusive term for the field of religious literature. The impact of this piece, and its further development in the *Cambridge History of Medieval English Literature*, is vividly felt within the scholarly milieu and it has led scholars to rethink their own preconceived views about mystical literature. However insightful his contributions and however inspiring they are to new generations of scholars, they are also the clear echo of advances in the field which were already on the move in the mid-eighties (see in particular the writings of Vincent Gillespie, J.R.R. Tolkien Professor of English Literature and Language at Oxford). Indeed, parallel to the feminist input, contextually based approaches to the field disentangled the mystical category by broaching a wealth of devotional and pastoral texts which, although not addressing a spiritual elite, were disseminated and reached a large popular audience in the late medieval period. The attention to such texts has for long been confined to a few specialists, but there is a move now for making such texts more readily available in affordable editions. Without omitting the intrinsic qualities of most of those texts, our understanding of medieval religious culture will greatly benefit from a focused attention on their cultural input.

A brief consideration of recent additions to *Ancrene Wisse* scholarship provides useful indications about the effect of new trends in medieval English religious scholarship. *Ancrene Wisse* scholarship of the twentieth century centered on complex issues related to the possible milieu which saw the production of this remarkable text, together with editorial questions which have now led to the forthcoming critical edition by the reputed *Ancrene Wisse* scholar Bella Millett and one of the Corpus Christi manuscripts by Robert Hasenfratz which, among its many qualities, is also affordable to students. No serious work on *Ancrene Wisse* and associated texts can dispense with those two works. Also, the recent input by Millett on *Ancrene Wisse* suggests new directions of research with a consideration of anchoritic culture within a broader context. *Ancrene Wisse* scholarship is now looking at continental expressions of anchoritic behavior and is gaining a lot from it. Anneke Mulder-Bakker, author of *Lives of the Anchoresses: The Rise of the Urban Recluse in Medieval Europe*, has forced *Ancrene Wisse* scholars to rethink anchoritic culture: to the typically British female anchoritic culture, usually opposed to the Beguines' continental communities, one now needs to add the continental tradition which Mulder-Bakker, among others, has brought to light. Via a different route, Millett herself has invited a consideration of the impact of continental pastoral practice permeated by Paris-trained bishops working in the West Midland area at the time of the composition of *Ancrene Wisse*. Further investigation in this area is currently under way and will appear in a published form in the near future. Also, even if anchoritic practice was not exclusively female, the English anchoritic material suggests a strong female involvement and hence a gender approach to those texts has usually offered significant results, allowed for a better understanding of this material, and contributed to the virginity discussion. *Anchorites, Wombs and Tombs*, edited by Liz Herbert McAvoy and Mari Hughes-Edwards, provides a good example of current developments in the field of anchoritic studies, with a mainly Gender Studies dialogue taking place between British and North-American literary scholars and continental historians and anthropologists.

Current developments in *Ancrene Wisse* studies show one of the ways forward for the field in general. Although the field appears more complex than it was twenty-five years ago, and invites investigations which rely on multidisciplinary approaches, it nevertheless points to an absence from recent active participation in those discussions on the part of theologians and church historians. Exceptions of outstanding quality can be found in the works of Barbara Newman and Ann Matter, for instance, even if the first is professor of both English and religion at her current university, while the latter's more recent contributions have taken a slightly less interdisciplinary approach than her work on the Song of Songs and her gendered approaches to her studies on women and sexuality in the context of Christian history.

This chapter has made reference to two female scholars in the field of theology and church history. The field has changed to an almost unrecognizable extent in the last twenty-five years or so and traditional male church historians and theologians may find it unfathomable today: they may have to tackle issues that their own scholarly practice has not equipped them to address. Provided that a fresh look at the new discoveries which those different perspectives have untangled allows them to readjust their own set of values, their contributions to the field will allow for considerable movements forward. The impact of the liturgy in shaping the consciousness of devotional and mystical writers is a major issue in the field: an interdisciplinary effort in this area, rather than solitary ventures on the part of literary scholars, would be salutary.

There is need for a greater and broader, collaborative and interdisciplinary effort. However, it cannot develop successfully without larger availability of the primary material. If a certain number of medieval English devotional texts will find paper to be edited on, many more will not be deemed financially viable pieces. The possible way forward is the production of an electronic corpus of devotional works in the major vernacular languages of the Middle Ages. Such an effort would require the man-power and financial support of an international team. The texts produced electronically would initially be selected from good manuscript exemplars, rather than being critical editions. For some of the more popular texts, hypertext editions would be added in the long term. The impact of the continental tradition on the Middle English religious tradition suffers from readily available editions of some of the most important texts. Although an edition of the Middle English version of Marguerite Porete's *Mirror of Simple Souls* exists, it is not easily available. Editions of the Middle English translations of Ruusbroec are equally difficult to find, and a serious study of his influence upon the Middle English mystical and devotional tradition is hampered by this fact. The thirteenth-century Latin text, *De doctrina cordis*, circulated widely in the medieval period (more than 200 Latin extant manuscripts) and was translated into English, French, Italian, Spanish, German, and Middle Dutch. The latter example provides evidence for the pan-European dimension of the field and makes a case for the need to be able to consult different vernacular versions of devotional texts. There is need for all of us to broaden our horizons and to open the field to even larger perspectives.

From an Oxonian solitary academic adventure my life has now become one in which my paternal self has had to find its bearing in the postmodern European context in which I live. There is not much room any more for the solitary, but not always incoherent, ramblings of my Oxford days, and the only survival approach for me is now the mixed life, not so much as understood by Hilton and his disciples, but rather that of a man who, from his office upstairs, must leave his supposedly elevated thoughts to care for the more urgent needs of a toddler preoccupied by the need of diaper change (I am not here making reference to the heraldic use of the term). The life which I live, here and now, affects importantly my way of engaging with the material that I investigate. Both my academic experience over the last twenty-five years and other aspects of my life impact on the way I choose material and how I interact with it. To write how my consciousness of the field has changed in those years would honestly require the writing of an autobiography which, I fear, would not find a very attentive audience. Suffice to mention that, as a result of both academic and personal experience, I have come to the recognition of the importance of contextualizing as much as possible the devotional and mystical material that I investigate. Also, and perhaps as a result of significant changes in my own life, I have developed a growing empathy for the more down-to-earth devotional material, learning to find ways in which those texts could speak simply to the ordinary Christian and nevertheless guide them to eventually reach the pinnacle of the Christian mystical tradition. Although I would not detract anyone from a consideration of the mystical texts, I believe that the way forward is in the systematic study of this still largely unexplored corpus.

Bibliography

Gillespie, Vincent and Samuel Fanous, eds. *The Cambridge Companion to Medieval English Mysticism*. Cambridge: Cambridge University Press, 2011.

Gillespie, Vincent. "Religious Writing." In *The Oxford History of Literary Translation in English*, vol. 1: 700-1550, edited by Roger Ellis, 234-83. Oxford: Oxford University Press, 2008.

———. "Vernacular Theology." In *Middle English: Oxford Twenty-First Century Approaches to Literature*, edited by Paul Strohm, 401-20. Oxford, 2007.

Hasenfratz, Robert, ed. *Ancrene Wisse*. TEAMS Middle English Series. Kalamazoo, MI: Medieval Institute, 2001.

McAvoy, Liz Herbert and Mari Hughes-Edwards, ed. *Anchorites, Wombs and Tombs: Intersections of Gender and Enclosure in the Middle Ages*. Cardiff: University of Wales Press, 2005.

Millett, Bella. *Ancrene Wisse: Guide for Anchoresses (a translation)*. Exeter, UK: University of Exeter, 2009.

———. *Ancrene Wisse, the Katherine Group, and the Wooing Group*. Cambridge, UK: Boydell and Brewer, 1996.

Mulder-Bakker, Anneke. *Lives of the Anchoresses: The Rise of the Urban Recluse in Medieval Europe*. Philadelphia: University of Pennsylvania Press, 2005.

Watson, Nicholas. "The Middle English Mystics." In *The Cambridge History of Medieval English Literature*, edited by David Wallace, 539–65. Cambridge: Cambridge University Press, 2002.

4

Reflections of an Historian of Early Modern German Protestantism

DOUGLAS H. SHANTZ

I WELCOME THIS OPPORTUNITY TO take stock of my life as an academic, considering new developments in my research field, the challenges and opportunities facing scholars of early modern studies, and some signposts on my own intellectual journey.

For the last thirty years my research has focused on the field of early modern German Protestantism, from 1500–1780. This period of European Christian experience has captured my interest for many reasons. It was a time of tumultuous change, politically, socially, religiously, and intellectually. German Radicals introduced a new paradigm to Protestant Christianity, reconceiving traditional Reformation Protestantism in terms of personal renewal and new birth, conventicle gatherings for Bible study and mutual encouragement, social activism, and post-millennialism. They created new forms of Christian community, such as the communal life and sharing of goods that one finds among the Hutterites in Moravia and Austria and among the Moravian communities under Zinzendorf in Herrnhut and Bethlehem.

From 1982 to 1992, during graduate study at the University of Waterloo and my early teaching career, my research focused on six-teenth century German radicals, especially Caspar Schwenckfeld and his humanist colleague, Valentin Crautwald.[1] Inspired by Erasmus and his

1. Shantz, *Crautwald and Erasmus* and Shantz, "The Role of Valentine Crautwald,"

emphasis upon inward piety and practical devotion, the Schwenkfelders promoted an innovative spirituality that also drew upon notions found in St. Augustine, Joachim of Fiore, Martin Luther, Ulrich Zwingli, and Sebastian Franck. During a research sabbatical in Marburg, Germany in 1992–1993, my focus shifted to late seventeenth- and early-eighteenth-century German radicals known as Pietists. The cradle of modernity can be found among these non-conformist Protestant groups whose writings, beliefs, and behavior pushed the limits of toleration within a homogeneous European society.[2] I continue to research and write on both the sixteenth century radicals and the later Pietists.

Pietism scholarship experienced a significant turning point almost thirty years ago with publication of Hans Schneider's literature reviews on the state of radical Pietism research in 1982 and 1983. Schneider described radical Pietism as *terra incognita et inexplorata*, unknown and unexplored territory.[3] Until that time, the field had been dominated by German theologians who tended to focus upon the thought and writings of Johann Arndt, Philipp Jakob Spener, and August Hermann Francke, ignoring the more radical, mystically-oriented groups. Schneider set an agenda for the field that has inspired numerous doctoral and habilitation students right up to the present time. Studies of figures such as Heinrich Horch, Johann Konrad Dippel, Johanna Eleonora Petersen and her husband Johann Wilhelm Petersen, Eva von Buttlar, Johann Christian Lange, Alexander Mack and the New Baptists, and my own work on Conrad Bröske have all benefited from Hans Schneider's mentoring.[4] Radical Pietism is now understood to have been essential to the Pietist movement from the very beginning, encompassing a broad spectrum of views, from mystical Spiritualists such as Gottfried Arnold, to Millenarians such as the Petersens, to founders of new communities and churches such as Alexander Mack and Georg Conrad Beissel. Even "Church Pietists" such as Spener and Francke continued to have close ties with the Radicals.[5]

287–307.

2. See my new book: Shantz, *A New Introduction to German Pietism*.

3. Schneider, *German Radical Pietism*, 207.

4. Examples of my recent work in the field of Radical German Pietism include: Shantz, *Between Sardis and Philadelphia*; Shantz, "The Millennial Study Bible of Heinrich Horch"; Shantz, "The Origin of Pietist Notions of New Birth and the New Man"; and Shantz, "Radical Pietist Migrations and Dealings with the Ruling Authorities."

5. See Strom, "Problems and Promises of Pietism Research," 542f.

The Pietism research agenda is now dominated by a new generation of scholars whose interests include social, gender, economic, and political questions.[6] Those pursuing this research come from a varied, interdisciplinary background and include women in ever increasing numbers. Pietism research has become truly an international phenomenon, including scholars on both sides of the Atlantic. In the last ten years the North American Pietism Studies Research Group, in association with the American Society of Church History, has brought together a critical mass of Pietism scholars on this side of the Atlantic. All of this augurs well for the field's future.

In terms of the scholarly agenda for the future, there is a constellation of questions surrounding collective memory and the self-understanding of the Pietists, including their uses of history, forms of communication, social background, and notions of family, marriage, and gender.[7] Schneider has called on researchers to unearth the wealth of literary material that Radical Pietists produced, much of it still hidden away in public and private archives.[8] Key figures still await much-deserved treatment such as Joachim Lange, the prolific Halle Pietist, Andreas Groß, a central figure among Frankfurt separatists, and the anti-Trinitarians Christian Fende and Christoph Seebach.[9]

Richard van Dülman has called for research into early modern worship and liturgical practices, into the common piety of ordinary people that crossed Catholic-Protestant boundaries, and into early modern and modern processes of secularization and de-christianization.[10] Of particular interest to me is his plea for investigation of subjectivity within early modern German culture and for study of "ego documents," the special genre of modernity.[11]

6. Volume four of the new *History of Pietism* provides thematic treatments of Pietism in relation to modern religion, culture, and society. See Lehmann, ed., *Geschichte des Pietismus*.

7. Schneider, "Rückblick und Ausblick," 463–66.

8. Ibid., 460.

9. Schneider, *German Radical Pietism*, 129, 132.

10. van Dülmen, *Historische Anthropologie*, 76. "Research interests are concentrating themselves today less on the marginal aspects of separatism and magic and more on everyday religious notions and practices . . . Archives are full of records concerning religious dissidents and deviant practices, but obviously there are no records concerning normal religious life."

11. Ibid., 47, 76–80.

In charting my personal journey and growth as a scholar, I find it helpful to consider the changes in my social setting and affiliations.[12] In the last thirty years my work setting has changed from the Bible school, to the Christian liberal arts university, to the public research university. I had a heavy teaching load in the early years, with seven or eight courses a year. I now teach two or three courses per year with more time for research, writing, and graduate student advising. My worship affiliation has changed from Baptist to Mennonite to Anglican. In each of these progressions I have experienced a more comfortable, less conflicted environment in which to pursue academic work as a Christian. While many see the public university as a threatening environment for people of faith, the evangelical world can also be a threatening place for the academic, one that is highly suspicious of the life of the mind. Mark Noll described the challenges of living "between faith and criticism."[13] I have come to see the public university as a *culture* that is marked by values such as curiosity, honesty, and intellectual discipline, one that has room for many perspectives and interests, including Christian ones.

Not surprisingly, my mind has changed over the years in significant ways: I have a new perspective on religious radicalism past and present, a new appreciation for the European Enlightenment, and a new sense of the role scholars can play in the academy and the larger world. What made early modern radical Protestants "radical" was their impatient rejection of the status quo, of institutional Christianity with its traditions, rituals, comfortable place in society, and low level of spirituality. The radicals saw the clergy as largely responsible for the miserable condition of the churches. Radical spokesmen were themselves often disillusioned clergy whose career path had been frustrated. One thinks of Andreas Karlstadt, Thomas Müntzer, Johann Wilhelm Petersen, and Heinrich Horch, all of whom were forced out of their churches by jealous clerical colleagues. Their personal frustration combined with an idealistic and charismatic personality to produce fledgling Christian movements, frequently dominated by women members. These early modern radical

12. Peter Berger observed: "Sociological consciousness moves in a frame of reference that allows one to perceive one's biography as a movement within and through specific social worlds, to which specific meaning systems are attached . . . We change our world views (and thus our interpretations and reinterpretations of our biography) as we move from one social world to another." See Berger, *Invitation to Sociology*, 64f.

13. Noll, *Between Faith and Criticism*.

groups were marked by anti-clericalism (egalitarianism), rejection of liturgies and creeds (anti-traditionalism), a return to simple biblical faith (biblicism), promotion of religious conversion experiences and direct communion with God (subjectivism), and hopes for a soon-coming age of vindication of the godly (millennialism). This Christian radicalism exerted a strong appeal in central Europe in the sixteenth, seventeenth, and eighteenth centuries.

There is much to commend in these early modern religious radicals, including their idealism, self-sacrifice, and moral zeal. But while the ideals of radical religion may work for a time, they cannot be sustained for long, as Richard Niebuhr and James Stayer have shown. The radical phase soon passes, and pass it must.[14] Early modern radicals were supremely confident of their own intimacy with God, their triumph over sin and evil, and their reading of the signs of the times. They saw themselves as a people apart, truly different from their surrounding society. In most cases they learned of their own fallibility through bitter experience. As radical leaders removed themselves from institutional accountability in their biblical interpretations, preaching, leadership style, and general behavior, they became vulnerable to a prophet complex, immorality, mental illness, social withdrawal, and extremism. Their rejection of tradition and society lasted a generation at most, the radical sect itself becoming an institutionalized tradition.[15] The Anabaptists, Hutterites, and Moravians developed their own liturgies, confessions, hymns, and institutional life. They soon successfully negotiated and integrated with the very societies their parents had rejected as evil.[16]

Such radical Christian piety is still with us today, guided by the same charismatic leaders and marked by the same condemnation of "religion" and religious institutions, the same triumphalism, and the same reliance upon private experience and personal Bible study. I hold in my hands a book by a pastor in the greater Toronto area entitled, *The End of Religion*.

---

14. See Stayer, "The Passing of the Radical Moment," 147–52.

15. "By its very nature the sectarian type of organization is valid only for one generation. The children born to the voluntary members of the first generation begin to make the sect a church long before they have arrived at the years of discretion. For with their coming the sect must take on the character of an educational and disciplinary institution, with the purpose of bringing the new generation into conformity with ideals and customs which have become traditional." Niebuhr, *The Social Sources of Denominationalism*, 19f.

16. See Packull, *Hutterite Beginnings*.

His church, the Meeting House, is "a church for people who aren't into church." The Meeting House promises an escape from ritual, creed, rules, institutional organization, and apathy and a return to true, biblical Christianity. "The Bible holds clues to a way out of human dependence on religious systems, while it simultaneously invites us into a direct connection with the Divine." The call is to "let the Jesus of Scripture be who he really was and not who 2,000 years of church history said he should be."[17]

The ironies here are many. For the Meeting House has already spawned satellite communities that are clones of the mother church. The different sites worship simultaneously by closed circuit, hearing the same sermon, singing the same songs. Talk about traditionalism! A church that began by escaping rituals and traditions has produced its own ritualized clones. The pastor has no need to consult church history to learn who Jesus is; he consults the Bible. Yet he expects that Christian people will heed his sermons and read his book along with the Bible. One must ask, Can one man act as a better guide than Augustine, Erasmus, Thomas Merton, and two thousand years of Christian wisdom? Can the Christian tradition simply be dismissed as so much "religion"?

My mind has changed in yet another way: I have a new appreciation for the European Enlightenment of the eighteenth century. Recent scholarship is showing that the age of reason was not generally anti-faith; indeed, in England and Germany prominent Enlightenment thinkers were Christian. One thinks of Isaac Newton, John Locke, Christian Thomasius, and G.F. Leibniz. "The Enlightenment originated in reformist-minded Christianity, both Catholic and Protestant" in Germany, Holland, and Scotland.[18] Reason served as a complement to faith in advancing social, religious, and legal reforms. The early modern period has much to teach us about how to negotiate issues such as the relation between Christianity and politics, Christianity and the academy, and Christianity and the world religions.

Our world has a pressing need for the self-critical, thoughtful mindset that Enlightenment reason can bring to religion in our day. It is ironic that many Christians who wish for a Muslim Enlightenment, for an Islam moderated by reason, are slow to recognize the advantages that Western society has gained from the age of reason. The end of religious wars did not

---

17. Cavey, *The End of Religion.*
18. Aston, *Christianity and Revolutionary Europe*, 93.

come about simply because of Christian charity. The benefits of Western pluralism, tolerance, and separation of church and state are not the result of religion alone. Indeed, as European governments pushed for toleration, Christian clergy typically pushed against it.[19] Even when radical Christians were in the majority, as in Puritan England and New England, the result was not peace and harmony. It was the Enlightenment's call for religious freedom in place of state-supported religious establishments and its recognition of a common human identity rooted in natural law that paved the way for Western democracy and human rights.

Finally, in recent years I have gained a fuller sense of the role scholars can play in the classroom and the larger community. Church historians in particular have much to offer in enriching our common civic and religious life.[20] Scholarship and teaching can become a source of wisdom, broadened perspective, and inspiration to our students and the wider culture. In my role as Chair of Christian Thought at the University of Calgary over the last twelve years, I have organized an annual roster of public lectures, hosted by Calgary churches. These events provide a platform in Calgary for leading Christian thinkers to pass on their hard-won insights. The enthusiastic response of Calgarians has convinced me that there is a bridge from the academy to the community, but it must be built and carefully maintained.

In the classroom I have sought to expose students to some of the significant people, movements, issues, texts, and ideas found in the Christian past. In taking students through John Bunyan's *Grace Abounding to the Chief of Sinners*, or Thomas Merton's *Seven Storey Mountain*, I ask them to consider the work's setting, purpose, key concepts, vocabulary, worldview, and social impact. I also ask Margaret Miles' question: Does the work offer "fruitful proposals for living a richly human life"?[21] Why or why not? I have found that students want to ask these questions. A few years ago, in the last week of my course in spiritual autobiography, the class met for breakfast at a restaurant near the university. One of the students posed a suggestion: "Let's discuss how reading these books has impacted our lives." What resulted was a lively, engaging, and memorable conversation.

19. Aston, *Christianity and Revolutionary Europe*, 143.

20. See my 2003 presidential address to the Canadian Society of Church History: Shantz, "A Usable Past," 171–92 and my Christian Thought lecture on February 7, 2011, "The Church and the Academy."

21. Miles, "Becoming Answerable for What We See," 471–85.

Jaroslav Pelikan observed that higher education can have highly unpredictable results. "The scholarly study of faith can be not only controversial, but contagious."[22] Mark Edmundson has challenged teachers of the humanities to realize that our disciplines have the potential to help us live better: "The purpose of a liberal arts education is to give people an enhanced opportunity to decide how they should live their lives." Our calling is to offer students "the best that is known and thought" and the opportunity to be transformed by what they find as they read and think about books.[23]

What I hope has not changed over the years is my intellectual curiosity and love of learning. As an undergraduate I came across Étienne Gilson's inspiring advice about the disciplined life of learning and teaching in the academy.[24] He quoted these words from William James, words that inspired Gilson's own life as a scholar:

> Let no youth have any anxiety about the upshot of his education. Whatever the line of it may be, if he keep faithfully busy each hour of the working day, he may safely leave the result to itself. He can with perfect certainty count on waking up some fine morning to find himself one of the competent ones of his generation, in whatever pursuit he may have singled out.[25]

Gilson called on scholars to be marked above all by humility, intellectual honesty, and a "scrupulous respect for truth." I still seek to follow Gilson's advice.

The professor's calling is an amazing privilege and joy with the opportunities it offers to read, learn, teach, write, and engage with colleagues around the world at conferences and colloquia. It is a betrayal of our calling when we allow it to be co-opted by narrow political and religious interests. When scholarship becomes predictable, when research and writing reinforce the same old conclusions, when there is no longer the surprise of discovery, I think the calling has been compromised. I derive hope from watching new generations of students as they catch the vision and pursue the life of learning and discovery.

22. Pelikan, *The Idea of the University*, 40.
23. Edmundson, *Why Read*, 5f.
24. Gilson, "The Ethics of Higher Studies," *Harvard Alumni Bulletin*, 127–30.
25. Gilson, "The Ethics of Higher Studies," *A Gilson Reader*, 28.

Bibliography

Aston, Nigel. *Christianity and Revolutionary Europe, 1750–1830.* Cambridge: Cambridge University Press, 2002.

Berger, Peter. *Invitation to Sociology.* Garden City, NY: Doubleday, 1963.

Cavey, Bruxy. *The End of Religion: Encountering the Subversive Spirituality of Jesus.* Colorado Springs: NavPress, 2007.

Edmundson, Mark. *Why Read.* New York: Bloomsbury, 2004.

Gilson, Étienne. "The Ethics of Higher Studies." *Harvard Alumni Bulletin* 30 (Oct. 27, 1927) 127–30.

———. "The Ethics of Higher Studies." In *A Gilson Reader,* edited by Anton C. Pegis, 24–30. Garden City NY: Image, 1957.

Lehmann, Hartmut ed. *Geschichte des Pietismus, vol. 4.* Göttingen: Vandenhoeck & Ruprecht, 2004.

Miles, Margaret R. "Becoming Answerable for What We See: 1999 AAR Presidential Address." *Journal of the American Academy of Religion* Vol. 68, 3 (September 2000) 471–85.

Niebuhr, Richard. *The Social Sources of Denominationalism.* New York: New American Library, 1929.

Noll, Mark. *Between Faith and Criticism,* 2nd ed. Grand Rapids: Baker, 1991.

Packull, Werner O. *Hutterite Beginnings.* Baltimore: Johns Hopkins University Press, 1999.

Pelikan, Jaroslav. *The Idea of the University: A Reexamination.* New Haven: Yale University Press, 1992.

Schneider, Hans. *German Radical Pietism.* Translated by Gerald T. MacDonald. Lanham: Scarecrow, 2007. 167–213.

———. "Rückblick und Ausblick." In *Der radikale Pietismus: Perspektiven der Forschung,* edited by Wolfgang Breul, Marcus Meier und Lothar Vogel, 451–67. Göttingen: Vandenhoeck & Ruprecht, 2010.

Shantz, Douglas H. "'Back to the Sources': Gottfried Arnold, Johann Henrich Reitz, and the Distinctive Program and Practice of Pietist Historical Writing." In *Commoners and Community: Essays in Honour of Werner O. Packull,* edited by C. Arnold Snyder, 75–99. Kitchener: Pandora, 2002.

———. *Between Sardis and Philadelphia: the Life and World of Pietist Court Preacher Conrad Bröske.* Leiden: Brill, 2008.

———. "The Church and the Academy: What an Historian of Christianity can offer the Church of Today." Christian Thought lecture at Christ Church, Elbow Park on February 7, 2011, available at: http://www.ucalgary.ca/christchair/2011_Events.

———. "Communal Diversity in Radical German Pietism: Contrasting Notions of Community in Conrad Bröske and Johann Henrich Reitz." In *Pietism and Community in Europe and North America, 1650–1850,* edited by Jonathan Strom, 65–79. Leiden: Brill, 2010.

———. *Crautwald and Erasmus: A Study in Humanism and Radical Reform in Sixteenth Century Silesia.* Baden-Baden: Valentin Koerner, 1992.

———. "Homeless Minds: the Migration of Radical Pietists, their Writings and Ideas in Early Modern Europe." In *Pietism in Germany and North America 1680–1820,* edited by Jonathan Strom, 85–99. Farnham: Ashgate, 2009.

————. "The Millennial Study Bible of Heinrich Horch: A Case Study in Early Modern Reformed Hermeneutics." In *The Practical Calvinist: Essays in Honor of D. Clair Davis*, edited by Peter Lillback, 391–414. Fearn: Christian Focus, 2002.

————. *A New Introduction to German Pietism: Protestant Renewal at the Dawn of Modern Europe*. Baltimore: Johns Hopkins University Press, 2012.

————. "The Origin of Pietist Notions of New Birth and the New Man: Alchemy and Alchemists in Gottfried Arnold and Johann Henrich Reitz." In *The Pietist Impulse in Christianity*, edited by Christian Collins Winn, 29–41. Eugene, OR: Pickwick, 2011.

————. "Radical Pietist Migrations and Dealings with the Ruling Authorities as seen in the Autobiographies of J.W. Petersen and J.F. Rock." In *Der radikale Pietismus: Perspektiven der Forschung*, edited by Wolfgang Breul, 211–27. Göttingen: Vandenhoeck & Ruprecht, 2010.

————. "The Role of Valentine Crautwald in the Growth of Sixteenth Century Schwenkfeldian Reform: A New Look at the Crautwald-Schwenckfeld Relationship." *Mennonite Quarterly Review* 65:3 (July 1991) 287–307.

————. "A Usable Past: Church Historians as Engaged Scholars who serve the Common Good." *Historical Papers of the Canadian Society of Church History* (2003) 171–92.

Stayer, James M. "The Passing of the Radical Moment in the Radical Reformation," *Mennonite Quarterly Review* 71:1 (January 1997) 147–152.

Strom, Jonathan. "Problems and Promises of Pietism Research." *Church History* (September 2002) 536–54.

van Dülmen, Richard. *Historische Anthropologie, 2. Auflage*. Köln: Böhlau, 2001.

5

Making Historical Theology

MARGARET R. MILES

T HE FIELD OF HISTORY has changed enormously in the last twenty-
five years. In the 1970s feminist historians, such as Joan Kelly, Gerda
Lerner, and Joan Wallach Scott, began to call scholarly attention to historical women's writings. Populist historians, like Carlo Ginzberg and
Robert Darnton, sought evidence of the lives of people who did not write.
More recently, "New Historicists" like Catherine Gallagher and Stephen
Greenblatt are proposing that anecdotes that interrupt or even contradict
the "great story" provide a more honest picture of past people and societies. These suggestions have opened the field of history beyond elitist,
intellectualist history, requiring more of historians than the traditional
skills of languages and hermeneutics. Gradually, historical theology is
beginning to reflect history's changed methods and content.

I can discuss these changes most concretely by reflecting on my own
career as an historical theologian. When I was in graduate school in the
mid-seventies, "Christian thought" was defined as the writings of a few
male theologians who, until the Early Modern period, wrote in Greek
or Latin. Although many historical theologians still focus exclusively on
texts, there is a new interest in historical social arrangements and practices, liturgies, and religious images and music. In *The Word Made Flesh:
A History of Christian Thought* (Blackwell, 2005), I argue that Christian
thought irreducibly includes the music, architecture, and images that
conceptualized and communicated Christianity to historical communities.

Using images and music, not as illustrations but as articulations of Christian thought, makes for a richer, more colorful, more accurate and more persuasive picture of how a small Palestinian sect quickly became a world religion and empire. Declining the unrealistic heroization of Christian leaders by including the "tasteless historical stories" that reveal Christian movements "in real life" contributes both to the liveliness and to the accuracy of Christian history. Moreover, the triumphal "great story" must be modified by acknowledgment of the terrible damage done to individuals and communities. This too is an undeniable feature of the past. A balanced history must insist on *both* the beauty and wealth of Christian thought *and* its abuses.

Perhaps my journey as an historical theologian could best be described as moving from intellectual history to a critical interdisciplinary hermeneutic. By "critical" interpretation I mean placing a text in the fullest possible context, not only the intellectual context of the author's Christian predecessors and cohorts, but also that of the social arrangements that informed his/her assumptions, the institutions that authorized and preserved (usually) his writings, the personal experiences that prompted her/his interests, and other relevant contextual features. In graduate school I was taught to read texts in the best possible light, endeavoring to discern author's intention. My dissertation sought to identify and discuss Augustine's ideas about human bodies from his writings. I argued that Augustine has been egregiously misunderstood and blamed for inserting disdain for bodies and the natural world into Christianity. But a critical interpretation also includes attention not only to the author's *intentions*, but also to the discernible *effects* of his/her assumptions, values, and teachings. I came to critical interpretation gradually. A decade after writing the dissertation, I wrote an article in which I examined Augustine's debate with the Manichaeans over what constitutes the community of human responsibility. Augustine said that the limit of human community is rational minds; the Manichaeans said that it must include all living beings. I suggested that Augustine's victory *effectively* supported the neglect and abuse that has led to the present ecological crisis. My most recent work on Augustine investigates what can be known about his partner of fifteen years (the mother of their son) by reconstructing her social niche as a lower class, (possibly) Christian, North African woman.

It is immediately obvious that my later projects, including *The Word Made Flesh* (described above), required a broader historical skill set than that needed to read Greek and Latin texts and explain what their authors "meant to say." Lacking formal instruction in the histories of gender, music, art, and architecture, it has taken decades for me to acquire even a modicum of ability to work responsibly with social history, gender theory, critical theory, and the history of art, architecture, and music. But then, scholars like to learn; that is why we enter the profession. Historical theologians presently in training will enter a social and intellectual world in which Christianity cannot be considered as a unified and isolated phenomenon. Rather, it must be seen as a cultural product that exists alongside other religions in religiously plural Western societies.

The question faced by institutions that train both teachers and clergy is how to provide an education that prepares students for the complexity of the situations they will face both in scholarship and in religious communities. The ideal curriculum would include more than superficial knowledge of other religions without entailing the sacrifice of breadth and depth in the study of Christianity. Moreover, the knowledge and skills necessary to the inclusion of material historical evidence could consume most of a student's curriculum at the expense of specialized knowledge. Yet I believe that students could receive more interdisciplinary training if the present preoccupation with technology were questioned and alleviated. For example, PowerPoint presentations, seen as indispensable in many fields, severely limit communication of complex and nuanced statements, reducing ideas to their "bottom line." Students accustomed to such presentations will not gain—they will actually lose—the ability to listen carefully to complex arguments. PowerPoint presentations also tend to reduce the lecturer's passion for her subject, focusing instead on the communication of information. The time, money, and energy currently spent by institutions of higher learning on the newest technology could be used for intensive workshops that would expose students to the content, methods, and skills of fields other than their own specialization.

If historical theology is to respond to and incorporate current changes in the broader field of history, the traditional training of future historical theologians must be revised. Presently, students trained as historians focus on social, political, and/or institutional history. Students trained as theologians are taught to read and analyze texts. Historians tend to minimize the social, political, and religious influence of ideas, while theologians ignore economic, social, and institutional circumstances, exaggerating the influence of ideas. A well-trained historical theologian for the future will need both historical and theological skills and sensibilities. It is not impossible to educate students in this way, but it will require faculty historians and theologians who can see beyond field loyalties to recognize the value of committed interdisciplinarity.

There has never been a time richer with possibilities for the making of historical theology. Historical theology, conceptualized as interpreting historical Christian authors in the best possible light, with the goal of defending Christianity from its "cultured despisers," cannot serve either the intellectual or the religious needs of the present or the future. But exploration of the complicated, ambiguous Christian past—the history of Christian *people*, including so-called heretics and dissidents as well as church leaders—is now an exciting challenge. Such a historical theology also provides the basis for the self-critical religious loyalty so needed in the twenty-first century world in which religious passions often fund social injustice, wars, and terrorism. A new history of Christian thought that includes artistic conceptualizations of Christianity can reveal the rich resources accessible to whole communities, sometimes enhancing, sometimes contradicting, but always enriching our recognition of the diverse modes in which people expressed their experience of God's activity in the world of bodies and senses.

6

Eastern Orthodoxy in the Twenty-first Century
Historic Faith, New Circumstances

JAMES R. PAYTON JR.

A s a Protestant and an intellectual historian, I have been teach-ing Eastern Orthodox Christianity for the past twenty-five years. During that time, Orthodoxy has changed dramatically. To be sure, Orthodox teaching and practice have not changed: Orthodoxy claims to stand in the footsteps of the apostles and the Church Fathers, maintaining but not altering the historic faith of Christianity. But with what has trans-pired within the last two decades, Orthodoxy finds itself in a new and unanticipated state of affairs. The new circumstances beckon Orthodoxy to reassess the way it sees itself and its role in the world. That process is underway, but much remains to be done. All this has demanded a sig-nificant reconsideration of and reckoning with Orthodoxy on the part of Western Christendom.

The collapse of the Communist Bloc in 1989 and of the USSR. in 1991 inaugurated a startling new situation for Orthodox Christianity. Prior to those dramatic events, some 80 percent of worldwide Orthodoxy found itself behind the Iron Curtain. Subject to persecution, manipulation, re-striction, and (at best) hostile tolerance, Orthodoxy contributed untold numbers to the list of Christianity's martyrs. Repression took a heavy toll on the churches within the Communist orbit. Through all this, the Orthodox experienced that dross is consumed but gold is refined by fire.

With the end of Communist tyranny, Orthodoxy found itself in a situation she had not experienced in more than half a millennium. With the medieval conquests of the Ottoman Turks, culminating in the conquest of Byzantium itself in 1453, most of Orthodox Christianity fell under Islamic rule. From that point onwards, the only Orthodox communion living in relative freedom was the one in the Russian state. Russian autocracy did not exactly allow Orthodoxy to flourish in its own right, however. Peter the Great and his successors tightly circumscribed the options for the Orthodox Church in the expanding Russian Empire. In the wake of the Bolshevik Revolution, the Russian Orthodox Church experienced far more than the restrictive oversight of civil rulers. After World War II, Communist Russia swallowed up Eastern Europe. The Kremlin was only too happy to encourage its willing subordinates throughout the region to repress the Orthodox (and other) churches.

Now that Communist domination has come to an end, both in Eastern Europe and in Russia, Orthodoxy faces an unfamiliar situation. Orthodox Churches can now worship, catechize, evangelize, engage in diaconal ministries, and speak to societal, moral, and cultural issues with a freedom they have not known for centuries. The new freedom entails new opportunities which Orthodoxy dare not miss. The new situation facing Orthodoxy is much more than simply freedom of initiative. For the first time, Orthodoxy must address the issues raised by modernity, and at the same time must also deal with the challenges of postmodernity. All this is a bit overwhelming, and it is hardly surprising that Orthodoxy is still finding its way through this unfamiliar terrain. But Orthodoxy is rising to the challenge. Of the various ways that this is evident, three strike me as especially significant.

The first of these is "The Basis of the Social Concept of the Russian Orthodox Church," adopted by the Jubilee Bishops' Council in 2000. In this document, for the first time in history, an Orthodox Church has addressed social and cultural issues in contemporary human existence. As the state of Russia moves into an uncertain political future, the Russian Orthodox Church has spoken in its own right, and not perfunctorily as a religious voice for the civil government. This remarkable pronouncement reveals a close understanding of the contemporary challenges it faces, addressing them forthrightly but sensitively from a nuanced and relevant appropriation of the Orthodox tradition. Among the issues it addresses are: "Church and Nation," "Christian Ethics and Secular Law,"

"Labor and its Fruits," "Personal, Family and Public Morality," "Problems of Bio-Ethics," "The Church and Ecological Problems," and "The Church and the Mass Media." The statement shows a vibrant, engaged Orthodoxy interacting with the issues of present-day society. It deserves much more attention than it has received to this point in Western Christendom.

Secondly, the neo-patristic movement within Orthodoxy continues to influence not only Orthodoxy itself, but also Western Christianity. Initiated in the early twentieth century by expatriate Orthodox members living in the West, this return to the Fathers has drawn Orthodoxy to a more conscious awareness and insightful appropriation of the Church Fathers. Indeed, this movement became and continues to be the dominant orientation within Orthodoxy. Within the last twenty-five years its practitioners have shown increasing awareness of the importance of the historical, and not merely the traditional, contexts in which patristic literature must be situated if that literature is to be handled responsibly. This neo-patristic scholarship has challenged some of the received wisdom in Western Christian approaches to patristics, helped spawn and stimulate the surprising development of interest in the field among evangelical scholars in the last twenty-five years, and has offered nuanced support to Orthodoxy's historic perspectives.

Thirdly, during the last twenty-five years Orthodoxy has proven attractive to many within Western Christendom. Books detailing the mass conversion of thousands of conservative Protestants, or the individual stories of clergy and laypersons of various Western Christian backgrounds, plus some with no previous religious connection living within the bounds of historic Western Christendom, offer abundant evidence of Orthodoxy's appeal in the West.[1] Whether that is owing to Orthodoxy's deep roots, its mystical practices, its embrace of symbols and icons, or its appeal to the five senses during the liturgy, Orthodoxy offers what many seem to be seeking in a postmodern world.[2]

Orthodoxy continues to face a considerable challenge. Both for "cradle" Orthodox members and for converts, Orthodoxy needs to make clearer than ever before how Orthodoxy shapes daily life, which St. John Chrysostom called, "the liturgy after the liturgy." This service of

1. See Gillquist, *Becoming Orthodox*; Doulis, ed., *Journeys to Orthodoxy*; Doulis, ed., *Toward the Authentic Church*; Nieuwsma, ed., *Our Hearts' True Home*; Gillquist, ed., *Coming Home*; and Mathewes-Green, *Facing East*.

2. For a discussion of such influences, see Payton, "Drawn Eastward," 53–67.

God outside the walls of the church includes not only acts of mercy and kindness, and much more than prayer and piety. In the past centuries of repression, with most adherents limited to peasant status, little needed to be said beyond what the faithful had long heard and experienced. In the hurly-burly of a globalized village piled high with technologies undreamt of by former generations and awash with opportunities for careers unimagined by their forebears, much more needs to be said. The Orthodox faithful need to see and sense how their Orthodox perspective shapes how they interact with a rapidly changing world. Unless Orthodoxy can demonstrate its relevance to the questions and issues of contemporary life in ways that intersect with the struggles individuals and families face in the present day, the Orthodox faithful will sense a disconnection between their faith and their life. This will undermine Orthodoxy's claim to speak to the whole of human existence. While it is essential that Orthodoxy build responsibly on its rich heritage, simply to appeal to what sufficed in the past as a worldview will no longer serve in the present. The implications of an Orthodox worldview must be spelled out for contemporary life.[3] There are resources for this in the Church Fathers that can be tapped as well as the guidance indicated by the Russian Orthodox Church's "Social Concept" document. If Orthodoxy does not rise to this challenge, it runs the risk of becoming what it has sometimes been accused of but has not yet been—namely, an outmoded relic of the Christian past.

Orthodoxy also confronts Western Christianity with a considerable challenge. Until the dramatic events of the late twentieth century, Western Christianity could largely ignore Eastern Orthodoxy. Seminaries in North America and Europe offered almost no exposure to Orthodox teaching or practice in the training they offered aspiring church leaders and theologians. Historical scholarship about Orthodoxy was notable for its misunderstandings and misrepresentation.[4] Aside from the occasional personal interest in iconography, most laypeople know next to nothing about Orthodoxy. With a vigorous Orthodox presence in the

---

3. For discussion of these concerns, see Payton, "Toward an Orthodox Worldview," 95–106; "Toward an Orthodox Approach to Higher Education," 57–66; and "Toward a Russian Orthodox Worldview," 299–318.

4. As one example, Orthodoxy was often judged to be profoundly shaped by Platonism, even though the history of Orthodox Christianity offers repeated condemnations of Platonic thought. For a fuller discussion, see Payton, *Light from the Christian East*, 19–42, 53–56.

contemporary world, Western Christianity must reckon with its Eastern sibling. Seminary curricula will have to expand to include consideration of Orthodox teaching and practice; theologians will find it necessary to interact with Orthodox perspectives; and the vast literature on personal piety will need to incorporate the contributions made over the centuries by the often neglected but irrepressible Orthodox tradition. This will not be easy for Western Christians, for Orthodoxy approaches Christian faith and practice with different assumptions than Western Christianity does, asks different questions, and consequently ends up with different answers. Incorporating distinctly Orthodox perspectives in such a way that we can appreciate and assimilate them enough to interact with them will be a steep learning curve for Western Christianity. The task must be faced; for those who succeed, the rewards will be rich.

I have found it so myself. As I reflect on the ways my mind has changed over the last twenty-five years, I trace much of my development to the influence of Orthodoxy. As an intellectual historian, inhabiting and incorporating the perspectives of those I am studying is part of my task. The variations within Western Christian thought, interesting in their own right, offer rooms in which the furniture was arranged differently but almost everything was familiar; my labors in this arena stimulated deeper insights but little in the way of perspectival transformation. Attempting to get inside the mindset of Orthodoxy, however, has required me to enter terrain I thought I knew but which I was now seeing from new vantage points. I have become much more appreciative of mystery and mysticism, and much less confident of the Christian mind's ability to discover and propositionally articulate truth. Orthodoxy has helped me see that answers are less important than openness, that wonder trumps understanding, and that faithfulness to tradition is better than originality in speculation.

Bibliography

Doulis, Thomas, ed. *Journeys to Orthodoxy: A Collection of Essays by Converts to Orthodox Christianity.* Minneapolis: Light & Life, 1986.

———, ed. *Toward the Authentic Church: Orthodox Christians Discuss Their Conversion.* Minneapolis: Light & Life, 1996.

Gillquist, Peter E. *Becoming Orthodox: A Journey to the Ancient Christian Faith.* Brentwood, TN: Wolgemuth & Hyatt, 1989.

———, ed. *Coming Home: Why Protestant Clergy are Becoming Orthodox.* Ben Lomond, CA: Conciliar Press, 1992.

Mathewes-Green, Frederica. *Facing East: A Pilgrim's Journey into the Mysteries of Orthodoxy*. San Francisco: HarperSanFrancisco, 1997.

Nieuwsma, Virginia, ed. *Our Hearts' True Home: Fourteen Warm, Inspiring Stories of Women Discovering the Ancient Christian Faith*. Ben Lomond, CA: Conciliar, 1996.

Payton, James R. Jr. "Drawn Eastward: The Attraction of Eastern Orthodoxy for Western Christians." In *The Practical Calvinist: An Introduction to the Presbyterian and Reformed Heritage*, edited by Peter Lillback, 53–67. Fearn, Ross-shire, Great Britain: Christian Focus, 2002.

———. *Light from the Christian East: An Introduction to the Orthodox Tradition*. Downers Grove, IL: IVP Academic, 2007.

———. "Toward an Orthodox Approach to Higher Education in 21st-Century Russia." In Высшее Образование в Контексте Русской Культуры XXI Века: Христианская, edited by Natalia Pecherskaya, 57–66. St. Petersburg: St. Petersburg School of Religion and Philosophy, 2000.

———. "Toward an Orthodox Worldview for the Third Millennium" (in Russian: "Третьему тыся елетию – православиое мировоззрение"). In *Man and the Christian Worldview: Conceptualizing the Normal and Abnormal in Medicine, Science and Society* (in Russian: Человек и христианское мировоззрение: Понятия "норма" и "отклонение от нормы в меди ине, науке и обществе), edited by Georges Carillet, 95–106. Simferopol, Ukraine, 1999.

———. "Toward a Russian Orthodox Worldview for Post-Soviet Society." In *Orthodox Christianity and Contemporary Europe*, edited by Jonathan Sutton and Wil van den Bercken, *Eastern Christian Studies* 3, 299–318. Leuven: Peeters, 2003.

7

Religion's Return

LAMIN SANNEH

IN 1966, NOT ONE contribution to the three *New Ways in History* issues discussed religion as an element in historiography. But it was clear by the end of the twentieth century that neither the rapid collapse of the colonial empires nor the surge of nationalist movements had been the decisive setback for religion that everyone believed. A sign of the resulting consternation came in the form of an invitation I received from the Russian Academy of Sciences, in the early 1990s, to a conference on "The Problem of Religion." The title was proof that the organizers were in what classical Islam would call "a state between two states" (manzila bayna manzilatayn), neither persuaded of the truth of religion nor completely willing to dismiss the fact of its return. But standing amid the debris of the collapse of the Soviet Empire, the organizers were clearly disconcerted by the improbable reality of religion having made a comeback against considerable odds.

The facts seem impressive enough. The total world population in 1900 was 1.6 billion; Muslims numbered just below 200 million, Christians 558 million. In 1970, total world population was 3.7 billion with a Muslim population of 549 million, and Christians at 1.2 billion. In 2006, out of a world population of over 6 billion, Muslims numbered 1.3 billion, and Christians 2.15 billion, including 1.3 billion Catholics. Buddhists and Hindus remained stable, with natural increase rather than conversion accounting for growth. The statistics for one year at the early phase of the return of religion, in the 1990s, showed that twenty-five million people changed their religious affiliation, of whom eighteen million were converts to Christianity and seven million defectors from Christianity to other religions, making Christianity the most active and most diverse religious frontier in the world. Religious expansion in Africa entered its most vigorous phase, following the end of colonial and missionary hegemony. In 1900, the Muslim population of Africa was 34.5 million, compared to roughly 8.7 million Christians, a ratio of 4:1. By 1985, Christians outnumbered Muslims there for the first time. Projections for 2025 are 600 million Christians and 519 million Muslims. The Christian figures represent a continental shift of historic proportions. Europe (including Russia) and North America in 1900 had 82 percent of the world's Christians. By 2005 Europe and North America's 758 million Christians were far fewer than the 1.4 billion for the rest of the world—a decline to thirty-five percent of the total.

Charismatic Christianity has been the engine of expansion and is largely responsible for the dramatic shift in the religion's center of gravity. In 1900 there were 981,000 Pentecostals; in 1970 over seventy-two million; and in 2005 nearly 590 million. Projections estimate that by 2025 Pentecostals/Charismatics will number nearly 800 million. Now exploding in Brazil, Mexico, Russia, and China, Pentecostals could in time become the most widespread Christian group, with as yet unquantifiable effects on mainline churches and on global politics. As David Martin has shown, in Latin America the prominence of women Pentecostals has affected the machismo culture of the traditional military-style establishment.

Female politicians are accordingly drawing on the energy of the Pentecostal movement to effect social change. Pentecostalism is also riding the wave of Latin American demographic flows, including immigration into the United States. The vast majority of Latino immigrants to the US are Pentecostal, with a strong Catholic overlay. Their convergence with US evangelical groups, such as the Christian Coalition, health-and-wealth adherents of the prosperity gospel, and the burgeoning mega-church phenomenon have raised the political stakes in mainstream America and impacted on the evangelical missionary agenda. The resurgence has coincided with radical Islam to upset calculations on a different front. Philip Jenkins, for example, sees a double jeopardy, with the onset of talk about new Crusades and a cultural clash with liberal Christianity. The spread of radical Islam across national boundaries has included areas of advantage

and mobility in the West, defying arguments adducing poverty, depriva-
tion, geographical alienation, and lack of access as causal factors.

Many observers discern a link between, on the one hand, intolerance and strife, and, on the other, resurgence and radicalism. Some see a
threat to civilization in the return of religion, while still others regard the
ferment as evidence of the ravages of rampant secularization in centers
of traditional religious life, confident that the drama of radicalism is but
the last gasp of religion. Max Weber observed that Islam is not a religion
of salvation, and so dropped it in his theory of modernization. Yet he did
not on that account say Islam had no future, which suggests accelerat-
ing divergence from secularization. Thus, these scenarios of intolerance,
conflict, and rampant secularism are united in the view that religion is
the problem.

At a crucial crossroad in relations with Islam, the West has been
weighing its options, as Pope Benedict XVI's Regensburg comments show.
The issue is not new, though the scale and the consequences of misunder-
standing are today far more serious. When in the 1740s Frederick the
Great of Prussia formed the first lancer unit from Tartar Muslim deserters
from the Russian army, with some 1,000 Muslim soldiers serving, he did
so from his commitment to Enlightenment ideals of religious toleration.
Frederick allocated a prayer room for the use of Muslim troops—but on
Sundays! Less clumsily, he later had a Muslim cemetery built in Berlin.
Through ups and downs, the Muslim community survived in Germany
and after 1951 it created an organization, the *Geistliche Verwaltung der
Muslimflüchtlinge in der Bundesrepublik Deutschland*, to administer the
affairs of Muslim refugees in Germany.

The Muslim prescription of the State as upholder of revealed law
constitutes a major obstacle in relations with the West. It forces such
questions as: Can radical outbreaks in the West be contained without a
fundamental diminution of human rights and a breach of the secular wall
of separation? Can the heartland of Islam be reformed from the margins
of the West? What role can the West play in the liberal reconstruction
of religion globally? After the bombings in Madrid and London, Europe
is on the defensive, with some Euro-secularists resolved to deploy the
European Union as a barrier against the return of religion, while, somewhat maladroitly, backing multiculturalism.

The religious awakening appears to have spread to China—at first
a surprising development, given the country's thoroughgoing program

of eradication of religion. In 1949, the year of the triumph of Mao Tse-tung's Marxist-Leninist Revolution, there were about 4 million Christians in China: three million Catholics and one million Protestants. Mao's antagonism to foreign agents did not spare Christianity, except briefly in the Hundred Flowers Period, which opened in May 1956. But a year later, in June 1957, that leniency was revoked as the Great Leap Forward campaign was launched. Buddhist, Christian, and other religious institutions were hit by new restrictions, with religious leaders reduced to playing cat's cradle with the overweening thicket of official decrees and measures directed at them. In the Great Proletarian Cultural Revolution, starting in 1966, seventeen million urban youths were deployed as Red Guards to stalk the countryside. They wreaked widespread havoc, sacking ancient Buddhist temples and Christian churches. Alarmed by the excesses of the Red Guards, Mao tried in vain in 1968 to rein them in. It took until 1976 to quell the uprising, by which time faith communities had retreated to the nether world of secret meetings, house worship, home Bible study, and nocturnal assemblies.

Meanwhile, many Western observers predicted the end of religion, saying nothing was more apt for China than for Christianity's God to be the one "who knew the way of the grave." China's Marxist success achieved the goals for which missions had striven in vain. Joseph Needham, the great authority on Chinese civilization, declared that China had accepted the spirit of Christ from another source, Marxism, and that "China is the only truly Christian country in the world in the present day, in spite of its absolute rejection of all religion." Weaned from faith in false absolutes and fortified with the aura of proletarian liberation, true believers must henceforth march to the chant of "What a comrade we have in Jesus!" The fiery chariot of Mao's Nationalist Revolution had overtaken the juggernaut of nineteenth-century missionary domination of China and would crush it.

Amid these galloping predictions, it did not occur to observers that religion might have a future. Official Chinese vacillations about religion, however, began to show cracks. As Party cadres became less starry-eyed about Mao, they were less doom-laden about religion. At the beginning of the Government's liberalization program in 1978, Deng Xiaoping announced an easing of restrictions on religion. The following year, to universal astonishment, Deng roused the Chinese Communist Party to "seek truth from facts": code for deserting Mao's legacy and opening the way for the return of religion.

Churches bounced back as the Government made good its promises of restitution for properties seized and wrongs committed. In the revised Constitution of 1982 religious rights were reaffirmed under article 36, followed by the publication of Document 19, concerning religious policy in China. The document essentially repudiated as a "leftist mistake" the excesses of the Great Cultural Revolution against religion. It did not take long for high-ranking officials to declare open sympathy for religion and by 1986 the thaw had created a stream of official endorsements, including subsidies for church reconstruction projects. According to a report in 2003, in addition to the 45,000 registered churches in existence, between 30,000 and 40,000 groups affiliated with the state-controlled Protestant community were still waiting for their turn to register. External pressure on the church combined with internal struggles between the "open" registered church as officially sanctioned and the unregistered "underground" church, under papal jurisdiction, to complicate the whole question of the return of religion in China.

There was expansion, but it carried the double burden of secret believers assembling in unauthorized places and of officially co-opted members in licensed churches. In *Global Catholicism: Portrait of a World Church*, the number of Catholics in mainland China is put at 7.5 million.

A generation of educated senior Chinese that grew up under the "open door" policy of Deng has been influenced by works such as R. H. Tawney's *Religion and the Rise of Capitalism*, resulting in revisionist changes in the ideology of a command economy. Similarly, the one-child policy of the Government has altered the basic family structure and is fueling a culture of individualism, which resonates with the message of individual salvation. Jiang Zeming, the Communist Party leader, is reported to have responded to a question in early 2002 about the kind of legacy he would like to leave in China, by saying he would propose to make Christianity the official religion of China, suggesting, perhaps in jest, replacing ideology with a faith-based order.

In an age of globalization, the return of religion and its radical strains has superseded the center-periphery historiography of postcolonial discourse. When he reflected on the crisis of the post-war world, Arnold Toynbee argued that the West could not wait for History, like an eighteenth-century Prussian drill-sergeant, to take it by the scruff of the neck and twist its head straight for it. Cleanthes once prayed to Zeus and Fate for grace to follow their lead on his own will without flinching, and one could do worse with respect to a religiously awakened world. One can explain away or even quibble with the resurgence, but one can scarcely deny that the ground has shifted and that the direction of historical inquiry must follow.

PART 2

Philosophical and Theological Issues

8

The Christian Philosopher Today

TERENCE PENELHUM

I WRITE THIS AS AN analytical philosopher with a special concern for the philosophy of religion. There has been a resurgence of activity in this field in recent years, much of it due to a renewed confidence among Christian philosophers, who used to feel a neglected minority in their profession. I think that this confidence, in spite of the excellent work it has produced, should be tempered by a recognition of some cultural realities that cannot be ignored. I shall try to explain my anxieties and suggest what issues Christian thinkers should address in our day.

First, however, a brief look at the recent past and the present. Analytical philosophy, as it developed in the first half of the twentieth century, was a much-needed return to the clarity and rigor characteristic of English-speaking philosophical thought in the eighteenth century, with the added impetus of a new sophistication in logic and the philosophy of language. It has brought us a very high level of philosophical discourse, notable for its clarity and exactitude. In its earlier years it also had built into it a deep suspicion of speculation and system, a suspicion that derived from the English empiricist tradition. For many of the disciples of Russell and Moore and Wittgenstein, and the influential "ordinary-language" philosophers of mid-century Oxford, this suspicion extended to the claims of the Christian religion, claims which remind us of supersensible realities that we ignore to our cost. As a result, analytical philosophy of religion of that era, when my philosophical career began, was obsessed by problems of the coherence and meaningfulness, rather than the truth, of these claims. Even some who thought themselves to be defenders of the faith were inclined to defend it by interpreting it in ways that minimized its supernatural teachings, or gave them a "non-realist" interpretation that reduced Christian proclamations to versions of a secular religiosity concerned merely with a liberated mode of living in this world.

In those years I was outside the church, but became ill at ease both with these skeptical criticisms of it and with these disingenuous forms of defense.[1] I took the neutral position that religious doctrines could be defended against charges of incoherence and meaninglessness, but that the philosopher is not able to show that they are true, even though adherence to them is a rational state of mind.

I subsequently abandoned the cozy neutrality of this position and rejoined the Anglican Communion in which I had been brought up. I ought, therefore, to be unambiguously pleased at the fact that analytical philosophy of religion has moved on from its mid-century phase to another, in which the most well-known figures are Christian thinkers who use the sophisticated tools of this tradition in the service of the faith (though not, of course, without vigorous opposition from philosophical skeptics, who have the same tools to use!). But I have more mixed feelings than one might expect.

The three most famous figures in Christian philosophy of religion in the last two decades have been Richard Swinburne in Oxford, and William Alston and Alvin Plantinga in the United States. All three are thinkers of truly formidable powers and achievement. I will first try to say a little, within the limits of this short piece, about their work. Swinburne is the outstanding natural theologian of our time: he argues that the claims of the Christian faith can commend themselves to our natural reason, and can be shown to have a high degree of probability by standards accepted in natural science.[2] Alston and Plantinga, in contrast, have developed a position often referred to as "Reformed Epistemology": they maintain that those who hear and accept the proclamation of the faith solely on the basis of its effect on their inner experience cannot be faulted if they

1. For what it is worth, my reflections of that time are to be found in two works, *Religion and Rationality* and *Problems of Religious Knowledge*.

2. Richard Swinburne has been immensely productive, but I would personally select the following works: Swinburne, *The Existence of God*; Swinburne, *Responsibility and Atonement*; and Swinburne, *The Resurrection of God Incarnate*.

have not also agreed to it on the basis of the external grounds that natural theology offers.[3] My sympathies are on the whole more with Swinburne, though the differences between these thinkers are perhaps less than they seem on the surface when we examine the details of their arguments. What they have jointly bequeathed to the Christian philosophers who follow them is a renewed confidence in the intellectual viability of the Christian message in an era dominated by a scientific culture.

This legacy is immensely to be welcomed, but my welcome of it is modified by my concern for the gravity of the challenges that Christian belief faces in our day. These challenges are addressed by all three and by those whom they have influenced. But the task of meeting them is greater than they seem to recognize and puts in question the theological conservatism that most Christian philosophers today find congenial. This has led to much work on traditional perplexities in Christian theism, such as the compatibility of divine foreknowledge and human freedom, the relationship between eternity and time, and the doctrine of impassibility. I find these as intriguing as anyone, but the new scholasticism that the debates about them have produced seems to me, if not anachronistic, then at least less urgent and religiously nourishing than the pursuit of answers to the challenges that our culture presents today to the Christian tradition. I single out three such challenges, all of which seem to me to put Christian conservatism at risk.

The first is the challenge of the world's religious ambiguity. To say that the world is religiously ambiguous is to say that it is a world in which it is rational both to adopt a religious interpretation of it and to adopt a wholly naturalistic one. A naturalistic world view is one in which all available explanations are scientific ones, and no recourse is ever felt to be necessary to supernatural or transcendent realities. To say such a world view is rational is not of course to say it is true, but merely to recognize that those (and they are many) who feel compelled to adopt it, or who have absorbed it from the culture in which we move, can point with truth to the immense advances in scientific understanding of our world and of ourselves in the last four centuries and can maintain without absurdity that religious interpretations of our world are unnecessary. Naturalism has its gaps and its puzzles; but these are matched by comparable puzzles and difficulties in religious understandings of the

3. William Alston's best-known apologetic work is *Perceiving God*. Alvin Plantinga's most famous work is *Warranted Christian Belief.*

world. Each side in this confrontation has resources to draw upon to explain why the other is unable to perceive the obvious truth of its own view. Our scientific culture has generated an ideological stalemate, and reflective persons confronted with it cannot be faulted for facing it with bewilderment and indecision. I think that lack of belief is often non-culpable. (In theological terms, they are not in every case to be blamed for the fact that to them, God may be hidden).

If faith and doubt are both rational states of mind in such an ambiguous world, two things follow for the Christian philosopher. The first is that we must come to an understanding of faith that recognizes the difficulty in Paul's claim in Romans 1 that unbelief is due to willfulness in the face of the obvious. The second is that the believing philosopher must seek always for the argument that *disambiguates* our world—that shows, after all, that it is not rational to disbelieve, and that at some level Paul was right. This was always the traditional task of natural theology. Hence my preference for the apologetic strategy of Swinburne, even though I remain unsure of his success in demonstrating that the probability of Christian claims is as high as he maintains.

The second challenge is that of religious diversity. While it is indeed rational, as the Reformed epistemologist says it is, for the Christian to say Yes to the gospel proclamation, the same seems to be true of the Muslim or the Hindu or the Buddhist who respond affirmatively to their prophet or sage. The ambiguity that seems to pervade the confrontation of the Christian and the naturalist seems also to exist in the relationship between one supposedly saving faith and another. Here too, each has resources within it to explain why the adherents of the other reject it. The plurality of faiths has always been a feature of the world. But our age has given it new urgency by making us familiar, both in the realm of scholarship and in daily living, with the realities of this diversity and with the depth of the spiritual lives of those who follow other traditions. If disambiguation here is possible for the Christian philosopher, it will be through the subtle and demanding work of the emerging study of comparative philosophy of religion, where one asks how far, and in what ways, the world faiths agree, how far and in what ways they are really at odds, and what resources each possesses to deal with the deflationary arguments of the naturalist. These are hard tasks with which Christian philosophers have begun to engage, but we need to do far more. Does the fact of the plurality of faiths put in question the truth of one's own? If not, are the others to be seen as competitive attempts to state the one truth, or as failed attempts to see what one sees oneself? Is salvation possible only for the Christian, or also for them? If the latter, on what basis?[4]

The third challenge I would especially emphasize is one that has been with us for some time, but seems to me to need deeper reflection than it has usually been given. One of the reasons for the power of naturalism in our time is the scientific entrenchment of evolutionary biology. The revolutionary discoveries of Darwin and his successors force us to rethink our understanding of creation and our place in it, not merely to concede that the Genesis creation story is not literally true. Evolutionary biology forces us to recognize that suffering and death have been integral to the history of all sentient life, and to acknowledge that the flaws in our natures that need redemption are not the result of a historical fall from a perfect paradisaical state. It also makes clear to us that we have a deep kinship with other species and that even if humans have a unique calling in the natural world, we are a part of that world and have neighborly duties to other species. The Christian tradition must therefore engage positively with the environmental movement in a way it hitherto has not. We must try to discover what renewed understanding of the traditional concepts of the fall and the kingdom of God our knowledge of our origins makes necessary.[5]

These issues are not the only ones the Christian philosopher faces; but they seem to me especially grave in our time. Yet, as so often before in history, those of us who find ourselves confronted with them also find ourselves the providential inheritors of a tradition that should enable us to address them in a way that is equal to the demands they pose.

4. Two works that make the challenges of ambiguity and diversity clearer than any others I know are Hick, *An Interpretation of Religion* and McKim, *Religious Ambiguity and Religious Diversity*. The recent work of Keith Ward, who is also a contributor to this volume, is an exemplary expression of a proper Christian attitude to other world faiths.

5. An excellent start for reflection on these matters is to be found in Ruse, *Can a Darwinian be a Christian?*

Bibliography

Alston, William. *Perceiving God*. Ithaca: Cornell University Press, 1991.

Hick, John. *An Interpretation of Religion*. New Haven: Yale University Press, 2005.

McKim, Robert. *Religious Ambiguity and Religious Diversity*. New York: Oxford University Press, 2001.

Penelhum, Terence. *Problems of Religious Knowledge*. Macmillan, London, 1971.

——. *Religion and Rationality*. Random House, New York, 1971.

Plantinga, Alvin. *Warranted Christian Belief*. New York: Oxford University Press, 2000.

Ruse, Michael. *Can a Darwinian be a Christian?* Cambridge: Cambridge University Press, 2001.

Swinburne, Richard. *The Existence of God*. Oxford: Clarendon Press, 1991.

——. *Responsibility and Atonement*. Oxford: Clarendon Press, 1989.

——. *The Resurrection of God Incarnate*. Oxford: Clarendon Press, 2003.

9

Christian Thought

Agenda for the Future

CLARK H. PINNOCK[†]

1. "How has Christian Thought in my field changed in the last twenty-five years?"

ONE WAY IN WHICH my field has changed relates to ecclesial demographics. There is now much more significant participation of evangelical scholars in teaching, research, and publication. Over a decade and a half ago (in 1994), historian Mark Noll wrote about "the scandal of the evangelical mind." The scandal, as he saw it, was that there is no evangelical mind to speak of, even though there had been such intelligence in earlier manifestations of the evangelical movement. Ironically, his book displayed the very kind of quality scholarship he was seeking. Noll proved to be a harbinger of an increase in serious evangelical scholarship; it did not take very long after the book appeared for the scandal to lessen. Evangelical scholarship—biblical, historical, dogmatic, scientific, and philosophical—has increased in quantity and in quality in the last two decades.

To get a feeling for this change, consider facts: over two thousand scholars belong to the (conservative) Evangelical Theological Society. Hundreds of more progressive evangelicals attend sections of interest at the American Academy of Religion and the Society of Biblical Literature. Hundreds more gather at the Institute of Biblical Research, at the Society of Christian Philosophers, at the Wesleyan Theological Society, and at the Society of Pentecostal Studies, just to mention a few academic societies. The demographic surge is supported by large publishing firms, by academic conferences held at large interdenominational and denominational colleges and seminaries, and thousands of keen students are encouraged to study theology by parachurch ministries such as the InterVarsity Christian Fellowship, Campus Crusade for Christ, Young Life, and Youth for Christ.

We have seen the rise to prominence of new and impressive voices in the evangelical / Pentecostal surge in North America, such as Miroslav Volf, Richard Hays, N. T. Wright, Veli-Matti Karkkainen, Alister McGrath, Alan G. Padgett, etc. The original post-fundamentalist movement, which spawned this present evangelical awakening, was initially headed up by theologians such as Carl F. H. Henry, E. J. Carnell, and Bernard Ramm. It is now populated by the second and third generation of scholars who are more numerous and better equipped to make challenging contributions to the theological discussions.

2. "How has my mind changed?"

My mind has changed theologically too, but not in isolation from larger movements in the evangelical coalition. One such grouping is now being called "post conservative evangelical" by Roger E. Olson and "the evangelical left" by Millard J. Erickson. Such labels are seldom satisfactory but they can alert us to some new thing that is stirring. The fact is that I do not consider myself "post conservative" and am certainly not "a man of the left" but, nevertheless, what they are seeing is worth comment. Critics point to a disparate group of "progressive" evangelical scholars who think "outside the box" and take greater risks in efforts to improve interpretations and reform the church's confession. Such evangelicals think of theology in terms of pilgrimage and of themselves as pioneers rather than guardians of orthodoxy. They desire "a generous orthodoxy" that avoids both narrow dogmatism and liberal relativism. They see value in constructive engagement and dialogue with our postmodern culture. They dislike doing conservative theology in "a high modern" way and are even prepared to question dogmas if they are just held for tradition's sake.

The term "post conservative" does not signify "anti-conservative" but the desire to move beyond the category of conservatism, insofar as it tends to tie us to the old and bad fundamentalist habits. They recognize that received tradition can be a form of bondage that hinders creativity and innovation. But they themselves honor God's word and respect the great theological consensus and are in that respect conservative also. So the pilgrimage continues and the work is still unfinished.

What places post conservative evangelicals in this camp is not any specific theme (their interests vary). What characterizes them and makes them fruitful is the richness of their method. Evangelical theologians have often followed the path of biblical summation, which renders their work superficial. But these fellows are self-critical and they recognize that all theological work is historically embedded. They appeal to Scripture, taking account of sound biblical scholarship, and they interpret it within a trilateral hermeneutic of tradition, reason, and experience. They also take account of mystery and know the limitations of their own under-standing. They see theology as a mystery-discerning enterprise; they do not approach the issues as problems needing to be solved but as mysteries to be discerned. My point is just to say that evangelical scholarship these days is much better than it used to be and there is more of it.

As for specific changes in my own thinking, mainly I went through a paradigm shift from theological determinism in the direction of celebrat-ing God's unbounding love. This Wesleyan turn has characterized most of my work and it shows up in what is called "the openness of God," which is a theology of divine love. In this model, God is not remote, closed off, and self-contained but rather is open to the world and to the future. It could be called "panentheism" because it embraces an ontological closeness un-common in Western theism. It imagines God holding the world "within himself" and relating to it "intimately and continually." God has a passion for freely chosen relationships of love and God's knowledge of this truly temporal world is both definite in regard to certainties and indefinite as regards to uncertainties. He knows what will be and what might be.

3. "What issues face Christian scholars today?"

One of these issues surely has to do with the dialogue between science and the doctrine of creation and the light which can be shed on it by ref-erencing the creator and creating Spirit of God. We need a theology of the ecology of the life-giving Spirit, first, because the doctrine of creation has been marginalized and subordinated to the doctrine of salvation. Being human, we naturally think anthropocentrically and view things from a human perspective, while neglecting the non-human. Secondly, the same impulse drives us to see the Spirit as an ornament of piety, not as the almighty power that launched the whole universe. We tend to neglect the cosmic dimensions of the Spirit's work who is, after all, at work everywhere in this world.

Modern science has given us a twenty-first century "creation story" in blazing technicolor. A stunning world has been opened up in the big bang cosmology and in evolutionary biology. All of us were made literally out of star dust. Every atom in my body originated in the furnace of the stars. It is high time to develop a theology of the creator Spirit that does not begin with Pentecost but with the origin of the universe. This is the larger story of the Spirit's working in creation literally from the first few seconds to a consideration of the Spirit's work among human beings that in turn culminates in the Christ event. The creator Spirit breathes life into the universe of creatures. The evolving universe with its remarkable features can only exist because of her empowering presence. She breathes fire into the equations and imparts life into the exuberant and interrelated community of living things. Spirit is the power that empowers a world in process and not only in predetermined ways but in dynamic and open ways. She is the immanent source of the new in an emergent universe. The Spirit embraces individuals and enables them to exist in an interrelated world of creatures, bringing them into the circle of divine love and leading them to their completion in God. Even when it comes to the dark side, to the realities of pain, predation, and death, the Spirit is the midwife in the midst of it all bringing about the birth of the new.

4. "What questions or problems would you list under the heading, "Agenda for the Future"?

Following from a theology of the creator Spirit, one detects the possibility of "a trinitarian panentheism." Like the openness model, God is not remote and distant but encloses the universe within the life of the Trinity. God and world exist in close inter-relationships and interactions. Creatures exist within the communion of three persons. In this picture, God is "other" than creatures but also interior to them. Transcendence and immanence are not polar opposites but are connected. Only because God is transcendent can God be immanent in creatures in the way no creature can be. Thus God can be closer to us than we are to ourselves, the One "in whom we live and move and have our being" (Acts 17:28). The Spirit can be understood as the One who makes space in the life of the three person God for a universe of entities both to be and to become and who empowers the process of an emergent life-bearing universe. God is not an isolated static ruling monarch but a relational dynamic tri-personal mystery of love fostering the dignity and freedom of the creatures. Through a free act of divine self-limitation, God entered into a relationship that affects both God and the creature. Some find shocking the idea that God can be affected by an event in the world. They worry lest God should be different from the God as he was before it. But God's essential nature would not be affected. Only his experiences would be affected. Perhaps a deity who exists apart from creation might be unaffected by it, but surely a God who holds the world within himself cannot view creation dispassionately. God may be different because you prayed, but that does not make God ontologically dependent on you. We must rid ourselves of the idea that any real relationship to the world would make God dependent on the world. Not so! He is not an absolute ruler living beyond the stars. Our God is in this world and this world is in God. It is a relationship not of weakness and dependence in any bad sense, but one of strength and freedom. He is with us in the midst of life. The God of the Bible does not exist in isolation from the world but acts in the midst of the world, and can be understood better in this way than in the light of Hellenistic and Medieval presuppositions.

10

Process Theology in Process

JOHN B. COBB JR.

PROCESS THEOLOGY CAN BE identified with a particular set of beliefs about God and the world. These have been derived from Alfred North Whitehead and Charles Hartshorne. The majority of those who today consider themselves process theologians subscribe to at least some of these beliefs. But process theology arose in a context that preceded the influence of these two philosophers and has played a more complex role than simply repeating these doctrines. Its emphasis that all things are in process works against understanding itself in an essentialist way. In this essay I will try to communicate its changing nature and roles.

When I was a graduate student in the years after World War II, what I understood to be mainstream Protestant theology was non-denominational and revisionist. We were all schooled in the German nineteenth–century tradition: Kant, Hegel, Schleiermacher, Feuerbach, Marx, Strauss, Ritschl, Harnack, Schweitzer, Barth, Brunner, Tillich, and Bultmann. Some knew this history in far more detail than others. Some were also interested, as was I, in the English-language tradition, especially pragmatism and naturalism of various sorts. We were aware also of the kind of ecumenical work done by the World Council of Churches, but that seemed somewhat specialized and not responsive to the intellectual problems posed by the modern world. Of course, we knew that there were those who worked intensively in their own denominational fields. We thought of Roman Catholic theology chiefly in that context although a few Catholics, such as Gilson and Maritain, were contributors to the broader conversation. We knew that there were some very conservative scholars who engaged in defending and rearticulating ideas that were little influenced by the figures I have cited, but precisely because they did not wrestle with what we considered the critical theoretical issues, we did not take them seriously.

We were all revisionists because we assumed, first, that the Christian tradition was important and, second, that only as it dealt with the problems of modern thought could it play a responsible role in the world in which we found ourselves. Some found a more or less Barthian return to the insights of the Reformers the way forward, but in those years more of us felt that Barth's way of bypassing the issues of the rational plausibility and credibility of traditional affirmations was not sustainable. Bultmann and Tillich, and, on the American scene, the Niebuhr brothers set the tone for much of the discussion. At the University of Chicago Divinity School, which I attended, American traditions of empiricism, pragmatism, and naturalism dominated, although we recognized that this separated us from the dominant currents of the mainstream. The neo-naturalist, Henry Nelson Wieman, was an influential figure there, whereas in the national mainstream he was not taken seriously.

In that context, I was one of a number of Chicago students who encountered the speculative, cosmological philosophy of Whitehead and the philosophical theology that it supported. Daniel Day Williams showed that from this perspective one could enter the mainstream discussion effectively and contribute significantly to it. I felt that Whitehead could also connect us with the natural sciences.

Nevertheless, speculative philosophy was largely regarded as unacceptable in the aftermath of Hume and Kant. Analytic philosophy, phenomenology, and existentialism were respectable and the latter played an especially large role in theology. The death of metaphysics in general, and of speculative philosophy in particular, was affirmed by both theologians and philosophers. Hence, what came to be known as process theology functioned at the fringe of mainstream theology. In general, in those days, process theology was viewed as the extreme left-wing of revisionist theology. This is one of the respects in which the context changed dramatically. In the mid-sixties, mainstream attention focused on the "death-of-God" theology. Each of the theologians in that movement was an independent thinker with distinctive reasons for challenging the "God-talk" that most revisionist theologians had previously agreed was central to the theological task. But their collective work resulted in the widespread abandonment of that language or at least the abandonment of the idea that it had any referential character.

With this shift of question, from how to speak realistically of God to whether to speak at all of a real God, process theology became conservative. The bright young thinkers who had previously gone into revisionist theology began to go instead into religious studies, but most process thinkers in the tradition of Whitehead and Hartshorne continued to do theology in service to the church, whether the church was interested or not. The focus of religious studies was not upon what scholars and others should themselves believe but the study of the phenomenon of religion in all its dimensions and relationships. They might study how people in various cultures have thought about God but not with the idea of coming to any normative judgment as to how today one *should* think of God. Process theology, however, continued to speak of God realistically, judging that how we think of God and what God is actually doing are matters of great human importance, and of special importance for the church.

In the seventies, theological excitement was directed to the various liberation theologies. These theologies proposed that the conversation partner of theology should be the social sciences rather than philosophy. They showed that revisionist theology, of which process theology was a part, belonged to the Euro-American university and reflected its bourgeois elitism or its racism and patriarchalism. The issues that have preoccupied liberation theologies have not usually included the ones dealt with by speculative philosophy.

Despite this fact, process theologians generally welcomed these developments. Even if the interests of liberationists did not include all of our interests, our interests did include theirs. Process theology, in part, grew out of the social gospel and its adherents recognized the validity and importance of what liberationists were saying. From the beginning there was some overlap between the process community and the various liberation movements.

In the case of Black theology, Henry Young was for some time a lonely figure in advocating Black attention to process theology. He was joined by Theodore Walker and now Karen Baker Fletcher, Monica Coleman, and Thandeka among others. The assumption that process thought is irrelevant to the needs of Blacks has largely been overcome. Meanwhile an African archbishop is establishing two centers for process theology in Congo, believing that the communication of Catholic theology in process terms will make a better connection with traditional African thought.

For some years the only visible overlap of Latin American liberation theology and process theology was George Pixley. Today, partly because of Pixley's work, interest among the Latin American heirs of liberation theology in process thought has grown.

Centers are being developed in Nicaragua and Brazil. The connection between process and feminist thought is more integral. Valerie Saiving's article is considered the initiation of feminist theology. She was working in the process tradition. Through the years eco-feminism and process thought have overlapped extensively in content as well as in adherents. The connection was confirmed recently when a leading feminist religious writer, Carol Christ, who had not studied process thought in school, discovered her affinities to this tradition and wrote a book, *She Who Changes*, that commends the thought of Charles Hartshorne to her followers.

Process thought gave some leadership in the emerging ecological movement, especially in the churches. Charles Birch, an Australian biologist and process theologian, gave the major address at the World Council of Churches, when it added "sustainability" to its goal of "just and participatory societies." My little book *Is It Too Late?*[1] has been kept in print by *Environmental Ethics* and credited by it as the first book on environmental ethics. Ian Barbour, a physicist and process theologian, has given major leadership in the field of science and religion and specifically in ecological thinking.

One development of the past few decades seemed on the surface to be peculiarly at odds with any continuing role for process theology: French deconstructionist postmodernism. This seemed to carry the rejection of speculative thought to its ultimate conclusion. However, this is not its only characteristic. What it deconstructs most thoroughly are substantialist concepts, including those of the self and the ideas of the Enlightenment in general. Process thought was an earlier form of such deconstruction. French postmodernism deconstructs our social reality also, removing the veil that leads so many to think that what *is* is simply natural and normal. By problematizing what is, writers such as Jacques Derrida and Michel Foucault paved the way for quite different visions

1. Cobb, *Is It Too Late?*

of what is possible, visions that include process theology. Although their work was generally non-cosmological, Gilles Deleuze found Whitehead's cosmology consistent with his sensitivities and recommended this vision as a "chaosmos." Deleuze thereby paved the way for process thinkers such as Catherine Keller and Roland Faber to make visible the large overlap between the two forms of postmodernism.[2]

For such reasons as these, process theology came to play a different role. Even though many of its new allies were not interested in its speculative philosophy, they shared many of its conclusions. As issues of the global economy and American imperialism came to the fore, the differences among those who opposed these developments seemed less important than joining forces for serious practical work.

Meanwhile, as the older focus on nondenominational revisionism faded, confessional theologies became much more important. These had a far more conservative cast. In general they spoke unabashedly of God in a realistic way, but without much concern to deal with the issues that had led to the demise of such speaking among the earlier nondenominational revisionists. Conservative evangelicals flooded seminaries and graduate programs in theology that were largely abandoned by the heirs of the revisionists, who now preferred objective study of religion.

For the most part, denominational confessional theologians and conservative evangelicals rejected process theology because of its sharp critique of traditional formulations. In this context, process theology was once again radical. But the fact that among conservative evangelicals there was a strong conviction of the reality of God and God's working in the world made it clear that they and process theologians were discussing the same topics. Debate then became meaningful.

But more than that, open-minded conservative evangelicals have come across some of the same problems that have influenced process theologians. Some have come to recognize the problem with affirming that God has all the power and determines all that happens. Some see that it is hard to reconcile human responsibility with the idea that God knows every detail of the future. Some acknowledge that in the Bible God is depicted as affected by what happens in the world and is therefore not impassible and immutable. Indeed, they notice the deep differences between biblical thought and later orthodox philosophical theology. Even if

2. See Keller and Daniell, ed., *Process and Difference*.

they do not accept all the solutions that process theology offers to these problems, conversation becomes possible and significant. In recent years there has been growing interaction between process theologians and that segment of the conservative evangelical community that has adopted "open theology."

Furthermore, although most conservative evangelicals tend to be socially and politically conservative, this is by no means true of all. Some take the Bible with *real* seriousness. The Bible is a countercultural book. Indeed, as our culture becomes more dominated by sex and the consumption of goods, our politics is more dominated by corporate wealth, and our international policy is dominated by the goal of total global hegemony, the Bible becomes more counter to this culture all the time. Process theology gains a countercultural stance both from the Bible and from its radically revisionist philosophy. There can be close and mutually appreciative relations between process theologians and those conservative evangelicals who really take the Bible seriously and are willing to criticize the Christian tradition in its light.

In all of this the central beliefs of process theologians about God and the world have changed little over the years. But the changing context has changed everything else about process theology. The threat to the survival of a livable world overwhelms other challenges, so that some of us measure all that we do in terms of its direct or indirect relevance to this overarching challenge. Process theology seems as important for what it implies about economics, politics, and global order as what it says about God and God's relation to the world. However, for process thinkers the two types of questions cannot be separated. The vision of the world for which we work is informed by what we believe about God and God's working in the world. Indeed, much of the world's difficulty in responding wisely to the many impending crises is to be found in bad theologies. Process theologians believe that our theology can help.

Bibliography

Christ, Carol P. *She Who Changes: Re-imagining the Divine in the World*. New York: Palgrave Macmillan, 2003.

Cobb, John B. Jr. *Is It Too Late? A Theology of Ecology*. Beverley Hills: Bruce, 1972.

Keller, Catherine and Anne Daniell, ed. *Process and Difference*. Albany: SUNY Press, 2002.

Saiving, Valerie. "The Human Situation: A Feminine View." *The Journal of Religion*. 40:2 (April, 1960). pp. 100-112.

11

Christian Theology in a Post-Christendom World

DOUGLAS JOHN HALL

THE EDITORS OF THIS volume have posed four questions to which contributors should respond. I shall forego any attempt at originality and simply answer the questions as honestly as possible in the space available.

1. How has Christian Thought in your field changed in the last twenty-five years?

Having attained the Biblical age (plus thirteen!), I find myself increasingly wary of generalizations of the sort implied in this question. Twenty-five years is a very brief space of time for *significant* change to occur. One can of course name certain twenty-five -year periods in history that constitute exceptions to that rule—for instance the periods 1517–1542 or 1914–1939, incorporating as they do watershed events (Luther's revolt and "The Great War," respectively) which, if they did not by themselves *effect* the change nevertheless made significant change conspicuous. As a rule, however, the mills of God grind more slowly, and, while some future observer of the period 1985–2010 may locate high significance in the course of "Christian Thought" during those two decades, I confess I am unable to do so.

To be sure, one could mention such subjects as (i) the growing awareness of ecological challenges to conventional Christian anthropology on the part of Christian thinkers—but Joseph Sittler and others were already writing about that concern in the 1960s; (ii) the necessity for Christian reflection on and dialogue with other world religions—but Wilfred Cantwell Smith, Hendrik Kraemer, Arthur Jeffries, and others spoke of this decades ago, and their pioneering work has not been much improved upon; (iii) the search for a biblical theology that is neither literalistic nor arbitrary—but Barth, Bultmann, Muilenburg and countless other theologians and biblical scholars were involved in that same search nearly a century ago.

The point is, the past twenty-five years, in my opinion, have not introduced any new and startling changes in Christian thought. At their best, these years have seen the working-out of *some* of the challenges handed over to us by the thinkers and scholars who preceded us—for instance, Walter Brueggemann and Phyllis Trible's imaginative biblical writings have helped both the academy and the church to delve more faithfully into the scriptures that were brought back into prominence by the generation of their teachers; Sallie McFague and Larry Rasmussen have furthered the work of those who, directly or indirectly, alerted Christians to the neglect of the natural order that characterizes much of Christian tradition. Other such contributions could be mentioned, for the period has not been without its luminaries. But if "change" implies a noticeable alteration in direction or emphasis, the period in question seems to me—at its best—to be more one of continuity than of change. The most inspired among us are still trying to take up the torch thrown to us by our forebears.

By our forebears I do not mean the Christian thinkers and writers of the decades immediately preceding the period in question (some of us ourselves belong to that period!) but the theologians of the first two-thirds of the twentieth century. We are all, I think, still working on the agenda they proposed. Far from exhausting it, we have hardly begun. As our continuing fascination with Tillich, Barth, the Niebuhrs and Bonhoeffer (especially in 2006, his 100th birth-year) indicates, there is a half-formed awareness among us that we have a long way to go before we have produced anything worthy of their challenge. Perhaps now that we have got out of our system some of the problems we have with theological conventions that are inherently patriarchal, parochial, racist, sexist, etc. (conventions still visible also in *their* work), we will be able to address the big tasks these giants of the past bequeathed us, some of which I will hint at in the fourth section of this piece.

2. How has your own mind changed?

The verb "changed" strikes me as a bit too dramatic for what my mind has been up to during these past two and a half decades. It is hard to assess one's own thinking—one's vantage point is pretty circumscribed! I believe, however, that what has taken place in my theological reflections since the mid-eighties would be more appropriately designated clarification than change. Some things have become clearer to me, even though they have been taking shape for a good deal longer than twenty-five years.

First, I know for certain now that Christian theology has to become far more *modest* than it has been throughout most of Christian history. I am speaking about *theology,* not just about theologians. What I mean has nothing to do with petit-bourgeois niceness, which most North American theologians manage all too well! Western Christian imperialism has been what it has been, not just because it was wielded by powerful imperial peoples, but because it was (and for the most part continues to be!) shaped by a very triumphalistic *theology.* This theology no longer speaks to human *experience* and its continuation can only spell disaster in a world where no one religion can claim ultimacy without courting violence. There are correctives to the bravado of Christendom's *theology of glory* in submerged aspects of Christian theological history. My own work over this period has been determined by my search for the contextual relevance of what Luther named "the theology of the cross."

Second, it has become clearer to me that serious Christian theology must be more comprehensive. Too much that passes for theological writing in North America, perhaps especially in Canada, is fragmentary, obscure, or driven by one-issue preoccupation. The contention that this is how it must be in a postmodern age is spurious. Precisely in a period of episodic and disconnected experiences and ideas, Christians have a responsibility to try to see life *whole.* When Christian scholars relinquish the quest for wholeness and produce only guarded little essays on this or that—contributions to *Festschriften* for one another!—then people looking for a way into the future will turn to sources that are much too ready to supply their needs. The rise of the Christian Right in the United States and (to a lesser extent, in Canada) is at least partly due to the withdrawal of serious biblical, historical, and theological Christian scholarship from the public sphere. One of the most eloquent essays I have read on the current political situation in the USA began in this way, "Where is Reinhold Niebuhr now that we need him?"

Concern for modesty and the quest for comprehensiveness are not contradictory aims. Modesty is a qualitative, not a quantitative virtue. There are very brief statements that trumpet highly presumptuous religious claims, and there are multi-volumed systematic theologies that exemplify genuine humility. A Christian theology that aims to be both helpful to the Christian movement in a time of uncertainty and open to dialogue with other faiths must be willing to explore the meaning of its central tenets for all aspects of human experience. It only does this immodestly if it assumes actual *possession* of the truth it contemplates from afar.

3. What issues face Christian scholars today?

On the one hand, one may well ask whether there is any area—problem, conflict, instability—of contemporary life in our much-threatened planet that is not, or should not be, an "issue" for concerned Christians, scholars or not! Whether one thinks about the degradation of the biosphere, or the disparity between the possessing peoples of the North and the dispossessed peoples of the southern hemisphere, or the so-called "clash of civilizations," or the rise of religious fundamentalism in all the major religions of the world, or the ethics of sexuality, gender, race, ethnicity, etc.—there is in fact no limit to the list of specific and pressing subjects with which responsible Christian thought must concern itself.

On the other hand, we must try to resist the habit of reducing the task of Christian reflection and action (including scholarly action) to "issues." What is most needed in Christianity today, I feel, is a lively, disciplined, and far-reaching exploration of what is basic—or *foundational*—in the Christian faith. What *is* Christianity? And, perhaps even more emphatically, What is it *not?*

We need such a foundational discussion for at least two salient reasons:

(1) We are emerging from a very long period in Christian history (at least two-thirds of Christian history, in fact) when the Christian faith was inextricably bound up with empire, one empire after another. Not only the behavior but also the *thought* of Christendom

was profoundly shaped by its relationship with Power. The two most pivotal doctrines of Christian theology (Christology and the Trinity) were worked out, as doctrines, *after* the official establishment of our religion by Constantine. Now, like it or not, we have entered the post-Christendom world. And we dare not do this without re-examining the manner in which our entire theology, as well as our behavior in the world (including mission), has been affected by our long co-habitation with empire.

(2) We are surrounded today by many *versions* of Christianity which, from the perspective of both responsible scriptural exegesis and the most profound theological traditions of this faith, can only be regarded as aberrations. Most notably on this continent, and in certain Third World settings, fundamentalist, apocalyptic, and militantly "evangelical" forms of the Christian religion have become so prominent—or at least so noisy!—as to pass for normative Christianity in much of the public arena. Unless the main historic streams (Catholic, Protestant, and Orthodox) are able to distinguish themselves from this kind of media-driven and politically-charged religious fervour, there can be no stopping the confrontation of Christianity with aggressive and intransigent forms of other religions, notably Islamic fundamentalism. Unfortunately, the old "established" churches had grown so accustomed to being-here, and so indifferent about theology, that they possess neither the wisdom nor the courage to offer an alternative to the simplism and militancy of the so-called "Christian Right."

This call for a serious recovery of basics is of course inseparable from the need for Christian intellectuals to come to the aid of the churches. Too much scholarly work on the part of those trained and equipped to think in profound and nuanced ways has been carried on in academic ghettos—and, often enough, in an attitude of condescension towards the churches. Theology exists first of all for the church, and even where Christian scholars are able to work in university and other settings that offer them economic independence, it is still the Christian movement at its forefront that they are called to serve.

Christian scholarship must certainly concern itself with all of the "issues" that impact contemporary life. But it will have no vantage point from which either to prioritize or to comprehend these issues unless the

Christian movement is informed and fed by an ongoing internal quest for the meaning of its message.

4. What questions or problems would you list under the heading, Agenda For the Future?

Obviously, I have just stated what strikes me as the most pressing item on such an agenda—the stimulation of a widespread, informed, and passionate conversation within all dimensions of the Christian movement aimed at recovering for this time and place what is of the essence—what is gospel. *Within* that overarching task, the following questions (and many others like them!) would have to find a place:

  i) *Theology:* How has the Christian conception of Deity been coloured by Western Christendom's imperial status, and what would a post-Christendom Theology (doctrine of God) look like?

 ii) *Christology:* How can Christians enter sincerely into dialogue with other faiths without jeopardizing the centrality of Jesus Christ (christocentrism) and thus begging the question of their own identity?

iii) *Anthropology:* In a world increasingly intrigued by machines and unimpressed by *homo sapiens,* "What are people *for?*" (Wendell Berry). An Iranian taxi-driver recently remarked to me, "Everything always gets more expensive. Only people are cheap."

 iv) *Ecclesiology:* Are institutional models of the church so entrenched that it is impossible for us to re-imagine the original conception of the Christian community as *movement*?

  v) *Eschatology:* Is there hope . . . *for the world*?

     And so on.

Bibliography

Finstuen, Andrew. "This American Mess: Where is Reinhold Niebuhr when we need him?" *Christian Century* (December 1, 2009).

———. *Original Sin and Everyday Protestants: The Theology of Reinhold Niebuhr, Billy Graham, and Paul Tillich in an Age of Anxiety.* Chapel Hill: The University of North Carolina Press, 2009.

Hall, Douglas John. *Bound and Free: A Theologian's Journey.* Minneapolis: Fortress, 2005.

———. *Remembered Voices: Reclaiming the Legacy of "Neo-Orthodoxy."* Louisville: Westminster John Knox, 1998.

PART 3

Encounters with Religious Pluralism and
the Frontiers of Science

12

A New Way of Being Christian

PAUL F. KNITTER

THE FOLLOWING ASSESSMENTS AND reflections are offered by a Christian theologian who, by reason of his professional identity, also strives to be a scholar of religion. To be the former, I believe, one must also be the latter. As a theologian, my job starts with a thorough understanding of the particular religious tradition to which I am committed; and it ends with a reinterpretation and recontextualization of that tradition that will enable me and my community to continue with our commitment. Between the beginning and end (never a final end) of that theological task, I have to bring to my job all the critical skills required by a scholar of religion. My "faith" seeks "understanding," but it can never dictate to my understanding.

I hope that such theological commitments and scholarly skills form the basis of the following analysis of what I believe are the most significant shifts over the past twenty-five years in my area of professional interest: interreligious theology, that is, theology done in conversation with other religions. This theology and this conversation have brought about some marvelous changes in the way the mainline Christian churches—in particular, my own Roman Catholic community—understand what it means to be Christian.

I take my cues from the title and contents of a book by Tom Fox, *Pentecost in Asia: A New Way of Being Church.*[1] Fox describes how the

1. Fox, *Pentecost in Asia.*

many facets of this "new way" boil down to one word: *dialogue*. The Asian Catholic Bishops, listening to their people and assisted by their theologians, have clearly and powerfully insisted that the Christian Church can be a church-in-Asia only if it is in authentic dialogue with other Asian religions *and* with the many Asian poor and marginalized.

In my own life as a Christian believer and in my labors as a Catholic theologian, I have come to realize that what is true of the local churches in Asia is just as true of the universal church. Pentecost, which might be called "the big bang" that launched the *ecclesia*, will continue rippling through the ecclesial universe of the third millennium mainly through the energy of dialogue. A growing number of Christians, mainly within the so-called mainline churches, are coming to realize that to be a truly *Christian* church, they have to be a *dialogical* church. Let me try to explain, briefly, what I mean.

Reasons for the Shift to Dialogue

The world that the Christian churches are called to serve, challenge, and transform is a world in dire need of dialogue. This need is rooted in two evident qualities of our present global reality: ours is a pluralistic world and it is a violent world.

Pluralism—the vast variety of peoples, cultures, religions—has, of course, always colored the fabric of human history. But today, mainly because of the push-button speed of communication and travel, those differing colors have become all the more evident. In fact, for many people, they have become bewildering or blinding. This is especially true of the multiple colors of religions. *Religious pluralism*—the abundant, persistent, exuberant diversity of religions—is confronting and perplexing Christians as never before. The shapes, colors, and even smells of other religions are no longer on the other side of the world. They often emerge from the house next door! In her highly regarded book, Diana L. Eck gives convincing data that there is *A New Religious America* and she describes "*How a 'Christian Country' Has Become the World's Most Religiously Diverse Nation*" (the subtitle).[2]

The many-ness of religions isn't going to go away. It seems that religious pluralism is "as it was it in the beginning, is now, and ever shall be." If that is the case, the simple, immediate conclusion is that Christians

2. Eck, *A New Religious America*.

have to learn to *co-exist,* to live with and be good neighbors to people who are Buddhists, Hindus, and Muslims, etc. But being good neighbors to each other means more than tolerance, more than just accepting the pluralistic state of affairs. Rather, it means learning about each other, appreciating and valuing each other. Pluralistic co-existence—that is, really living and thriving together as different religions—requires dialogue.

But co-existence is not enough. We have to do more together because our world is not just a pluralistic world; it is also a violent world. I am talking mainly (but not only) about the violence that erupts from the barrel of a gun, the impact of a missile, the explosion of an airplane crashing into a building. I am talking about military or terroristic violence. The dreams of a new age of peace after the fall of the Soviet Union have turned, it seems, into nightmares. Besides the multiple, rampaging conflicts of ethnic and/or religious groups, the world is witnessing the "clash of civilizations"—a clash fueled by the terrorism of scattered movements pitted against the military might of a world power. All too often, religion is used to fuel such violence.

But if such "use" of religion for violence is a "misuse," then the religions of the world are going to have to do something to prevent that misuse. And they are going to have to do it *together.* So, besides co-existence, we also need *cooperation* among the religious traditions of the world. Speaking as a Catholic Christian, I feel the need to cooperate with persons of other religions in order to prove that religions are a much more powerful tool for peace than they are a weapon of war. But such cooperation can be realized only through dialogue. The well-known dictum of Hans Küng rings true: "There will be no peace among nations without peace among the religions. And there will be no peace among the religions without dialogue among the religions."[3]

The Newly Felt Demands of Dialogue

But what do we mean by dialogue? That is an important question, since dialogue is a term that gets thrown around facilely and sloppily. As it is generally understood in interreligious encounters, dialogue can be described as follows: a relationship among differing parties in which all parties both speak their minds and open their minds to each other, in the hope that through this engagement all parties will grow in truth

3. Küng, *Global Responsibility,* xv.

and well-being. Dialogue, therefore, is always a *two-way street* that can lead all who travel it to greater understanding and cooperation. All participants in a dialogical encounter have to be ready both to listen and to speak, to teach and be taught. A true dialogue is always a "give and take"—one gives witness to what one holds to be true and at the same time accepts the witness of what the other holds true and dear. Everyone seeks to convince and is ready to be convinced. And if in the dialogue I come to see and feel the truth of your position, then I must also be ready to clarify, correct, even change my views. Dialogue is always exciting; it can also be threatening.

And it is just this kind of dialogue that one of the most cautious and conservative of the mainline Christian churches has been trying to foster over recent decades. This, I believe, constitutes a milestone in Christian awareness. I'm talking about my own Christian community, the Roman Catholic Church. Since the Second Vatican Council in the 1960s, the Catholic Church has held up interreligious dialogue as an ideal—one might even say, an obligation—for all Christians.

In 1965, the bishops at Vatican II called on all Catholics to "engage prudently and lovingly in dialogue and cooperation" with other religious traditions.[4] In 1984, this gentle invitation became a requirement when the Vatican Secretariat for Non-Christian Religions (later called the Pontifical Council for Interreligious Dialogue) announced that dialogue is an essential part of the Church's mission.[5] Then in 1991, the meaning of dialogue was boldly clarified in Pope John Paul II's Encyclical *Redemptoris Missio* (RM)[6] and in the Declaration *Dialogue and Proclamation* (DP) from the Pontifical Council for Dialogue.[7] These official statements expressly acknowledged that the intended fruits of dialogue are in the "mutual enrichment" of *all* sides (RM # 55, DP # 9), that in the dialogue Christians should allow themselves to be "questioned," perhaps "purified," (DP # 32), maybe even "transformed" (DP #47). Surprisingly, the Vatican document even goes so far as to recognize that in a true dialogue, all the participants (including Christians) must be open to being "converted," that is, open "to leave one's previous spiritual or religious situation in order to direct

4. *Nostra Aetate*, par. 2.

5. Secretariat for Non-Christian Religions, *Attitude of the Church toward Followers of Other Religions*.

6. Pope John Paul II, *Encyclical Redemptoris Missio*.

7. Pontifical Council for Dialogue, *Dialogue and Proclamation*.

oneself to another" (DP # 41). Clearly, Christians have finally begun to recognize dialogue as a *two-way street.*

Catholic = Dialogical

So as Christians step into the new millennium, many of them (certainly not all!) in the mainline churches are doing so with a new and quite different understanding of how Christians are to relate to other religions and other philosophies. They are coming to a deeper, more adequate understanding of what the word "catholic" means. (With a small "c" and without "Roman" in front of it, "catholic" was used in the early creeds to describe all the Christian communities.) Literally, "catholic" signifies "universal"—related to and sent into the whole world with its many peoples and cultures and religions. But for most of their history, the churches have understood this universal relatedness as a one-way street. Christians bring the truth and salvation to others; they give, the other religions receive. Such was the understanding of "Christian mission."

But "catholic" understood as "dialogue," and "dialogue" understood as Pope John Paul II and the Pontifical Council for Dialogue do, mean that the relationship between Christianity and other cultures and religions must be *two-way.* If the Christian churches are to grow and be faithful to the gospel of Jesus, they must not only deliver the Good News but also be open to whatever Good News God may be providing through other religious traditions. Christian mission now requires not only "teaching all nations" but also learning from all nations. Only then can Christians cooperate with other religions in the work of overcoming violence and bringing justice to the poor of our planet and to our poor planet suffering from environmental devastation. To call themselves "catholic Christians" means that the community of Jesus followers must be in a genuine, dialogical relationship with *others*—with people and religions who are really different. Dialogue is becoming a meaningful, challenging "new way of being Church."

Remaining Challenges

But this is only half the picture of what is new in my field of interreligious theology. This new understanding of what it means to be church contains some profound, unsettling challenges for Christian theology and self-understanding, challenges which, I'm sad to say, are not being sufficiently taken up or even recognized. Briefly stated: there are definite tensions, if not downright contradictions, between the new ecclesiology that extols dialogue as the new way of being church and the traditional Christology that extols Jesus as the one and only savior and as the bearer of God's full, definitive, and unsurpassable revelation. Unless these tensions or contradictions are squarely faced and resolved, I fear that Christians' dialogue with other religions will not be honest and successful and may well turn out to be exploitative.

How can Christians carry out a dialogue with other believers that is genuinely a two-way relationship—as Pope John Paul II said, a conversation in which Christians are truly open to learning as much as they want to teach, in which they are ready to be "questioned . . . purified . . . transformed, even converted"—if they believe that God has given them the one source of salvation and the full, final, normative truth over all other truth? They hold, as it were, the divinely-given trump card for all other religious truth. It would seem, therefore, that within the mainline Christian churches today, there is a tension between the *practice* of dialogue to which Christians are being called on the one hand, and the *theory* of traditional Christology. This, I believe, is one of the most serious and pressing challenges facing the Christian churches today.

It is a challenge that calls Christian theologians to the task that has so often driven theology throughout the centuries of church history—how to resolve the tensions that naturally arise as the church moves through different times and different cultures between the *practice* of Christian living and the *theory* of Christian believing. The particular challenge I am pointing to in these reflections calls theologians to work out a Christology, an understanding of Jesus the Christ, that will preserve his distinctive message without subordinating the distinctive identities and message of other religious figures. It will be a Christology that enables and requires of Christians an ongoing, full commitment to the gospel of Jesus and at the same time a genuine openness to the truth that may be challenging them in other religious traditions.

Some such challenge—how to be committed to one's own identity and at the same time truly open to that of others—faces all religious communities. My hopes are that in the coming decades we Christian theologians can offer some good examples of how that challenge can be met.

Bibliography

Eck, Diana L. *A New Religious America: How a 'Christian Country' Has Become the World's Most Religiously Diverse Nation.* San Francisco: HarperSanFrancisco, 2002.

Fox, Tom. *Pentecost in Asia: A New Way of Being Church.* Maryknoll, NY: Orbis, 2002.

John Paul II, Pope. *Encyclical Redemptoris Missio* (1990). Available at Vatican website: http://www.vatican.va/edocs/ENG0219/__P1.HTM

Küng, Hans. *Global Responsibility: In Search of a New World Ethic.* New York: Crossroad, 1991.

Paul VI, Pope. *Nostra Aetate: Declaration on the Relation of the Church to Non- Christian Religions* (October 28, 1965) par. 2.

Pontifical Council for Dialogue. *Dialogue and Proclamation.* Vatican City: Pontifical Council for Dialogue, 1991. Available at Vatican website: http://bit.ly/oucC7v

Vatican Secretariat for Non-Christian Religions. *The Attitude of the Church toward Followers of Other Religions.* Vatican City: Secretariat for Non-Christian Religions, 1984.

13

Comparative Theology

KEITH WARD

O NE OF THE MOST important factors to affect modern theology is globalization. By this I mean that virtually every part of our planet can
now be in instant communication with every other part, that it is possible
to travel to any part of the globe in hours, not years, and that there is
unprecedented access to previously inaccessible information through the
use of the Internet.

The main impact of globalization on Christian theology has been
to open Christian thinking to many different strands of thought, not as
something alien and exotic, but as immediately present on a screen in
front of an enquirer's eyes. In the first half of the twentieth century if I
had wished to read a Tibetan Buddhist text I would have had to learn a
difficult language, travel laboriously to Tibet, and even then would probably have been denied access to the documents I wanted to see. Now, at
the beginning of the twenty-first century, I can call that text up in English,
with a commentary by a competent scholar, in the comfort of my study.

Of course it is not true that everything is available in this way, but a
huge and growing number of texts. And I can certainly call on scholarly
resources to help my own researches in ways that would have been unthinkable just a few decades ago. Because of increased ease of travel, there
is also little excuse for me not to go to meet an expert in a topic in which
I am interested, to hear first hand exactly what he or she thinks.

This means that Christian theology can no longer be done in isolation from all the resources of human knowledge and opinion. All the
vast diversity of Christian beliefs, and the changes Christian faith has undergone throughout its history, can quickly be made apparent to all who
are prepared to learn. That makes a certain sort of Christian education
obsolete—and not only obsolete, but indefensible. The sort of education I
have in mind is one that says, "This is the one and only Christian truth. It
is theoretically certain and unchangeable, and has always been so. Other
Christian views are simply mistaken, and are probably due to willful mis-
understanding or malice. As for other religions, there is nothing in them
to teach us anything. They can safely be ignored."

Perhaps there is no longer such Christian education. If so, I am
extremely glad. But we need to be clear about what it is in the modern
situation that has rendered such education indefensible. It is that having access to intelligent people who have different views from your own
brings sharply into focus the fact that theoretical certainty is rarely, if ever,
available in matters of religion.

The paradigm of theoretical certainty is found in the natural sciences. We can be theoretically certain of the boiling point of water at
sea level, because we can repeat, test, and verify that on innumerable
occasions, and everyone will agree on the result. What is theoretically
certain is what is beyond reasonable doubt. Anyone who takes the trou-
ble can verify it for themselves, and no competent observer will ever
disagree. No rational person can doubt what is theoretically certain, for
it is publicly verifiable.

Hardly any important religious claim is publicly verifiable in this
sense. If I believe there is a God, thousands will deny it. If I insist that
Jesus was crucified, every Muslim will deny it. If I even think that at least
Jesus existed, a quick search of the Internet will reveal many who do not
agree with me. Religion is a realm of innumerable disputes, and there
seems to be no way of resolving them.

Of course we always knew that. But in the past we were rarely
forced to confront the fact. We could just mix with people who agreed
with us, and not take seriously the opinions of others. It is still possible
to do that—but not if we are making any serious claim to be concerned
about truth. A serious concern for truth requires that we examine all the
available evidence as carefully as we can, unless we know it to be spurious. And now there is just so much more available evidence. Atheists and

polytheists are not just remote possibilities we never actually come across. There are huge groups of them, commanding our attention in our own homes through various media of communication.

Diversity of religious belief has become a real problem in a globalized world, for when we really pay attention to what other people are saying, we realize that the sorts of reasons they have for their beliefs seem to be more or less as strong as the sorts of reasons we have for ours. This has become clear in the case of the relation of Islam and Christianity in the modern world. If I, as a Christian, say that the Bible is the Word of God, and I know that because the Spirit tells me so, I can now see that Muslims say that the Qur'an is the Word of God, and they know it because God tells them so as they read the text. We disagree, but our reasons seem more or less equally reasonable to both of us, and we cannot resolve our dispute.

One main theological problem globalisation raises is how to account for the huge diversity of religious beliefs on the planet, and for the fact that none of them can establish itself with anything like the sort of theoretical certainty the natural sciences have. This is a new situation, because in past ages we did not realize just how great the diversity was, or how sophisticated alternative religious beliefs were, or how different from scientific knowledge religious beliefs are. We did not realize it because we lived in a cozy tribal world in which all sensible people agreed on basic religious beliefs, except for heretics and infidels, who were intellectually or morally unsound. The beliefs of heretics could readily be stereotyped as they were not allowed to voice their own views too publicly, and so could be described as deviant in terms of a dominant religious system they did not accept. Globalization has blown the tribal world apart, and each tribe has henceforth to justify its beliefs in the face of informed encounter with the beliefs of others.

The fairly new discipline of comparative theology is theology in a global context. Such a theology does not take the beliefs of one religious tradition for granted. Its field of enquiry is the global range of religious beliefs. One of its main aims is to gain a sensitive and informed understanding of such beliefs, explain their diversity, and articulate a rational basis for holding (or for rejecting) beliefs that are not publicly verifiable.

The first academic appointment in the field was that of James Freeman Clarke, who was appointed Professor of Natural Religion and Christian Doctrine at Harvard Divinity School in 1867. He wrote *Ten*

Great Religions: An Essay in Comparative Theology in 1871. At about the
same time in Oxford, Max Müller, who held a post in comparative philology, was working on an *Introduction to the Science of Religion,* published
in 1873. These were both early attempts to see religion in a global context.
They took a fairly positive view of the diversity of world religions, and
their theological ancestor was Friedrich Schleiermacher, whose *Speeches
on Religion* of 1799 saw different religions as different ways of relating to
the one Supreme Infinite.

Schleiermacher held that the heart of religion lay not in intellectual
dogmas or in moral rules but in what he called intuition (*Anschauung)*
or feeling (*Gefühl).* There is some debate about exactly what he meant by
these terms, but it is clear that he was speaking not of a purely subjective
inner state that is unrelated to the nature of objective reality but of an
affective state of mind that is a response to something objective that can
only be apprehended through some appropriate affection or feeling. In
Speeches on Religion he speaks of a "sense and taste for the infinite." It
seems to be a sort of apprehension, but not of a particular material object
and not one that is dispassionate and analytical. It is more like a way of
responding to objective experience in general that is sensitive to an element of "depth" or "transcendence," of totality or unity.

Though Schleiermacher's thought is often placed in opposition to
that of Georg Wilhelm Friedrich Hegel, who lectured in Berlin at the
same time, there is a definite affinity between them. Hegel published lectures on the philosophy of religion in which he treated all the religions
of which he knew (though his knowledge at that time was very restricted
and often inaccurate). Hegel did so in the light of his general philosophy
of Absolute Idealism.

According to that philosophy, the whole of history is the self-man-
ifestation of Absolute Spirit (*Geist),* which is the ultimate reality. Spirit is
the Infinite and includes all finite reality in itself, unlike the infinite God
of Thomas Aquinas, which excludes everything finite. So time and history are included in Spirit, which expresses itself in them. They become
objectified and alienated from Spirit, but through a historical process of
dialectic, of conflict and resolution moving on to a higher level of manifestation, time and history are eventually reconciled to Spirit again. At
that point Spirit becomes fully conscious of its own manifested nature.
History is that which actualizes the potentiality of Spirit, and Spirit is that

in which all history is taken up, purified, and integrated into one fully self-conscious reality.

Within this ambitious metaphysical scheme, the various religions can be seen as phases of the realization of Absolute Spirit, often placed in dialectical opposition to one another, yet always moving towards a fuller synthesis at a higher level of understanding and then generating a new phase of dialectical progress. Hegel was insistent that this process was a manifestation of pure Reason and could in principle be intellectually understood. Indeed, he was usually taken to be saying that his philosophy was superior to any specific religion. Absolute Idealism revealed each religion to have its place in a dialectical process whose true nature and fulfilment were to be found in Hegel's own philosophy. This is probably unfair, since Hegel thought of himself (at least most of the time) as a Lutheran philosopher, and indeed as the first truly Christian philosopher.

Nevertheless, Schleiermacher was sceptical of Hegel's apparent claims to complete intellectual understanding of reality. Schleiermacher agreed that there was an Infinite Spiritual reality, and that all finite things were parts or manifestations of it. But he denied that Reason could grasp it and stressed instead a sort of direct non-cognitive apprehension of the Infinite. Various religions give different apprehensions of the Infinite—after all, if it is truly infinite, we might expect that there would be an infinite number of ways of apprehending it. So each religion has its own validity as a way of intuiting the infinite and religions are to be distinguished by their different models of the Infinite. The more such models there are, Schleiermacher suggested, the more adequate our knowledge of the Infinite might be. So the diversity of religions is a good thing. Our intellectual uncertainty is a consequence of the inadequacy of Reason to understand fully the final truth of things, a consequence of the ineffability of God.

Schleiermacher was quickly accused of pantheism. In his later book *The Christian Faith* (1821), he defined the essence of religious faith as "the sense of absolute dependence"— more clearly separating the being of God from every finite and dependent thing. He also asserted that (Protestant) Christian faith was "the perfect religion." So, though it might be a good thing that there are many religions, they are all destined to reach their perfection in Christianity.

I have spent some time on Schleiermacher and Hegel because they still set the agenda for approaching the basic problems of diversity, change, and the public unverifiability in religion. If God is not a specific natural object, then the methodology of the natural sciences does not apply to God. Apprehension of God will be a matter of personal experience or intuition and at any specific stage of the historical process no such intuition will be final or complete. None will be publicly verifiable, though we can explain divergences of apprehension by learning about the different conceptual models and analogies that exist in specific cultures. If God is infinite, there will be many possible ways of apprehending God and we might hope that these may in a sense converge as people realize how limited and complementary their basic models are. Of course, the paradox is that, once you have stated this view, it has itself become the "true" view of religious faith and as such it excludes alternatives. It is not the case that any religious view is just as good as any other.

The views that come out as "best" are views that affirm the infinity and ineffability of God as "ultimate reality," the limited nature of all religious perspectives, and the importance of continued changes in religion as they respond to new insights and new knowledge. The views that come out as "worst" are those that claim final and unchangeable knowledge of what God is, that claim an absolute certainty of faith, and that insist on retaining ancient formulations as irreformable.

It seems that truth does not belong to any one religious tradition as such. It belongs to the way in which any religious tradition is interpreted. Today this view is known as "pluralism." It was defined by John Hick in 1989, in *An Interpretation of Religion*, as the view that "the great post-axial faiths constitute different ways of experiencing, conceiving, and living in relation to an ultimate divine Reality which transcends all our varied visions of it" (235). This definition does not assert that all ways are equally good, but it does assert that all relate to the same divine Reality and that no way gives a fully adequate vision of that Reality. Clearly there remain many issues to be resolved in comparative theology. Is it true that all the post-axial faiths claim to experience the same reality, or that they actually do so? By what criteria can one decide that some religious beliefs are more acceptable than others? Is it possible to make neutral judgments on this issue, or do we each necessarily belong to some one tradition of belief? Is it even possible to compare different belief-systems, or are they in some important sense incommensurable?

These are all important subjects of debate, but the modern situation dictates that they be intellectually addressed and that the only way to resolve them is to examine and compare diverse religious traditions as sensitively and accurately as possible. Comparative theology does not suggest one set of agreed answer to the problems, but it does insist that informed, sensitive, yet critical comparison of global religious beliefs is necessary to a comprehensive theological education.

There are various methods of approach to comparative theology. Some scholars concentrate on detailed comparative work in two traditions. Wilfred Cantwell Smith and Kenneth Cragg have worked on Islam and Christianity, Raimundo Panikkar and Francis Clooney work on Hinduism and Christianity, and Paul Griffiths and Donald Mitchell write on Buddhism and Christianity. In such work, surprising affinities and overlaps between diverse traditions constantly appear, but it is also plain that the more detailed one gets, the more differences and contradictions also appear. Such work is essential if one is to avoid over-generalization, the bane of comparative religion in the past, and achieve a sound basis for the study of human religious beliefs in all their complexity.

Another approach is more general and seeks to achieve a systematic overview of religious beliefs. Mircea Eliade and Hans Kung, John Hick and Ninian Smart, Huston Smith and Robert Neville, are just a few of those who have attempted to pursue the general programme of Schleiermacher and Hegel in light of more detailed knowledge of religious traditions and in ways less dependent upon philosophies of nineteenth century German Romanticism. I would place my own *Comparative Theology*[1] here.

It is not an accident that such analyses of religion have usually been written by Christian theologians of a broadly liberal disposition. The development of Christian theology in the last 150 years has led to acceptance of a critical historical approach to the Bible and acceptance of a need to reformulate traditional beliefs in the light of the modern scientific view of the universe. This has both weakened the force of any simple appeal to pre-critical theological tradition and made clear the necessity of reformulating traditional beliefs by assimilating the best knowledge from outside the tradition. The Christian theologian now has need of modern historical and scientific knowledge. It is a short step to realize that knowledge of the general history of religions might also have an important contribution to make to theological understanding. We become less defensive about

1. See Keith Ward's multi-volume comparative theology: *Religion and Revelation, Religion and Creation, Religions and Human Nature, Religion and Community*, and recently, *Religion and Human Fulfilment*.

the absolute truth of our own religious understanding when we realize how much we need constantly to re-think this understanding in the light of new knowledge from other areas of human experience.

There is no need for comparative theology to be a *Christian* discipline, however. It should include a range of religious practitioners, as well as those who do not have a religious practice at all. Comparative theologians will find themselves variously committed to specific religious traditions. I regard myself as a fairly mainstream Anglican. By that I mean that I value the main definitions of the first seven ecumenical councils of the Christian church, especially with regard to the Incarnation and the Trinity. I also support free and informed critical enquiry into all religious beliefs, I value freedom of conscience and belief, and I hold that even Popes and church councils are liable to error. I believe that the orthodox Christian faith was formulated by the encounter of Jewish Messianic beliefs with Hellenistic philosophy. A re-thinking of Christian faith for our own day will require an encounter with a range of modern philosophies and worldviews, both religious and secular. What will result from such an encounter it is impossible to say in advance. But, speaking for myself, I have found that my understanding of Christian faith has been both deepened and widened by my attempts to understand the Indian religious traditions. I have not found myself cast out into a wilderness beyond any tradition, for my own part of Christian tradition is open to change by creative encounter with other insights into the being and nature of God.

Some comparative theologians will be concerned about the nature of Christian relations with Judaism and Islam, relations that have been filled with misunderstandings and hostility in the past. Perhaps it is because I am a philosopher that I have been attracted to the broadly Idealist religions of India. In those traditions I have found a stress on compassion for all sentient beings, an insistence on the religious path as one of non-attachment and mindfulness, an acceptance of many paths to one supreme spiritual reality, a sense that all things exist within the reality of the divine, and a belief that all persons can know God in "the cave of the heart."

These things are not alien to Christian tradition, but they have been neglected in Christian practices that tend to be overly concerned with personal salvation (a sort of long-term selfishness), to be overly judgmental about those who hold different views (despite Jesus' teaching that we should love even our enemies), and to be overly pessimistic about the depravity and horrifying destiny of most human beings (despite the fact that the gospel is the good news of forgiveness and eternal life for all).

I hope this gives a sense of how exposure to other religious traditions can and will affect understanding of one's own tradition. I also hope that in the twenty-first century theologians of many religious traditions will cooperate to construct many comparative theologies, by detailed, sensitive, and informed exposure to a range of religious beliefs. This will undoubtedly change their own beliefs to some extent, but it will not lead to any sort of new syncretistic super-religion. It will lead comparative theologians to a range of religious views that incorporate and learn from other traditions, even as they follow their own distinctive insights in a non-aggressive and non-defensive way.

Will it happen in the future? In 2006 the American Academy of Religion had a section on comparative theology for the first time. In an age of growing global communication and contact, the prospects for comparative theology seem good.

Bibliography

Clarke, James Freeman. *Ten Great Religions: An Essay in Comparative Theology*. 2 volumes. Boston: Osgood, 1871, 1883.

Hick, John. *An Interpretation of Religion: Human Responses to the Transcendent, Second Edition*. New Haven: Yale University, 2004.

Müller, Max. *Introduction to the Science of Religion*. London: Longmans, Green, and Co., 1873

Schleiermacher, Friedrich. *On Religion: Speeches to its Cultured Despisers*. 1799 text tr. Richard Crouter. Cambridge: Cambridge University Press, 1996.

Ward, Keith. *Religion and Revelation*. Oxford: Oxford University Press, 1994.

———. *Religion and Creation*. Oxford: Oxford University Press, 1996.

———. *Religion and Human Nature*. Oxford: Oxford University Press, 1998.

———. *Religion and Community*. Oxford: Oxford University Press, 2000.

———. *Religion and Human Fulfilment*. Norwich, UK: SCM, 2008.

14

Science and Religion in the Twenty-first Century

JOHN POLKINGHORNE

CHRISTIANS ARE CALLED TO love God with their minds as well as with all other parts of their being. This duty calls for an engagement between Christian understanding and all other forms of truth-seeking endeavor. In particular, the dialogue between science and religion is a necessary part of this activity. During the twenty-five years in which the Chair of Christian Thought has been in existence, the interaction between science and religion has been one of increasing intensity and fruitfulness.

The spirit of the conversation has been one of seeking complementary understanding rather than confrontational engagement. Neither side can dictate to the other how to answer its own proper questions, but if both are searching for truth about the one world of human encounter with reality, the two perspectives must bear some congruent relationship to each other. There will not be entailment either way between science and religion, but their insights must be expected to bear some form of complementary relationship to each other.

Science has purchased its great success by the modesty of its ambition, restricting itself to asking a single set of questions (essentially, how things happen) and a single dimension of reality (its impersonal aspect, open to experimental manipulation and interrogation), and bracketing out all else (questions of meaning and purpose in what is happening; the personal aspect of reality in which testing has to give way to trusting).

One important point of contact between religion and science lies in the former offering responses to those limit questions that arise out of our experience of doing science, but whose answers demand a form of insight going beyond the self-limited power of science to supply. Why is it that the physical world is so transparent to our inquiry, to a degree far exceeding that needed for everyday survival? Why is the deep order thus discovered so rationally beautiful that it evokes in the scientist a feeling of wonder? Why is the universe so finely tuned in its given physical fabric in just the fashion that was necessary if it were to be capable of producing carbon-based life anywhere within it? It does not seem intellectually satisfactory to treat these questions as unanswerable, but for science itself the facts about the world to which they point can only be treated as happy accidents. Christianity can make these facts intelligible, seeing them as signs of the divine Mind and Purpose that lie behind a universe understood as God's creation. This understanding is not logically coercive, but it is deeply intellectually satisfying and it has been the basis for a contemporary revival of a form of natural theology.

In its turn, science can offer theology some help with its deepest problem, the suffering present in the world. From the publication of Darwin's *Origin of Species* onwards, there have been theologians willing to accept evolutionary insight as pointing to a creation not ready-made in character, but one in which creatures had been given the gift of making themselves. Science, however, has also made it clear that this great good has a necessary cost. The shuffling explorations of potentiality cannot be without their shadow side. The same processes that allow germ cells to mutate and produce new forms of life, will also allow somatic cells to mutate and become malignant. The presence of cancer in the world—anguishing fact that it is—is not gratuitous, something that a Creator who was a bit more competent or a bit less callous could easily have avoided. It is the inescapable shadow side of a creation in which creatures make themselves. This insight from science does not remove all theological perplexity about the problem of suffering, but it is certainly helpful.

These kinds of exploration of the frontier between science and religion have undoubtedly been valuable and detailed discussion of these issues will continue. However, by itself the understanding gained is as consistent with the spectator god of deism, as it is with the Christian God who is providentially active in the unfolding history of creation. The science and religion discussions of the 1990s concentrated on the further issue of divine action. If one takes with due seriousness all that science can tell us about the regular process of the world, is it still possible to believe in a God who acts providentially, for example in response to prayer? If the scientific account were simply that of a world of cosmic clockwork, the answer would surely be No. We would be left with the deistic picture of a divine Clockmaker. However, twentieth, century science saw the death of a merely mechanical view of the world, made obsolete by the discovery of *intrinsic* unpredictabilities present in nature. They were first discovered at the level of atomic physics, subject to quantum uncertainty, and then at the everyday level of the chaotic theory of exquisitively sensitive macroscopic systems, uncontrollably affected by the slightest disturbance.

Unpredictability is an epistemological property (you cannot know what will happen), but those committed to a realist philosophical stance will interpret this fact as the sign of an actual ontological openness to the future. Science's reductionist account cannot claim to soak up all power of causal influence. The world is not only more subtle than mere mechanism; it can be understood also to be more supple, affording room for the operation of agency, both human and providential. The detailed proposals made for how this might work out were varied, and matters were too complex for anyone to be able to claim to possess a complete theory of agency. Nevertheless, it was clear that the defeaters had been defeated. A just account of science's insight did not demand denial of the exercise of will, either personal or divine. This particular discussion has probably been carried as far as is possible with present knowledge.

So what of the future? There are three specific issues that I believe will be significant in the further development of the dialogue between science and religion:

(1) *Theological agenda.* So far, most of the agenda for the conversation between science and religion has been set by scientific discovery. Theologians have been told about big bang cosmology, or about evolutionary biology, and invited to say what they make of that. Of course, this is a valuable component in the discussion, but theology has its own autonomy and insight and it is beginning to play a more proactive role in the discussion. The last twenty-five years or so have seen the increasing recovery in theology of a recognition of the central significance and fruitfulness of trinitarian thinking. One of the books that played an initiating role in this process was *Being*

as Communion, by John Zizioulas.[1] At the same time, in a more spo-
radic way, scientists have been recognizing the remarkable degree to
which relationality is woven into the fabric of the universe: general
relativity's integration of space, time, and matter into a single unified account; the phenomenon of quantum entanglement (the EPR
effect), in which entities that have once interacted remain effectively
a single system however far they subsequently may separate; the
sensitivity of chaotic systems to the slightest influence from their
environment that renders them incapable of being treated properly
in isolation from their surroundings. One could paraphrase the title
of Zizioulas's book as *Reality is Relational*, and science is discovering that this is indeed the case. I believe that this means that specific
theological insights, such as trinitarian thinking, will come to play
an increasingly important role in the science and theology dialogue.[2]

(2) *A credible eschatology.* The universe will not remain fruitful forever. Ultimately it will die, most probably in the whimper of ever
increasing cold and dilution. What does this imply for a theology of
creation? Christian hope embraces the concept of a destiny beyond
death, both for human individuals and for the whole of creation.
This belief is grounded in the everlasting faithfulness of God, which
Christianity sees manifested in the resurrection of Jesus Christ. But
can we make sense of such a hope today? Doing so requires ideas
of both continuity (so that Abraham, Isaac, and Jacob really live
again, not just new characters given the old names) and disconti-
nuity (so that the patriarchs are not just made alive again in order
to die again). Discussion of these issues is beginning to become an
active topic in the science and religion community.[3] A key issue is
how to think about the soul, if human beings are indeed psychoso-
matic unities as so much scientific insight suggests. This has led to
a modern version of the Aristotelian-Thomistic concept of the soul
as the form, or information-bearing pattern, of the body, held in the
divine memory at death and re-embodied in God's eschatological

1. Zizioulas, *Being as Communion*.

2. Polkinghorne, *Science and the Trinity* and Polkinghorne, *Exploring Reality*.

3. Polkinghorne and Welker (eds), *The End of the World and the Ends of God*;
Polkinghorne, *The God of Hope and the End of the World*; Peters, Russell and Welker
(eds), *Resurrection*.

act of resurrection. Clearly work will continue in this area that is so critical for Christian thinking.

(3) *Interfaith dialogue.* The world-wide universality of science contrasts perplexingly with the regional diversity of the world faiths. They all witness to the human experience of encounter with sacred reality, but they say such different and apparently conflicting things about the nature of that reality. This is a problem likely to be on the religious agenda, not just in the twenty-first century but for the third millennium. Serious dialogue among the world's faiths is only just beginning in a truth-seeking and mutually respectful way. The process will be long and, I fear, painful because of the deeply held convictions that are under scrutiny. Initial meetings have to be concerned with serious issues, but simply to go straight to confronting the deepest cognitive clashes (the status of Jesus, the authority of the Qur'an) would be likely to prove too difficult and challenging a starting point. Mutual discussion of how the faiths respond to the discoveries of modern science would provide one possibility for worthwhile, but not too threatening, encounter. The recently founded International Society for Science and Religion seeks to offer a world-wide setting for just such kinds of interfaith meeting.

We live at a time of great potential for gaining insight from the meeting of science and religion in respectful dialogue. Activities such as those fostered by the Chair of Christian Thought in Calgary and the associated lecture program are an important element in this quest for truth. I am grateful for the privilege of having participated in that program and I wish it well for the future. It is work that is much needed.

Bibliography

Peters, Ted, Robert John Russell & Michael Welker (eds). *Resurrection: Theological and Scientific Assessments*. Grand Rapids: Eerdmans, 2002.

Polkinghorne, John and Michael Welker (eds). *The End of the World and the Ends of God: Science and Theology on Eschatology*. Harrisburg, PA: Trinity Press International, 2000.

Polkinghorne, John C. *Exploring Reality: The Intertwining of Science and Religion*. New Haven: Yale University Press, 2005.

———. *The God of Hope and the End of the World*. New Haven: Yale University Press, 2002.

———. *Science and the Trinity*. New Haven: Yale University Press, 2004.

Zizioulas, John D. *Being as Communion: Studies in Personhood and the Church*. Crestwood, NY: St Vladimir's Seminary Press, 1985.

15

Bioethics

A Forum for Finding Shared Values in Twenty-first Century Society

MARGARET SOMERVILLE

MY MARCHING ORDERS FROM the editors of this volume were to reflect on how my research field has changed in the last twenty-five years, and how my mind has changed. Where do I see my field going in the next twenty-five years? What are the issues that will be occupying scholars in the foreseeable future? So, where to begin?

Bioethics is a sub-category of applied ethics. It is one of the most *avant-garde* and exciting fields of theory and practice in terms of the variety, novelty, importance, depth, and breadth of impact of the issues people in this field are called upon to address on a daily basis. But here I will not concentrate specifically on any of these issues. Rather, I want to look at where the field has come from, where it is now, where it might go, and what it needs to get there.

You do what . . . ?

Let me start by telling the story of my entry into bioethics, which at the time was, at best, an amorphous, unnamed, unrecognized field of study. My academic background is in pharmacy and law. In 1975 my then husband and I were living in Sydney, Australia, when he accepted an offer to come to McGill University to undertake post-graduate medical research.

As a "dutiful wife" I came with him for, as we agreed it would be, one year. I decided that I would spend the year putting my backgrounds together by studying for a master's degree in medical law.

Unknown to me, one of the few people in the world at that time with qualifications in medical law, Professor Paul-André Crépeau (d. 2011), was at the Faculty of Law at McGill. During my first meeting with him, he said, "You should be studying for a doctorate, not a master's." I protested strongly and explained that I was only doing a master's to keep myself occupied during my year in Montreal. But, he prevailed, eventually, and became my thesis supervisor.

Professor Crepeau was chairing an unprecedented committee set up by the Medical Research Council of Canada (the forerunner of the present Canadian Institutes for Health Research) to look into the ethics of medical research involving human subjects. This topic was almost entirely unexplored in academic research and there were few formal guidelines. We sometimes forget that the vast medical research complex, as we know it today, is almost entirely a creature of the late twentieth century. My doctoral (DCL) thesis was entitled *Medical Experimentation on the Person: A Survey of Legal and Extra-Legal Controls*. I found little relevant law in carrying out my research. I turned, therefore, to other sources, in particular moral philosophy and ethics. And so began my career as an ethicist.

There is folklore in bioethics, which like much folklore is based in fact. The story is that, in 1970, there were seven articles in English published in the world in the area we would now call bioethics. In 1980, there were fourteen specialty journals in this area. And in 1990, there were over two hundred centers in North America. In 1978, when I completed my doctorate and was appointed to the academic staff at McGill, the word ethicist was at best a neologism. When people asked me what I did and I'd say, "Applied ethics," "Bioethics," or "I'm an ethicist," they would invariably exclaim, "You do what?" or "What's that?" It's hard to imagine such a response today.

The search for ethics . . .

Today the search for ethics seems to be everywhere. One has only to pick up the daily newspaper or watch TV to see the perceived relevance of "ethics talk" to much of what goes on in our lives as individuals and communities. We now explore the ethics of politics, politicians, judges, and police; the ethics of public policy, governmental bureaucracy, and public accountability; ethics in academia, business, industry, and health care; the ethics of our treatment of animals; environmental ethics; ethics in the media, communications, and documentary film-making; cross-cultural ethics; ethics in sport; the ethics of armed conflict; and the ethics of scientific and medical research and the new technologies resulting from that.

Initially, we examined ethical issues at the individual level, for instance, in the individual physician-patient relationship. Over the last twenty-five years major developments in institutional and organizational ethics and in societal ethics have emerged. This widespread search for ethics can be seen as a revolution in consciousness and conscience, in the sense of a rapidly expanding awareness of the need to ask the question, "Is it right?" and, even more importantly, its companion question, "Is it wrong?" in a wide variety of contexts.

Recognition of the need for the development of applied ethics at individual, institutional, and societal levels, and most recently the global level, was initially precipitated by unprecedented medical advances—in particular, the first heart transplant. We were astonished that a person could be alive and walking around because he had the heart of a dead person beating inside him—the organ whose functioning was seen, up to that time, as the principal indicator marking the line between life and death.

After the first heart transplant, ever more mind-altering scientific and medical breakthroughs continued to raise ethical questions we have never faced before. Such questions continue to play an important and challenging role in the development of the field of applied ethics. For instance, advances in reproductive technologies that offer the prospect of precise laboratory manipulation of the genetic makeup of human embryos do exactly that. Likewise, the possibility of making gametes (sperm or ova) from stem cells presents unprecedented ethical issues, since this technology opens up the possibility of two same-sex people having their "own genetically shared" baby. The same technology might make it possible to create a "one parent" baby who is not a clone—for instance, a woman's ovum could be fertilized with a sperm made from one of her stem cells. With the legal recognition of same-sex marriage, which carries the right to found a family, the ethics and law that should govern this technology are brought into sharp focus in the public square. I believe that to transmit human life other than by the union of a natural ovum and a natural sperm is profoundly unethical, both in terms of respect for the transmission of human life (a new form of respect for life that we now need because of possibilities opened up by reprogenetic technologies) and, most of all, it is unethical *vis-à-vis* the resulting child.[1]

The convergence of nanotechnology, artificial intelligence, robotics, genetics, and information technologies challenges us with unprecedented powers and unprecedented ethical issues that no humans before us have faced. They allow us to hold the essence of life, including human life, in the palm of our collective human hand and to intervene to change it in ways that were never before possible. Advances in the life sciences that could be used for bioterrorism confront us with the issue of how best to prevent the life sciences from becoming the death sciences in the hands of bioterrorists. Ethics could be used as one weapon to counter bio-terrorism.[2] Synthetic biology, with its capacity to allow us to make organisms that don't exist in nature, faces us with never-before-encountered risks. It also raises ethical problems because of its possible diversion to perpetrate intentional harm and because it presents unknown but potentially very serious threats to public health, other species, and the environment.

Even advances that we have come to accept as "everyday" fall within an "ethics alert zone." For example, the high costs of advances in such areas as transplantation medicine, genetics, and new cancer drugs raise important ethical issues about the extent to which public health insurance should provide access to them at the taxpayers' cost.

In secular, liberal societies, which include Canada, where individual autonomy is often seen as the preeminent value when values conflict, and in which an *ethos* of intense individualism prevails, questions about the ethics and law that should govern euthanasia and physician-assisted suicide are now clearly on the political and public policy agenda and ethicists are involved in the debates about them that are taking place. In my view, the combination of an aging population, scarce health care resources, and euthanasia would indeed be a lethal one.

But interest in applied ethics in medical and biological sciences and healthcare, in general, now extends far beyond just what is required within

---

1. Somerville, "Children's Human Rights to Natural Biological Origins and Family Structure."

2. Somerville and Atlas, "Ethics: A Weapon to Counter Bioterrorism," 1881–82.

those areas to ensure that they function ethically. That has occurred because we have recognized that our decisions about ethics in those areas have implications far outside them. Those decisions can often have an impact on some of our most important values; our sense of what it means to be human and how we find meaning in life; and our cultural identity as both individuals and a society. Humans have always formed their most important values around the two great events in each and every human life, birth and death. Bioethics is intimately involved with twenty-first century birth and death. In short, bioethics is an important forum in contemporary Western democracies—and increasingly in other kinds of societies such as China and Iran, where a strong interest in bioethics is emerging—for finding human values and meaning.

In contemporary secular societies[3] such as Canada, we engage in "ethics talk" especially in Parliament and the courts, the main cathedrals of a secular society, to either reaffirm old values, lay them to rest, or articulate new ones. This is the process through which the societal-cultural paradigm—that is, the shared story composed of the values, principles, attitudes, beliefs, and myths that we all buy into in order to bind together as a society—is formed and re-formed.[4] We now speak not only of genes passing from generation to generation, but also of units of deep cultural information (sometimes called "memes") being handed on to those who will follow us. When societies were more or less homogeneous, especially religiously homogeneous, the transmission of such values from generation to generation was a major function of religion. I believe that religion still has a very important role to play in this regard in contemporary societies, although secularists (fundamentalist neo-atheists) such as scientist Richard Dawkins and journalist and the late author Christopher Hitchens would adamantly disagree, but certainly religion is no longer "the only game in town."

Holding foundational values on trust for future generations will require conscious effort, because never before in history have they been open to the possibility of such major and rapid change. Whether we look

---

3. I hasten to explain this term does not mean that religion is unimportant or irrelevant or that many people are not religious. Rather, it indicates a society in which there is separation of church and state, that is, there is no established state religion and religious voices are valid ones among the wide variety of voices that have a right to be heard in the public square. See Somerville, "Birth, Death and Technoscience," 99–115.

4. Somerville, *The Ethical Canary*.

at current advances in communications and genetic technologies, or the possibilities being opened up by nanotechnologies and human-machine interfaces, the impact on our values and culture is enormous.

Paradoxically, these incredible advances in human knowledge are causing us to face the most fundamental questions about our sense of human identity: What does it mean to be human and to act humanly and humanely towards others? And, in a globalized world, who are those others? Clearly, they are our fellow Canadians. But what are our ethical obligations to people from whom we are separated by thousands of miles, national borders, or boundaries of other kinds? It is the task of applied ethics to help the people who must decide on such issues to do so ethically, which often requires addressing them proactively and across the broadest possible spectrum of perspectives. Doing that is very often not easy and usually requires sophisticated methodologies.

The need for structures and processes for "doing ethics"

As applied ethics developed it became clear that we needed not only good research on the substantive content of applied ethics but also on the development of structures and processes that would support "doing ethics," whether in an academic research context or in practice in the real world. Factors that combined to give rise to the recognition of this need for more comprehensive and coherent structures and processes included:

- the foundational concepts on which ethics centers, such as the McGill Centre for Medicine, Ethics and Law, were established—namely, that research, teaching, and community service in applied ethics are interdependent, must be integrated, and can be mutually reinforcing—proved to be exceptionally fruitful in generating work and interest from a wide variety of sources;

- the nature of the work undertaken at such centers—they were called upon by a wide variety of people and institutions to help to address many leading-edge, high profile ethical issues facing society—was very broad-based; and

- the process and methodologies that were developed in "doing ethics," in particular transdisciplinarity, became widely accepted and used and themselves required further research.[5]

5. See, for example, Somerville and Rapport, ed., *Transdisciplinarity.*

We need structures in which scholars, students, members of various professions, politicians, those in the public service, leaders of industry, the cultural communities, the media, and the public can engage in "ethics working conversations" in an atmosphere of respect, integrity, freedom, and excitement. Among many other requirements, this requires training people as applied ethicists who can facilitate, but never take over, these conversations. There has been a severe shortage in Canada and worldwide of people trained in this field, but with many programs for graduate studies in ethics now available, this shortage is being alleviated. Applied ethics continues to require educating all who participate in "ethics working conversations" how to do so most effectively.

The need for transdisciplinary research and scholarship in a broadly based field of applied ethics is now fully recognized. The research must be structured to attract researchers from a wide range of disciplines (for example, biotechnology, science, communications, economics, journalism, cultural studies, law, management, medicine, philosophy, political science, religious studies, science, and the social sciences, to name just some fields that should be involved) at all levels of seniority and, without sacrificing academic integrity, must be open to participants from outside the academy. To achieve that has required restructuring universities in several respects, and will continue to do so, a daunting task. For instance, in the past many universities paid lip service to transdisciplinarity, but their administrative structures were and often are still set up on exclusively traditional lines and, as a result, militate against it. People can be punished in terms of tenure and promotion for not shining in a traditional discipline in a traditional way. If bioethics is to flourish, that situation must be corrected.

Protecting one's academic turf is a legendary activity in academia; as the former Secretary of State of the United States, Henry Kissinger, put it, "University politics are vicious precisely because the stakes are so small." In a field such as bioethics, it is essential to overcome such conflict because the field's very existence and further development depend on being able to cross many different kinds of boundaries. To meet the challenge that presents itself, we must design structures that can hold in creative tension the crossover of disciplines. It is at these margins that the most exciting advances in knowledge, whether in the sciences, the social sciences and humanities, or the arts, are occurring and that is as true of bioethics, neuroethics, and genethics as other recently emerged areas of research and study.

Daily media reports show the high level of public interest in applied ethics in a broad variety of contexts, from politics to *avant-garde* science, sport, media, and communications. The public needs to have a strong and readily heard voice in applied ethics, in particular, in relation to societal and cultural ethics, and ethics in government and politics, in non-governmental, corporate and professional institutions, and in academia. There is an ethical obligation to inform the public and involve its members in decision-making that goes to the very heart of societal values and ethical standards. One of the major challenges is to establish forums and modes of discourse that will allow the voices of individual members of the public and the public voice itself to be heard. That will not just happen spontaneously; rather, we need to research the ways in which such participation can be best achieved and implement them.

In particular, the public needs to participate in "ethics talk" in the public square. One requirement for them to be able to do so is ethics information. Ethicists fulfill an important public service role in providing the public with such information and that requires providing those involved in applied ethics with access to the media. Ethicists as commentators in the public square have become an increasingly familiar phenomenon over the last two decades.

It could be argued that there is nothing new about the need for "ethics talk" in the public square. I would respond, however, that two sets of developments have made the need especially acute at present. First, globalization has meant that cross-border connections of various kinds have increased exponentially, whether they involve trade, investment, migration, or communications or, indeed, our direct involvement in the affairs of other countries, whether Libya, Somalia, the former Yugoslavia, Haiti, or Afghanistan. This means that our actions inside and outside of Canada must always be evaluated in terms of their effects beyond our borders as well as within them. Second, and more particularly, the expanded reach of mass broadcast communications and the explosive growth, since roughly 1995, of the Internet and more recently of social media mean we must confront with renewed urgency the question of *what kind* of public square we want. Our choice in that regard is not ethically neutral; it will affect the form of our "ethics talk" and the substance of our ethics.

For example, one source estimates that at the peak of the show's popularity a billion people around the world watched *Baywatch*. North American and European television reach into the remotest corners of the world. This means not only the global diffusion of the idea of a consumer society that many consider to be unsustainable even for the minority of the world's people who now enjoy it, but also that ownership of major media outlets carries with it an unprecedented degree of political power. On the other hand, the Internet has diffused power by providing a relatively low cost means of virtually instantaneous communication and publication. For example, the campaign to roll back the price of antiretroviral drugs to treat people with HIV infection and AIDS in developing countries almost certainly could not have been coordinated without the Internet. And web-based information sources have created new possibilities for disintermediation in a variety of relationships: not only those between business and consumers, but also those between doctors and patients, news seekers and news generators, or those who would like to be news generators. The full text of many official announcements and publications is often available almost immediately. In spring 2011, we saw the so-called "Facebook Revolution" in the uprisings of citizens demanding governmental change in Middle-Eastern and North African countries. If Facebook were a country, it would now be the third most populous country on our planet. Hard thinking about the *kind* of Virtual Public Square we want has, however, lagged far behind the technologies for providing it.

How have I changed my mind in the last twenty-five years?

For me, this is the most difficult question the editors have asked. There are a few instances where I've radically changed my mind, for instance, I initially thought that infant male circumcision did not raise any important ethical issues and should simply be a matter of choice by a baby boy's parents. I no longer believe that. It should not be undertaken, with the possible exception of where it is carried out in fulfillment of an absolute religious obligation to do so.[6]

Like the development of applied ethics, in general, and bioethics, in particular, I too have changed over time as I have learned more and, as a

---

6. See Somerville, supra, note 3, 202–19.

result of that learning, realized that there is even more that I don't know. I hope and have every expectation that that process will continue.

None of us who were in bioethics at its beginnings could have imagined, even in our wildest dreams, how the field would expand, indeed, explode, over the last forty years. Many of us thought at the time that the first organ transplant took place, that it was an historic event, which indeed it was. But we also thought that it was unique and we would never see anything so radically "outside of nature" again, at least not in our lifetimes. How wrong we were as so many extraordinary developments have shown: Dolly the sheep and cloning; putting spider web genes in goats and recovering a substance from their milk that is stronger than steel; "pharming" in general—genetically altering cows or goats and obtaining therapeutic products from their milk; xenotransplantation, putting human complement genes in pigs in order to be able to use their organs or tissues for transplant to humans; and in the future, pharmacogenomics, personally designed therapies on the basis of each person's genetic make-up and the possibility of creating artificial life. It is indeed a wondrous world of technoscience. It is the job of bioethics to ensure that it remains a wondrous world of the natural and Nature, in particular, human nature.

So, where do we go from here?

There is now increasing recognition that the search for ethics, including in bioethics, is a search for one or more new cultural-societal paradigms. Whether we can find any universally shared values, no matter how few, on which a global paradigm could be constructed is a crucial question. Certainly we will need vision and leadership and a very broad search if we are to have any realistic chance of achieving such a goal.[7]

Such a paradigm must be neutral in the sense that it can accommodate a wide variety of beliefs or non-beliefs without compromising either. It must be acceptable in a multi-cultural, pluralistic, postmodern, secular, Western democracy such as Canada, and in a theocracy such as Iran. That might seem an impossible quest at first glance, but my experience "in the trenches" in many countries has been that open-minded, moderate people of good will from very different cultures can find consensus on many important values. To achieve that experience of belonging to the same moral community with respect to at least some issues, however, requires

7. See, in general, Somerville, *The Ethical Imagination*, pp. 270, 71.

establishing structures that will help us to identify the values we hold in common and to deal in a peaceful and constructive manner with those we do not share. That, in turn, requires advancing research, teaching and learning, and the involvement of the public in each of our countries in the broad field of applied ethics. In short, we must actively engage in an ongoing process of developing a "shared values vision" for both the present and future world. We must continue to engage in "ethics talks" and "doing ethics" to achieve that outcome. Facilitating those processes is, I believe, the primary function and goal of the field of bioethics and of ethicists for the foreseeable future.

What role, if any, does Christianity have in the construction or identification of the shared values and good-will needed to find consensus and deal in a peaceful and constructive manner with the range of scientific advances that we now face?

Contemporary debates around the ethics of the new technoscience are the crucible in which some of our most important shared social values will be forged. As I explained above, we have always formed those values around the two great events in each human life, birth and death. The new science has the potential to radically change both those events. Whether it will and to what extent depends on our decisions about the ethics that should govern it.

Religion has always been engaged in forming those values and religious voices are now even more crucial to that decision-making than in the past. But if they want to be heard by all who should hear them, they must learn to translate what they say into generally accessible, non-religious, language. That is not to sell out religion, anymore than speaking Chinese to a Chinese person who doesn't understand English is to sell out English. If we think of the great world religions, including Christianity, as the repositories of our most important human wisdom and present them in that way, in my experience what they have to say is considered by open-minded people of good will. Those who have a hatred of religion in any form will oppose any religious voice in the public square, even if it is not speaking the language of religion. Indeed they will oppose even what they perceive as a religious voice, that is, somebody who happens to be religious, whatever the topic they are addressing, even if they do not disagree with that person's position. Likewise, they will oppose positions on ethical issues that coincide with those taken by a religion, even though a person's reasons for adopting those positions are not religious. But it is a huge mistake to concentrate on trying to "convert" those people to listeners. It is a waste of resources that would be more ethically, and perhaps even more religiously, employed elsewhere.

Bibliography

Crépeau, Paul-André. *La responsabilité civile du médecin et de l'établissement hospitalier.* Montréal: Wilson & Lafleur, 1956.

———. *La responsabilité médicale et hospitalière - Évolution récente du droit québécois.* Éditions Intermonde, 1968.

Somerville, Margaret. "Birth, Death and Technoscience: Searching for Values at the Margins of Life." In *Recognizing Religion in a Secular Society*, edited by Douglas Farrow, 99–115. Montreal: McGill-Queen's University Press, 2004.

———. "Children's Human Rights to Natural Biological Origins and Family Structure." *International Journal of the Jurisprudence of the Family* 1 (2011) 35–54. HeinOnline *IJJF* library 2011 http://heinonline.org/HOL/Page?handle=hein.journals/ijjf1&id=1&collection=journals

———. *The Ethical Canary: Science, Society and the Human Spirit.* Toronto: Viking/Penguin, 2000.

———. *The Ethical Imagination: Journeys of the Human Spirit.* CBC 2006 Massey Lectures. Toronto: House of Anansi Press, 2006.

Somerville, Margaret and Ronald Atlas. "Ethics: A Weapon to Counter Bioterrorism." *Science* 307 (2005) 1881–1882.

Somerville, Margaret and David J. Rapport, ed. *Transdisciplinarity: Recreating Integrated Knowledge.* Oxford, UK: EOLSS Publishers; Montreal: McGill-Queen's University Press, 2000.

PART 4

The Academy and the City

16

"But Have You Kept the Faith of Your Ancestors?"

Musings on the Writing and Teaching of the History of Christianity in a Secular Canada

MARGUERITE VAN DIE

A S A CHILD NURTURED on religious patriotic literature extolling Dutch resistance to the sixteenth-century Spanish occupation, and later to the Nazis, I thrilled to the words of hymns such as "Stand Up, Stand Up for Jesus," and "Faith of our Fathers, living still, in spite of Dungeon, Fire and Sword." The words might be in English, belted out in a Christian Reformed basement church in Canada in the 1950s, but in my mind they placed me in touch with a heroic tradition, one as fascinating in the past as it remained alive in the present. Later, when I enrolled at Victoria College, University of Toronto, where life did not revolve around faith and church, I saw no need to abandon my fascination with Christianity. University life in the 1960s did test old boundaries, but for those so inclined there was comfort in the Protestant ethos still evident in Victoria's residence life, and more widely in Toronto the Good and its thriving churches. History courses, though challenging my earlier bent towards the heroic and patriotic, became opportunities to examine the teachings and practice of the institutional church in settings as varied as medieval Germany and early twentieth-century French Canada. These were not considered marginal topics but rather key approaches to the period under consideration.

No doubt insulated by the religious values of an immigrant society and by those vestiges of a Christian past still evident in university life, I remained blind to the dramatic seismic shift the Canadian church was undergoing at the time.[1] More prescient was the observation in 1967 by John Webster Grant, Canada's pre-eminent church historian: "The image of Christian Canada—churchgoing, moral, and devotedly partisan—strikes both believers and unbelievers today as somewhat archaic. Whether we like this image or not, it is unlikely that the church will have sufficient authority in our time to replace it with another."[2] In the four decades that have since passed, it has become unequivocally clear that Grant's image of a Christian Canada has indeed vanished without a trace. Yet, like Alice peering through a looking glass in which everything appears upside down, we continue to look for something familiar, something that once warmed our hearts as did those now so politically incorrect "triumphalist" hymns of my youth.

More recently, with the generous assistance of the Pew Charitable Trusts, my colleague David Lyon, Professor of Sociology at Queen's, and I had the opportunity to explore through a series of conferences the historical place of religion in Canada's public life and to compare this country's secularization to that in the United States and Europe.[3] The invited speakers, primarily sociologists and historians, were part of a revisionism that challenged the enduring post-Enlightenment assumption that religion represented an immature engagement with reality and was destined to vanish with the advance of science and technology. As eminent sociologists such as Jose Casanova and David Martin analyzed places as varied as the United States, the Middle East, and Latin America, they pointed out that religion remains a vital way for many to engage modernity.

The questions examined at these conferences, especially as they relate to our own Canadian context, continue to surface in public and private discussions. How secular is Canada today? Does a secular society by its nature devalue religion or can it provide room for diverse religions to flourish within an inclusive framework? How can we value the diverse religious beliefs and practices that have been and continue to remain

1. For the prevalence of a Protestant ethos in Canadian university life until well into the 1960s see Gidney, *A Long Eclipse*.

2. Grant, "The Church and Canada's Self-Awareness," 164.

3. Publications issuing from these conferences include Lyon and Van Die, ed., *Rethinking Church, State and Modernity;* Van Die, ed., *Religion and Public Life in Canada.*

important in the lives of new Canadians? To what extent is Canada's public life impoverished without the presence of religious voices and values?

These were also some of the questions that I addressed at the University of Calgary in the 2002 Iwaasa Lectures in Urban Theology. By this date, like the old image of a Christian Canada, my youthful fascination with a heroic Christian past had long been cast aside. In the course of my research and writing as a historian of evangelical Protestantism in nineteenth-century Canada, the warts and wrinkles of that religious movement had become clearer. Entitled "The End of Christian Canada: Past Perspectives, Present Opportunities," the lecture ended with the observation that it would be ahistorical to wish for a return of the past. In the discussion that followed I came to realize, however, that the lessons of history are often persuasive only to historians. To a number of the evangelical, highly committed students in the audience that evening, to proclaim, let alone accept, the loss of Christian cultural authority revealed the myopia of someone living not in Alberta but in Ontario and perhaps also an admission of a loss of faith. Their response has led me to face once more the words of the title of this brief essay: how, if at all, can we today "keep the faith of our ancestors"?

My answer is at best provisional, for it is developing slowly in bits and pieces, but like anything tentative it begins with the personal. Hence, the autobiographical approach to this writing, an approach mandated by the nature of this collection, for which I now, despite earlier misgivings, thank the editors. The first part of my response revisits my earlier musings on the writing and researching of the history of Christianity, this time moving from the heroic and the institutional to a brief discussion of current approaches. The second part is likewise shaped by the personal: my joint appointment as a professor in a secular department of history at Queen's University and as a church historian at Queen's Theological College (in 2009 renamed the Queen's School of Religion), dedicated to preparing candidates for the ministry of the United Church of Canada.

As the students in Calgary perceptively pointed out, the site of the observer does indeed influence the diagnosis. Many years ago I changed my denominational identity, but each time that I worship with my mother in the Christian Reformed congregation that helped shaped my youthful enthusiasm for a Christian past, I am made aware of how much of that past still remains. Scores of blond-haired, blue-eyed children flock to the front of the pulpit each Sunday for the children's story. Meanwhile, their parents and grandparents settle in for a half-hour of theological and biblical sermon reflection, followed by a lengthy congregational prayer. Laying out the needs and joys of the community, the prayer is followed by a different from of public witness: well-funded collections for local and church causes, ranging from the needs of a city mission or the local Christian school to famine relief in drought-stricken Africa. Fifty years after its founding by Dutch immigrants, this church, and so many like it, continues to reflect many of the facets of the image of a Christian Canada that historians and other observers, including most of the media, have long since considered vanished.

Nor is it entirely absent in my own United Church congregation. The contours remain, evident in the aging congregation's intense concern with "faith and justice" issues, but also in its reenactment of a social and communal identity at variance with today's fragmented, busy, and individualistic urban lifestyle. And, having recently launched for theology students a course on church renewal with the provocative title "Evangelism for Non-Evangelicals," I know from the presentations offered by ministers that there exist today many vital and vibrant congregations within the old mainline denominations.

Nevertheless, while the extent of the loss of Christian cultural authority may vary with the location of the observer (a point underscored by the high level of religiosity in the United States), few would deny that a chasm separates us from the experience of a half century earlier. Again, I refer to personal observation. In 1985 when I was first appointed to Queen's, I could expect that most of the undergraduates who chose to take my history course in religion and North American society had some personal connection to organized Christianity and understood its basic terminology. Twenty-six years later this is no longer the case. For many "spirituality" has replaced any coherent religious tradition, and conventional narratives such as the development of a Christian Canada are of marginal interest, if not politically objectionable. The historian's craft has reflected this sea change. Beginning in the 1970s with a shift in methods and interest from political and institutional history to the social sciences and gender, the carefully constructed narratives of the Christian church in Canada by John Webster Grant and his generation of church historians came to an end.[4] At the same time, a younger group of trained historians,

4. Grant's work was sufficiently appreciated, however, to call for a second edition: Grant, *The Church in the Canadian Era*, 2nd. ed.

informed by new perspectives and questions, began to flesh out the older story of Christian Canada with fine-grained analyses of such varied topics as women's missionary work, the nature and impact of urban revivals, and the symbolic significance of Canada's Centennial celebrations.[5]

Some of these changes have been beneficial. The recent historical method of "lived religion" is especially useful for teaching students who have had little or no personal religious socialization. Pioneered by American historians such as Robert Orsi, David Hall, Colleen McDannell, and Leigh Schmidt, and shaped by the insights of post-structuralism, this approach emphasizes religion's dialectical relationship with the social.[6] Like anthropologists seeking to understand an unfamiliar society, these scholars of religious history in a secular age take as their guide ethnography rather than institutional or intellectual history, as was once the case. Institutions, denominations, theologies, and doctrinal teachings are indeed part of the context from which lived religion is extrapolated, but the focus is not on these but on what people actually make of them. This forces historians to become aware of the idiomatic possibilities and limitations within the culture under investigation, of what people were able to desire, express, fantasize. Why, for example, did the rich imagery of a heaven figure so prominently in nineteenth-century accounts of death, to disappear almost entirely in our own time? Related to this is an openness to the prevailing knowledges of the body: what was it that people in a certain period of time and place tasted, felt, smelled, heard?

Asking such questions, historian Robert Orsi has been able convincingly to reconstruct for readers the lush rituals and feasts of Italian American immigrants in early twentieth-century Harlem, while Canadian historian James Opp has published a magnificent description of faith healing.[7] For both historians, one writing in the context of a post-Vatican II Roman Catholicism critical of devotionalism, and the other in a highly secular academic environment, the body becomes the site of religious belief and practice rather than the institution or the intellect. Excavated with care, skill, and observation, practices that could easily be derided or criticized instead become the subject of informed understand-

5. For a sampling of these studies, see the long list of titles published in the two McGill-Queen's Studies in the History of Religion.

6. Hall ed., *Lived Religion in America: Towards a History of Practice*; Schmidt, *Consumer Rites*; McDannell, *Material Christianity*.

7. Orsi, *The Madonna of 115th Street*; Opp, *The Lord for the Body*.

ing. In such a method, students are encouraged to recognize that religious idioms, symbols, and institutions do not simply reflect a world (as was the assumption in the older approach to history), but that they also *make* a world, a world with all its tensions, contradictions, and ambiguities.

To the students reading such new histories, the emphasis on religion as dynamic experience in dialogue with its context also has implications for their own self-awareness. As researchers and writers, they begin to recognize their personal implication in the study and writing of human history, and hence to realize the importance of their own spirituality and their own religious formation or lack thereof. Rather than seeing the religious past as dead and its actors as "other," they are encouraged to explore to what extent their own circumstances as thinking, feeling people, caught in the complexities of daily life, can provide at least an entry into the religious experience of, for example, Pentecostals in the early twentieth century. In short, along with the usual reading and analysis of texts, students become more aware of the kinds of religious worlds people have made and of the scholars, including themselves, who study these worlds.

Such an approach would not have been possible if the moral authority of the old Christian Canada were still in place. Rather than being forced to take a creative, multifaceted approach to excavating the religious experience of an earlier time, students (and their instructors) would have simply assumed that a knowledge of institutions and theology alone was needed. Overlooked would have been the messiness, the contradictions, and the tensions that were (and are) part of lived religion, as they are of life more generally.

How then does this pertain to the matter of "keeping the faith of one's ancestors" in a secular society? In the first place, by approaching the religious past through the lens of "lived religion," historians and their students recognize how intimately religion has been part of people's social, economic, and intellectual experience. At the same time, by sharpening our perception of the presence of religion within the warp and woof of daily life in the past, this historiographical method also raises awareness of the many ways in which the quest for the sacred continues to shape people's negotiation of daily life. Faith is then seen never to be static but always sensitive to the context of its practitioners. I have tried to make this same point at some length in a recent study examining the religious ife of one nineteenth-century evangelical family over three generations.[8] The study's concluding observation that "the world that parents bequeath to their children is not the world their children inherit," is a matter of common sense, sometimes forgotten, but pertinent to the present discussion. Just as the faith of the third generation of this particular family as they stepped into twentieth-century Canada could not replicate that of the parents, so too mine at the dawn of the twenty-first is not "the faith of our fathers." The massive de-Christianization of the intervening period has permanently displaced such an option.

What it has also done, however, is open a space in the academy for a more perceptive approach to religion, one that recognizes the ambiguity of life, the tensions and contradictions that are part of living within the given structures of our own place and time.[9] In the nineteenth century, sometimes referred to as Canada's "Christian century," the doctrine of the atonement, Christ's sacrificial death, provided the basis for moral and social action for evangelical Protestants and ultramontane Roman Catholics.[10] A century later, in a secular society it is the doctrine of the incarnation, the Word made flesh, which for me has become a compelling symbol of the way religion is now lived through and under the structures of daily life. So often unnoticed in our midst, the Word made flesh is a symbol of the intricate and (to my limited vision) often ambiguous ways in which the sacred and the secular are, and have always been, scrambled together. Where once in my youth, and in our country's youth, the history of Christianity was seen as a heroic enterprise, today its study is more complex. Yet as I grow older, I see it as more rewarding, as demanding a deeper self-knowledge and a keener awareness of the fragility and ambiguity of every day life, in the past but also in the present.

---

8. Van Die, *Religion, Family, and Community in Victorian Canada.*

9. To explore "lived religion" does not call for a confessional position. Historian Robert Orsi, for example has been clear that for him there can be no return to the Roman Catholic piety of his youth, nor to any confessional faith. At the same time, in an insightful essay on the way the personal and the historiographical have been linked in his work, he has acknowledged how his insight into the lived experience of devout Roman Catholics has sharpened his own self-insight as a human being. Orsi, *Between Heaven and Earth*, 146–76.

10. For the concept of "Christian Canada," see Noll, *A History of Christianity in the United States and Canada*, especially 540–53.

Bibliography

Gidney, Catherine. *A Long Eclipse: the Liberal Protestant Establishment and the Canadian University, 1920–1970*. Montreal/Kingston: McGill-Queen's University Press, 2004.

Grant, John Webster. "The Church and Canada's Self-Awareness." *Canadian Journal of Theology* 13, no. 3 (1967) 155–64.

————. *The Church in the Canadian Era*, 2nd. ed. Burlington, ON: Welch, 1988.

Hall, Robert N. ed., *Lived Religion in America: Towards a History of Practice*. Princeton: Princeton University Press, 1997.

Lyon, David and Marguerite Van Die, ed., *Rethinking Church, State and Modernity: Canada Between Europe and the United States*. Toronto: University of Toronto Press, 2000.

McDannell, Colleen *Material Christianity: Religion and Popular Culture in America*. New Haven: Yale University Press 1995.

Noll, Mark. *A History of Christianity in the United States and Canada*. Grand Rapids: Eerdmans, 1992.

Opp, James. *The Lord for the Body: Religion, Medicine, and Protestant Faith Healing in Canada, 1880–1930*. Montreal/Kingston: McGill-Queen's University Press 2005.

Orsi, Robert. *Between Heaven and Earth: The Religious Worlds People Make and the Scholars Who Study Them*. Princeton: Princeton University Press, 2005.

————. *The Madonna of 115th Street: Faith and Community in Italian Harlem, 1880–1950*. New Haven: Yale University Press 1985.

Schmidt, Leigh Eric. *Consumer Rites: The Buying and Selling of American Holidays*. Princeton: Princeton University Press, 1995.

Van Die, Marguerite. *Religion, Family, and Community in Victorian Canada: the Colbys of Carrollcroft*. Montreal/Kingston: McGill-Queen's University Press, 2005.

————. Ed., *Religion and Public Life in Canada: Comparative and Historical Perspectives*. Toronto: University of Toronto Press, 2001.

17

The Spiritual Quest, Christian Thought, and the Academy

Challenges, Commitments, and Considerations

CHARLES NIENKIRCHEN

OVER THE PAST THREE decades I have taught an array of "spirituality" courses at Canadian and American Christian colleges, seminaries, and universities. In response to student demand, these institutions are offering an increasing number of courses dealing with issues of spiritual experience. In several instances the intensity of student interest outstripped the capacity of schools to create appropriate curricular classification for the courses I taught.

The evolving nature of students' questions has been particularly revealing. Traditional concerns about the big ticket items of right doctrine, belief, and justifications for one's denominational allegiance have been overtaken by a host of queries and comments such as these: "How can I be connected to the spiritual world?" "What is spiritual direction? Can you tell me how to find a spiritual director? "Can a person hear God through dreams and if so how does one interpret them?" "I need to recover a sense of sacredness in my life." "I would like to learn how to meditate." "Will you tell me about discernment?" "How can I become more spiritually empowered?"

A growing number of students enrolled in Christian Thought programs have the sense that they are living in an emerging post-denominational age of spiritual and ecumenical collaboration that is displacing the age of triumphalistic promotion of denominational identities. This sense has spawned students' desire to be informed about and to draw from the spiritual treasures present in a broad spectrum of Christian traditions. They realize that a full-orbed Christian spirituality can only be developed if the positive contributions of the various historic Christian "spiritualities/pieties" are appreciated and incorporated.

This search for an inclusive, pristine Christian spirituality, uncontaminated by schism, has given many Christian Thought students a hunger for roots and a new appreciation for Christian antiquity. Implied in all of this is a rejection of what might be termed "Enlightened," rationalistic, doctrinally defined, business-styled Christianity. In contrast, the ancient Christianity of the Fathers with its openness to the supra-rational spiritual world, its respect for mystery and symbol, its reverence for liturgical traditions of worship, and its sense of aesthetic beauty appears more interesting and satisfying. In short, Christian Thought as it exists within the academy must make room for spirituality as a discipline.

Spirituality scholars have made concerted attempts over the past twenty-five years to establish the credibility of their discipline in the face of charges of "flakiness." The creation of spirituality-focused scholarly societies with associated journals and the appearance of a growing number of accredited graduate and PhD spirituality programs in reputable universities have done much to raise the profile of spirituality as a legitimate academic discipline. Spirituality scholars have served the broader academic community, church, and society through their translation of classic texts, their study of the reception of these texts, and their reflection on the spiritual implications of these texts, thereby ensuring their continued existence as sources of spiritual direction. All of this work has been going on in the midst of an animated, in-house debate over the relationship between spirituality studies in the academic sense and spiritual formation as practiced by individuals and communities. It remains unresolved.

The dual matters of defining spirituality and resolving the tension between theory and practice are the paramount sources of conflict and challenge in the spirituality field. Defining spirituality is an immensely complicated and contentious affair. Popular attempts to give the term semantic clarity are ever changing and confused. Scholars wrangle over whether the term should have any subjective, applied element as an intrinsic part of the definition.

While spirituality defined theoretically certainly has a rich, documented past, the growth of spirituality studies in recent decades has mostly been in the experimental direction, thus giving the term a much more expansive scope than ever before. Presently, academics, theologians, ministerial professionals, and popular practitioners all have a vested interest in spirituality. Thus it is an open competition as to who should have the right to define it. The growing body of literature on the problems of definition and disciplinary methodology has reached voluminous proportions.

If defining the term is problematic, then the status and perception of faculty who teach spirituality within the academy is equally so. Is the Professor of Spirituality one who engages in a detached, objective presentation of the subject as seen through the lenses of research, description, and critical analysis, removed from any kind of praxis? Is scholarship to be segregated from one's personal spiritual pilgrimage? Or does the most authentic teaching of spirituality occur when there is cross-pollination between one's academic profession and one's personal spiritual quest? Where do theory and praxis meet, if at all?

As a Christian in the Methodist tradition, who teaches Christian spirituality in conservative Protestant institutions, my approach to the discipline is predicated upon several *a priori* commitments. The following premises constitute the cornerstones of my teaching of Christian spirituality:

1. The term "spirituality" acknowledges the primacy of the creating and restoring work of the Holy Spirit among humankind. At the same time, it affirms the innate self-transcending capacity of all human beings which enables them to enter into relationship with the divine and to connect with the spiritual world which exists beyond the realm of empirical reality. Humans have the ability both to be recipients and transmitters of spirituality. Everything which pertains to this synergistic divine-human relationship falls under the rubric of spirituality. This definition necessarily precludes attempts to reduce spirituality solely to the domain of the human spirit with no otherworldly frame of reference.

2. Spirituality, notwithstanding its association with a search for transcendence, also has a conspicuous "this-worldly" social and cultural dimension. This is expressed in the variety of ways in which those

seeking to live with spiritual integrity enter into a network of relationships with various communities throughout the course of their lives. Factors such as gender, family of origin, ethnic identity, religious affiliation, and socioeconomic status all play a role in lived, spiritual experience. The relationship between spirituality and culture is a fluid, dynamic one which can and should be investigated and analysed by the social sciences. The study of spirituality is naturally and necessarily interdisciplinary.

3. All traditions of Christian spirituality ultimately derive from the teachings of Jesus of Nazareth and have been disseminated over the centuries both by individuals and organized communities of faith. Christian spirituality has a necessarily communal dimension in which traditions of belief and practice are transmitted from generation to generation. A spirituality without tradition is a spirituality without either a memory which gives a sense of rootedness or a stable base which provides a reasonable prospect for future survival. It is not in the interest of the social good for religion and spirituality to be allowed to go their own ways. A privatized spirituality which eschews dependence upon organized religious life is to be discouraged. It harbors the risk of spawning a spirituality which deteriorates into destructive aberrations of thought and practice against which a knowledge of and respect for time-tested tradition offers some protection.

4. Since its inception, Christian spirituality has always had life transformation as a foundational objective. The primary consequence of the encounter of humans with divinity is a call to conversion and the realignment of one's life by the empowerment of the Spirit of God. Gaining recognition within the academy should not allow the inextricable link between epistemology, pedagogy, and ethics which Christian spirituality espouses, to be broken. Prickly as the issue is for relating to the secular academy, this calls for fortitude on the part of Christian Thought programs, especially in public institutions. If the engaged teaching of spirituality is suspected by a secular academy of compromising the critical distance needed by scholars to conduct their objective analysis it is also true that the detached teaching of spirituality at arms length equally runs the risk of skewing or impairing scholarly interpretation and judgment.

In conclusion, a brief consideration of the benefits of including Christian Spirituality within the orbit of Christian Thought as it is taught in institutions of higher learning in Canada and the United States seems in order. Firstly, the injection of spirituality into Christian Thought will go a long way to revitalizing this field of study at a time when in both countries many are making their exodus from Christian churches and opting instead for seemingly more attractive spiritual alternatives. The current explosion of spiritual curiosity at a time when many faith communities are declining has spurred the growth of religious pluralism and publicized the availability of a panoply of esoteric spiritualities as never before. There exists a tidal wave of experimentation on which Christian spirituality can surf. In the postmodern era both the unchurched and the lapsed could be induced to give Christianity serious consideration if it were seen to be responding to the spiritual needs of the populace. Without compromising its unique truth claims and commitment to prayer, Christian spirituality in secular public institutions should readily participate in hospitable, open dialogue with non-Christians and spiritual seekers who do not evidence any faith or belief or espouse any brand of theism.

In its original New Testament form, Christianity was essentially about being on a spiritual pilgrimage in mystical union with the resurrected Christ, electrified by the supernatural charisms of the Holy Spirit and grounded in the epistemological certainty that the spiritual world beyond space and time is immanent. One of the earliest designations for the Christian movement was "The Way." Early Christians knew nothing about an abstract "truth" devoid of the lived way.

Secondly, the recovery of Christian spirituality holds the possibility of initiating a new, robust trend toward the unprecedented convergence of Christian spiritualities involving whole families of churches—Orthodox and Catholic churches which emphasize apostolic succession and sacramental order, Reformation churches (Calvinist, Lutheran, Methodist ,and some strains of Anglicanism) which shift their attention to the priority of correct doctrine and the authority of Scripture over tradition, and Restorationist churches, descendants of the Radical Reformation (Mennonites, Baptists, Pentecostals) who broke completely with apostolic succession and advocated a restitution of the apostolic church based on Scripture rather than a reformation of the existing one.

The old ecumenism, preoccupied with discussing differences in dogma, liturgy, and organizational structures, is largely a spent force. Nor was it as inclusive as it might have been since it was rejected by some families of churches on doctrinal grounds. By contrast, an emerging new ecumenism, which strives for Christian unity based on respect for a doctrinal and liturgical consensus derived from antiquity, already has much vibrancy at the grassroots level. Recent Orthodox/Catholic/ Evangelical Protestant dialogues, in which discussions of spirituality have played a prominent role, are a vibrant indicator of the dynamic of this new ecumenism and its potential for fostering a new kind of mutually respected, lived, Christian unity. Christian Thought scholars who pursue spirituality studies along these convergent trajectories can only further abet this process.

Lastly, beyond the boundaries of inter-church dialogue lies the much larger, exceedingly complex and tangled world of inter-faith relations in which I claim no expertise. Dialogue among the world's great religious traditions for the dedicated purpose of raising levels of global civility has never been more urgent. Religious-instigated violence in many countries seems to hold world peace hostage. The academy has vigorously debated the merits of Huntington's thesis regarding the "clash of civilizations." One wonders if the study of Christian spirituality as an academic discipline coupled with the realization that all the religions of the world give rise to their own version of the spiritual quest might encourage a consideration of the "convergence of civilizations" around the theme of humanity's search for a common path. Empowered by a commitment to peace, which lies at the original core of Christian spirituality, and sensitive to those primal spiritual values which they share with other religions, Christian scholars who are personally in touch with all that is really spiritual in Christianity could encourage those in the academy of other faith traditions to move in the same direction. At the same time they would have their own spiritual insights enhanced and their blindspots addressed by inter-faith conversations. This would do much to demonstrate that the spiritual quest, Christian Thought, and the academy do indeed belong to the same fraternity.

18

Ecstatic Nerve

Fiction, Historical Narrative, and Christian Theology in an Academic Setting

PETER C. ERB

I N THE EARLY 1980s I moved laterally from an English to a Religious Studies department. After a decade as a philologist, teaching Old and Middle English, my identity struggles appeared resolved. Trained in the study of medieval spirituality, I could at last settle down to teach courses in Christianity as a broad support for my scholarly interest in historical theology. But any relief I felt in my new position was soon dissolved. My career path now included responsibilities as managing editor of *Studies in Religion / Sciences Religieuses*. As I faced the challenges arising word by word, comma by comma, in the arguments my new-found colleagues were making, I recognised that I had unwittingly shifted into a world which seemed to be casting off religious ecstasy (as my former department had the aesthetic variety) while suffering a colossal "failure of nerve."[1] Indeed, my favoured area, Christian theology, was excoriated and effectively excommunicated by the secular rites of a renovated low-church priesthood, unknowingly intoning its arch-enemy Karl Barth: "A 'pure' science of religion is one which does not make any claim to be theology. [I]ts procedure [is] more sober and instructive and promising than the adulterated science of religion of theologians, who spoil the peaceful

1. See Davis, "Wherein," 393–400 and Wiebe, "Failure," 401–22.

course of this investigation by suddenly taking account of revelation, and give evidence, by the philosophic standards of assessment and value which they apply, that they are dealing with something that they are in no position either to understand or to take seriously."[2]

"What have I got myself into?" I wondered. In large part, the debates struck me then as marks of an adolescent identity crisis. I should have known better, of course: religious studies had been undergoing an identity crisis from birth, and there is good reason to argue that its struggles were a continuation of nineteenth-century Christian concerns in a re-structured language,[3] centered either on the "mystical" and the hope for "ecstasy" (in tracing some underlying unity in all religions), or on "positive" a-theistic terms, courageously pursuing an "academic" or "social scientific" study of religions as pluralities, reduced to a unity only by the most objective standards.[4] What I should also have known then was that long-standing crises are likely to be long-lived. "This too will pass," I supposed, as I reviewed the interminable debates over the definition of "religion" ("theology," strikingly, remained undefined, static, and monolithically Christian) and watched wide-eyed as my field laid imperial claim with post-colonial rhetoric over every popular phenomenon from Star-Trek parties to paint-ball battles, from Eminem to Harlequin romances. What I did not expect was that in the next decade the continuing self-critical debate would turn to masochistic self-abuse, in much the same way as it did in those Christian communities that earlier gave rise to religious studies. One practitioner described the field as having no language and speaking "only a mongrel, polyglot jargon."[5]

But stranger things were in store. Had someone suggested in the late 1970s that in less than a decade the study of Barth on the Trinity and Aquinas the theologian (sic) would be considered *avant-garde* and that theology would soon seek revenge on its cultured despisers by re-addressing the historical narrative and laying claim as elder parent to a

---

2. Barth, *Church Dogmatics*, 1/ 2, 295.

3. Compare the argument of Smith, *Drudgery Divine*.

4. Compare the insightful comments of Barth, *Church Dogmatics* 1/ 2, 317–25, regarding this "religious" turn.

5. For details see Matter, "Academic Culture," 383–89. Note the parallel pattern among Christian writers of various groups: Spong, *Why Christianity must Change*, Wills, *Papal Sin*, and, more directly, Harpur, *Pagan Christ*.

rightful place in its former household,[6] I would have shrugged and deferred the prediction to the better keeping of some absent transcendental signifier. But by the mid-80s, at the very time religious studies scholars were endeavouring to remove all traces of theology from their work, theology took on new life. I increasingly found myself present at prescribed secular rituals by day and poring over theological aesthetics, political theology, postliberal exegesis, and, eventually, the wild imaginations of Radical Orthodoxy by night.

Two examples offer a more concrete view of the changes I am noting. The first relates to theological aesthetics, an avocation that brought me to Calgary as a guest of the Chair of Christian Thought for the first time in 2000.[7] Almost twenty years had passed since I first began to teach in a Religious Studies department, and when I was asked to offer a popular lecture on a topic of my choosing I was immediately drawn to the growing use of Christian theological themes that I had noted in the popular novel from the mid-1980s. They were everywhere. My own interest focused on the work of P. D. James, in whose books High Church Anglicanism is ever-present and who began to explore the religious dimensions of human life more explicitly in *A Taste of Death* in 1986. She was not alone. A half decade earlier similar questions were taken up in *The Name of the Rose* by Umberto Eco (1980). These questions were explored in other ways by James' fellow Oxonians, Ian Pears in *An Instance of the Fingerpost* (1997) and Colin Morris in *The Remorseful Day* (1999). On the American side of the Atlantic the same pattern was clearly evident in the Baptist John Grisham's *The Street Lawyer* (1998) and *The Testament* (1999). It was not only the mystery/thriller that exemplified the turn to religion and certainly not only Christians or religious practitioners.[8] A good representative of quite different work is the evangelical atheist, Jim Crace, who explores humanity's striving beyond its limits in his first collection *Continent* (1986), through to his life of Jesus, *Quarantine* (1997), and after.

6. With respect to the United States, for example, see the analyses of Marsden, *Soul,* and Hart, *University,* and compare Milbank's defense of the rightful place of theology as an academic discipline in his *Theology.*

7. See my "Murder, Espionage, and other Christian Mysteries," University of Calgary, January 25, 2000, and my *Murder, Manners, and Mystery,* the final result of the paper originally given at Calgary and in a much expanded form for the John Albert Hall Lectures at the University of Victoria in 2004.

8. For British Catholic and Anglican writers of the late 80s and 90s see my "Reappropriating."

These and other works had been largely ignored by religious studies scholars and, if considered, were viewed primarily in the older frameworks of the 1960s—a sort of "religious themes" approach. Film proved more attractive to the academic study of religion, but there again it was largely viewed thematically (crucifixion themes, the use of water images), psychologically (charting developmental needs in a character), or sociopolitically (tracing patterns of hegemonic control). Christian theology took a different tack, rooted as it was in the doctrine of the Incarnation: no separate element in a text could be considered apart from the whole nor the whole "created" structure apart from its meaning. The word in which and through which all was created bespoke the Word. Whether for Protestant, Orthodox, or Catholic, the relationship between nature and grace was a central issue in any discussion of beauty. Aesthetic and theological concerns were necessarily linked, whether considering a conversion experience in Janette Oke's "Christian Fiction" or Ian McEwan's *Black Dogs* (1992). Neither Hans Urs von Balthasar nor Karl Barth offered a final word, although both provided a wide range of possibilities for students of the literatures of the great Western and Eastern religions, the study of which was sadly limited by the exclusion of theology from academic halls.[9]

Historical theology affords a second dimension worth considering, and again I limit the treatment to a specific interest. For twenty-five years now I have been working on a critical edition of the correspondence from 1833–1890 between the British Prime Minister William E. Gladstone and the former Anglican priest, later Catholic Archbishop of Westminster, Henry E. Manning. From the beginning I found myself immersed in historiographical problems of two sorts. Just as I was beginning the project the study of Anglican theology and history was undergoing a revival. In 1987 Christopher Haigh edited a volume that marked a new era in Anglican Reformation studies.[10] The growing number of detailed monographs on the sixteenth century in turn stimulated work into the Caroline/Laudian period. This brought attention to the differing readings of the Church of England's past found among nineteenth-century adherents

9. Among other examples not so hampered, consider Kroeker, *Remembering the End*, and more recent wide interest in works such as that of Hart, *The Beauty of the Infinite*.

10. *English Reformation Revised*, edited by Haigh. Note as well the popularity of Duffy, *Stripping of the Altars*, MacCulloch, *Thomas Cranmer*, and the ongoing popular debate arising out of their disagreements over the necessity of the Anglican Reformation.

to Low Church, Broad Church, Old High Church, Tractarian, Ritualist, Evangelical, and Roman Catholic principles. Later historical and contemporary theological debates shaped the understanding of earlier eras. At the same time J. C. D. Clark forced a reconsideration of the central place of religion in British political life in the long century following the Glorious Revolution.[11] Shortly thereafter, Boyd Hilton directed attention to the close relations between theology and social and political thought.[12] In these and similar cases several things were immediately evident. In the first place, the anthropological self-reflective turn of the historian aided, rather than hindered, the work and insight of the scholar.[13] Announced theological or personal partisanship benefited scholarship, even when it appeared to distract from it. However one might disagree with Clark's political concerns, they played an important role in directing the reader to an understanding of the central place of theology in the development of political and social life in eighteenth-century England and the need to recognise that element in other eras as well.[14]

Neither a prophet nor the son of a prophet, I will make no predictions. But perhaps one conclusion might be drawn: the study of theology, particularly Christian theology, has proven an important element in much scholarly activity over the past twenty-five years of work in many scholarly disciplines and fields and continues to do so. Indeed, it might be said that the attempted elimination of theology[15] may have impoverished rather than aided the academic study of religion, especially considering the importance of Christianity as the largest global religious phenomenon and of Christian theological categories as the root of secular modernity.[16] We can be thankful for secular institutions with the nerve to continue

11. Clark, *English Society.*

12. Hilton, *The Age of Atonement.*

13. For a striking work in this respect see Harris, *Lourdes.*

14. Cf. Brent, *Liberal Anglican Politics* and Nockles, *The Oxford Movement.*

15. See McCutcheon, *Manufacturing Religion.* There is no reason according to my argument to reduce the study of any religion to a Weberian reading, although it is worthy of note that some recent introductions to religious studies appear uncomfortable with Weber, perhaps as a result of their desire to distance themselves from theology generally. Note, for example, Pals, *Seven Theories.*

16. Even popes and Marxists are in agreement on this issue. See the papers of Habermas and Ratzinger, *Dialectics.* For background see Schmitt, *Political Theology* and Löwith, *Meaning in History,* and the reservations of Blumenberg, *Legitimacy.*

their support of explicitly-defined Christian studies without fear of some inevitable ecstatic theological infiltration.

Bibliography

Barth, Karl. *Church Dogmatics*. Edited by G. W. Bromiley and T. F. Torrance, translated by G. W. Bromiley. London: T&T Clark, 1956.

Blumenberg, Hans. *The Legitimacy of the Modern Age*. Translated by Robert M. Wallace. Cambridge: MIT Press, 1983.

Brent, Richard. *Liberal Anglican Politics: Whiggery, Religion, and Reform, 1830–1841*. Oxford: Clarendon, 1987.

Clark, J. C. D. *English Society, 1688–1832: Ideology, Social Structure, and Political Practice During the Ancien Regime*. Cambridge: Cambridge University Press, 1985.

Davis, Charles. "Wherein There Is No Ecstasy." *Studies in Religion / Sciences Religieuses* 13 (1984) 393–400.

Duffy, Eamon. *The Stripping of the Altars: Traditional Religion in England, c.1400-c.1580*. New Haven: Yale University Press, 1992.

Erb Peter C. "Reappropriating the Catholic Past: British Catholic Novelists in the 1990s." Aquinas Center Symposium on Catholic Fiction, Emory University, Atlanta, Ga., February 20, 1998.

———. "Murder, Espionage, and Other Christian Mysteries: Contemporary Christian Novelists in the Secular World." The Rev. Howard Bentall Lecture on Education and Theology, University of Calgary, Calgary, AB, January 25, 2000.

———. *Murder, Manners, and Mystery: Reflections on Faith in Contemporary Detective Fiction. The John Albert Hall Lectures, 2004*. London: SCM, 2007.

Habermas, Jürgen, and Joseph Ratzinger. *The Dialectics of Secularization: On Reason ad Religion*. Translated by Brian McNeill. San Francisco: Ignatius, 2006.

Haigh, Christopher (ed.). *The English Reformation Revised*. Cambridge: Cambridge University Press, 1987.

Harpur, Tom. *The Pagan Christ: Recovering the Lost Light*. Toronto: Thomas Allen, 2004.

Harris, Ruth. *Lourdes: Body and Spirit in the Secular Age*. New York: Viking, 1999.

Hart, D. G. *The University Gets Religion: Religious Studies in American Higher Education*. Baltimore: Johns Hopkins University Press, 1999.

Hart, David Bentley. *The Beauty of the Infinite: The Aesthetics of Christian Truth*. Grand Rapids: Eerdmans, 2003.

Hilton, Boyd. *The Age of Atonement: The Influence of Evangelicalism on Social and Economic Thought, 1795–1865*. Oxford: Clarendon, 1988.

Kroeker, P. Travis. with Bruce Kinsey Ward. *Remembering the End: Dostoevsky as Prophet to Modernity*. Boulder, CO: Westview, 2001.

Löwith, Karl. *Meaning in History; the theological Implications of the Philosophy of History*. Chicago: University of Chicago Press 1949.

MacCulloch, Diarmaid. *Thomas Cranmer: A Life*. New Haven: Yale University Press, 1996.

Marsden, George. *The Soul of the American University*. New York: Oxford University Press, 1994.

Matter, Ann. "The Academic Culture of Disbelief: Religious Studies at the University of Pennsylvania." *Method and Theory in the Study of Religion* 7 (1995) 383–89.

McCutcheon, Russell T. *Manufacturing Religion: The Discourse on Sui Generis Religion and the Politics of Nostalgia.* New York: Oxford University Press, 1997.

Milbank, John. *Theology and Social Theory: Beyond Secular Reason.* Oxford: Blackwell, 1990.

Nockles, Peter B. *The Oxford Movement in Context: Anglican High Churchmanship, 1760-*Cambridge: Cambridge University Press, 1994.

Pals, Daniel L. *Seven Theories of Religion.* Oxford: Oxford University Press, 1996.

Schmitt, Carl. *Political Theology: Four Chapters on the Concept of Sovereignty.* Translated by George Schwab. Cambridge: MIT Press, 1985.

Smith, Jonathan Z. *Drudgery Divine. On the Comparison of Early Christianities and the Religions of Late Antiquity.* Chicago: University of Chicago Press, 1990.

Spong, John Shelby. *Why Christianity Must Change or Die: A Bishop Speaks to Believers in Exile.* San Francisco: Harper, 1998.

Wiebe, Donald. "The Failure of Nerve in the Academic Study of Religion." *Studies in Religion / Sciences Religieuses* 13 (1984) 401–22.

Wills, Garry. *Papal Sin: Structures of Deceit.* New York: Doubleday, 2000.

19

Athens and Jerusalem

Facing Both Ways in Calgary

ALAN P. F. SELL

T HE CONTEXT IN WHICH John Bunyan introduced Mr. Facing-both-ways makes it clear that this character is not to be emulated. But, as if in defiance of Tertullian's celebrated expostulation, "What indeed has Athens to do with Jerusalem? What concord is there between the Academy and the Church?" the incumbent of the University of Calgary's Chair of Christian Thought was required to be a Mr. Facing-both-ways in the nicest possible way.

It was precisely the challenge implicit in this requirement that brought me to Calgary at the end of 1987. University Chairs at the University of Calgary were designed to bring to Calgary scholars able to contribute to the research profile of the University and to teach graduate students. Facing the Academy, I taught a graduate course every semester and conducted an extensive program of research and writing. In addition, I volunteered to teach a number of undergraduate courses. With a view to stimulating debate among members of a number of faculties, I inaugurated the University's Eighteenth-Century Studies Group. In order not to remain aloof from the extra-disciplinary tasks that are the lot of all academics, I served on a number of committees, and chaired the University Students Academic Appeals Committee during what proved to be a bumper period for appeals.

Facing the Church and the wider community, I gave two series of "town and gown" public lectures,[1] alternating the venues between the campus and a local church. In these lectures I tackled a diversity of subjects in what, I hoped, was an informative, challenging, and entertaining way. I still remember some of the stimulating questions posed by members of the audiences. I conducted worship in a number of Christian denominations, addressed church assemblies, and spoke at meetings religious and secular. My articles appeared in Christian magazines across Canada, and, from time to time, graced the religion pages of the *Calgary Herald*.

In such ways I sought, over a period of almost five years, to honor the convictions of those who inaugurated the Chair, namely, that Christian Thought not only can, but needs to, carve out an unprivileged path in the disciplinary jostle which is academia, and at the same time communicate with the believing and secular world around. It was a privilege to serve in this way and I look back upon the period with much pleasure and gratitude to the many who supported me in the work.

I am now asked by the editors of this volume to indicate the changes that have taken place in my fields of interest since the Chair was inaugurated twenty-five years ago. In philosophy of religion analytical questions continue to be pursued and one could wish that more systematic theologians paid heed to them. It is interesting, and in a way disquieting, to observe that some of the most stimulating works on such subjects as theodicy, the divine attributes, and immortality are written not by theologians but by professional philosophers—a significant departure from the derision which many of that ilk heaped upon religious topics when I was a university student. One can still find persons of a Wittgensteinian or a Thomist kind, and the latter are much more visible on the stage of general philosophical debate than they were prior to Vatican II. In addition, we now find those known as Reformed epistemologists (some of whom are not, ecclesiastically, Reformed) and, to the delight of some and the dismay of others, the phenomenon of continental philosophy and that elusive catch-all (purloined from the arts), "postmodernism." Among the more encouraging signs is the retreat by many philosophers from the analysts' complaint, "That is history, not philosophy," and the realization that there is much to be gained from reading philosophers in their intellectual context. By this means we may be spared the mistake of

---

1. Sell, *Aspects of Christian Integrity* and Sell, *Commemorations*.

supposing that when Schleiermacher or Charles Wesley spoke of "feeling" they had in mind subjective, emotional, "cozy glows." We shall also avoid the abstractions of those who, for example, are content to write on John Stuart Mill's utilitarianism without noting that to Mill, utilitarianism was intended as the creed of his desired Religion of Humanity.[2]

In historical theology there has been, in recent years on the Protestant side, a growing appreciation of the insights of medieval thinkers; and, conversely, some of the best scholarship on Luther and Calvin is now contributed by Roman Catholic scholars. In constructive and systematic theology, the Barthians are ever with us and the process theologians continue to ply their trade. But increasing attention is being paid to liberation, African, Asian, and other theologians, and also to feminist theology. All of these in their different ways have raised issues of theological importance, many of which have been overlooked for too long; but, as with any brand of theology, all of them can, in incautious hands, become sectarian badges of separation from those of other theological persuasions. Fundamentalists come in many guises. On occasion the theological curriculum itself can contribute to unhealthy partisanship. How unfortunate, for example, if courses on feminism are taken by the converted only and by women only; or if Hispanics alone pay heed to writings on liberation theology. A proper catholicity needs to be reflected in teaching, too. We do not expect Augustine to be taught only by North Africans. We shall, perhaps, have come of age as theologians when we grasp the fact that the manifold aspects of theology can be taught with integrity, zeal, and knowledge by scholars regardless of their race and sex.

In ecumenical theology there have been many advances during the past twenty-five years. These have accrued especially from international and regional dialogues among members of the several Christian communions. There is an unfortunate time-lag, however, between the publication of dialogue findings and the discussion of those findings in systematic theology classes. Nor can it be said that the recommendations of dialogue commissions have been fully implemented, or in some cases even discussed, at the grassroots level. It is understandable that many of the dialogues have focused upon church-dividing issues such as ministry and sacraments, but positions adopted on these matters in turn depend

---

2. See further Sell, *Mill on God.*

upon diverse understandings of the development of doctrine, on which hard work remains to be done.[3]

Where Christian apologetics is concerned, it is still possible to find Christians engaging in "cult-bashing" on the one hand and a lopsided critique of the Enlightenment in favor of a frequently elusive, and sometimes incoherent, postmodernism on the other. There are many available works on theodicy, religion and science, and pluralism—indeed, these are veritable industries. But there are fewer writers who are willing to ask second-order questions concerning the presuppositions of Christian apologetics—a doomed discipline in the eyes of some within the theological circle and of others who are critical of, and in some cases hostile to, the theological enterprise as a whole.[4]

Similarly, one finds in Christian ethics that a considerable number of life and death, and socio-economic issues are being addressed but, again, discussion of the presuppositions of Christian ethical discourse is all too frequently bypassed.[5] Moreover, in church circles the pursuit of ethical issues (I almost wrote, "the embarking upon ethical crusades") can, as with theological "isms," take a sectarian turn: "If you are not on my moral platform you are not a *bona fide* Christian." This appears at its most gruesome in those church assemblies where highly politicized, and sometimes well financed, pressure groups promote their wares, on occasion wielding the Bible as a weapon. All too often the objective of seeking unity in Christ is rendered unattainable.

I turn, finally, to some general concerns. The first is the instrumentalist attitude towards education in many parts of the academy. Where modular systems hold sway the situation is exacerbated, for without careful controls there is no guarantee of progression in depth as a student's degree course proceeds. This is especially damaging to theology, the foundational disciplines of which—languages, logic, historical method—cannot be acquired in single twelve-week modules. The situation is aggravated in the seminary context, where professional as well as classical academic courses have to be accommodated within

---

3. See further on the themes briefly indicated here, Sell, *Enlightenment, Ecumenism, Evangel*, chapters 6, 10, 11.

4. For my contribution to the discussion of the prolegomena to Christian apologetics, see the trilogy: *Philosophical Idealism and Christian Belief; John Locke; Confessing and Commending the Faith*.

5. See Sell, *Testimony and Tradition*, chapter 9.

the available three or four years. I sometimes fear that students do not linger long enough with a subject to begin to master it, still less to enjoy it. We may even be giving them such small doses that we inoculate them for life against particular subjects.

Secondly, there is that creeping quantitative managerialism exemplified in academic staff assessments that require a certain number of publications per person and per department if adequate funding is to follow. This not only rules out the life-time project, or puts enormous pressure upon those committed to such work who may be made to feel that they are traitors to the fund-raising cause, but it also raises the possibility that we shall breed a race of scholars who are not widely read even in their own disciplines. Their reading is all "hand to mouth"; that is, they simply read for their next article. From such a pernicious treadmill, good Lord deliver us.

Thirdly, there are institutions of higher education, and even departments of Religious Studies, where Christian theologians (or, for that matter, theologians of any other religion) are not welcome. Faith and reason are deemed to be incompatible and faith is presumed to be "blind." The sphere of the reasonable is restricted, sometimes to such an extent that all the more important questions are ruled out. As I said above, fundamentalists come in various guides, and the secular fundamentalist is a not unknown phenomenon. The church's primary task is the worship of God, while universities should be places where argument flourishes. In the absence of living representatives of traditions, both secular and Christian, it is all too easy for protagonists to set up straw men for the sole purpose of knocking them down. Such victories are hollow indeed. In a pluralistic age there are bound to be conflicting truth claims, both religious and secular. Christians, for example, claim that in Christ, God has "visited and redeemed his people." This at once brings us up against the scandal of particularity and the fact that the Cross is an offence to some. How, if at all, may such a stance be justified in present circumstances? Such questions as this deserve to be subjected to the closest scrutiny. What more appropriate location for such scrutiny than the university? If such debate is to be as lively as it ought to be, a goodly supply of atheists and agnostics will be required. There is reason to think that the overall calibre of these has declined in recent years: some are not as well versed in their "enemy" as the best of them used to be and they lack the wit of the ablest Victorian secularists. It is my conviction that, for the health of both, the church and the academy need one another. Neither is necessarily hostile to the other, but there is ample scope for principled disagreement. So let us *all* face both ways, and the intellectual sparks will fly.

Bibliography

Sell, Alan P. F. *Aspects of Christian Integrity*. Calgary: University of Calgary Press and Louisville: Westminster/John Knox Press, 1990. Reprinted Eugene, OR: Wipf and Stock, 1998.

————. *Commemorations. Studies in Christian Thought and History*. Calgary: University of Calgary Press and Cardiff: University of Wales Press, 1993. Reprinted Eugene, OR: Wipf and Stock, 1998.

————. *Confessing and Commending the Faith. Historic Witness and Apologetic Method*. Cardiff: University of Wales Press, 2002. Reprinted, Eugene, OR: Wipf and Stock, 2006.

————. *Enlightenment, Ecumenism, Evangel. Theological Themes and Thinkers 1550–2000*. Carlisle: Paternoster, 2005.

————. *John Locke and the Eighteenth-Century Divines*. Cardiff: University of Wales Press, 1997. Reprinted, Eugene, OR: Wipf and Stock, 2006.

————. *Mill on God. The Pervasiveness and Elusiveness of Mill's Religious Thought*. Aldershot: Ashgate, 2004.

————. *Philosophical Idealism and Christian Belief*. Cardiff: University of Wales Press: 1995. Reprinted, Eugene, OR: Wipf and Stock, 2006.

————. *Testimony and Tradition. Studies in Reformed and Dissenting Thought*. Aldershot: Ashgate, 2005.

20

The City and the Church

WESLEY A. KORT

CHRISTIAN THOUGHT IN THE twenty-first century will be forced to take the city more seriously. The tendency of populations, not only in the Western world but globally, is toward increased urbanization. Christian thought, however, is ill-prepared to meet this challenge.

I

To respond adequately to urbanization, Christian thinkers must first of all face the fact that it is not the city but their own negative appraisals of cities that cause the problem, appraisals that find support in the wider culture. We inherit these appraisals most immediately from the aftermath of the First World War. That war was seen by many people, artists and social/political theorists as well as theologians, to be a culmination of unfortunate developments in Western history beginning at the end of the eighteenth century. These developments were tied to rapid urbanization in Western countries, especially in England. During the nineteenth century England changed from an agricultural and rural to a dominantly urban society, with all of the accompanying consequences of dislocation, concentrations of population, and the domination of personal life by industrial environments. Cities were primarily commercial and industrial centers, and they developed networks of relations not so much with their immediate contexts as with other cities. Imperialism and the desire to control raw materials and markets all contributed to the growth and character of urban life, and the First World War was a culminating event in a history that had the city at its center.[1]

After the First World War negative attitudes toward modern history and its principal product, the city, became a period style. Economic and political critics and theorists decried the exploitation and alienation of peoples in urban environments. Artists recoiled from the crudeness of life revealed by war and from the submersion of the populace in ordinariness. And theologians, none of them more widely influential than Karl Barth, saw the war as revealing the pretentiousness and delusional character of the human, cultural enterprise. These attitudes persist. In a recent book on the city, theologian Graham Ward, self-identified as "radical orthodox," condemns the modern city by claiming its most characteristic and revealing institution to be its pornographic shop. What is impressive about Ward's argument is that he can find so much support for it, and he offers a long list of widely known people who, in one way or another, agree with him, theorists, cultural critics, and artists.[2] T. S. Eliot, we recall, invoked language from Dante's "Inferno" to describe the denizens of London, and Graham Greene liked walking around the bombed places in London because the destroyed facades of buildings revealed their seedy interiors, suggesting that war uncovered the ugly and concealed truth of human life. Indeed, theology has made remarkable inroads in the university because, in its neo-orthodox and evangelical forms, it gives Christian support to the anti-modernist and anti-urban thrust of most cultural, economic, and political analyses of the West and its hallmark, the city.

Christian critics, while influenced by these cultural critiques of the city, also employ biblical warrants. Many of the writing prophets, beginning with Amos, denounced the city because they saw it as an occasion of pride, a display of human strength and skill, and a site for political and economic ties with other peoples. Micah and Jeremiah denounced Jerusalem for the comfort and protection that people thought it provided, and they predicted its ruin. This attitude toward the city finds its New Testament culmination in the depiction of Rome in the Book of Revelation as the epitome of human pride and degradation, the new Babylon. While Christianity developed in the West largely in and from

1. For a more complete account of this history see the Introduction to my book, *Place and Space in Modern Fiction*.

2. See Ward, *Cities of God*.

urban centers, its evaluation of the city remained at best ambivalent and always potentially negative.

Aggravating Christian critiques of the modern city is the fact that the city stands as a contrary in modernity to the rise of personal interiority as a religious source and theological focus. Modernity can be defined not by the city alone but by the split between the modern in its massive, external, and physical form, namely, the city, and the modern in its personal, internal, and spiritual form, namely, the resources for religious creativity and experience within the person. While many theologians have resisted this attachment of Christianity to personal preoccupations, the overwhelming portion of Christian people today are influenced by the culturally pervasive fascination for the internal capacities of persons as sites of divine presence or revelation. This fascination comes to religion in the modern period not from religious but from philosophical and aesthetic sources, the idea, in Kant and in Coleridge, for example, of the genius, especially of art and the artist as instruments or occasions of epiphany. This role of the genius stands behind the elevation of charismatic and creative religious people, whether as in Wellhausen's theory of the primacy of the individual prophets in ancient Israel or in William James' theory of the privileged religious position of the visionary.

Religious and cultural condemnations of the city warrant, ironically, the patterns of further decline and exploitation of the city. Viewed as evil, cities get no more than they deserve. Cities are seen as opportunities for the exercise of power by people who, rather then live in them, use them. Cities are more often than not shaped by commercial, profit-making motives, and negative, cultural and religious views of the city condone this neglect and abuse. There is much about urban life that is deplorable and alarming, but the situation is not helped by theorists, artists, and Christian theologians in the twentieth century whose negative image of the city warrants exploitation. The city, while a victim, is blamed for its own condition.

It should be noted, also, that Christian thought in the period after the Wars was affected by the dominant paradigms of theories of religion. One example is the influential work of Mircea Eliade, especially his theory of sacred space. Eliade defines sacred space by means of his analysis of modern history, which he condemns. A displaced Romanian, Eliade evidenced a deep distrust of modern history. Under the banner of what he called the "terror of history," he advocated a reinstatement of sacred space as an antidote to the consequences of dislocation, alienation, and trauma caused by modern history in general and by the World Wars in particular. He defined sacred space primarily as the opposite of profane history. As he put it in one of his most widely read books, "The first possible definition of the *sacred* is that it is *the opposite of the profane*."[3] However different from one another they otherwise may be, radical orthodox theologians and the many religious theorists who are influenced by Eliade agree that the sacred (for the radical orthodox, the church) should be defined first of all as the opposite of the profane, and the profane, with whatever else it is, is most of all the modern city.

II

If a more positive image of the city can arise from Christian thought, one that sees the church not as a refuge from or antagonist to the city but as, at least to some degree, continuous with it, where should it begin? To put the question differently, is there a place for the church in the city or is the church in the city only an anachronism, a sentimental gesture, or, worse, a heavenly warrant for exploitation?

In his widely influential *The Production of Space*, Henri Lefebvre gives us a hint, it seems to me, as to why the church has a place in the city, although such a use of his work is not one that he anticipated. Lefebvre argues that social space is constructed primarily not physically and visibly but tacitly and invisibly. What he means is that social space is based on assumptions and directives that create boundaries and limits, thereby determining where people may or must go and be or where they may not. These boundaries and limits are not only restrictive; they are also enabling. For example, if work of some kind needs to be done, it is important that it not be disrupted by people who have no contribution to make to it. Boundaries and limits bring people together as well as separate them from one another. Finally, he points out that these boundaries and limits, some of which are fixed by laws and maintained by force, are for the most part hidden. The structure of social space, then, is largely achieved and maintained by invisible demarcations.

All of this is preliminary to Lefebvre's principal point, namely, that urban spaces need what he calls "monumental space." He indicates with this term those aspects of cities that are most familiar to us, especially in

3. Eliade, *The Sacred and the Profane*, 1.

our roles as tourists. We are attracted to and impressed by the great buildings and squares for public events that are found in urban spaces, and we
are meant to be impressed by and attracted to them. What monumental
space does is to compensate by means of visibility for the invisibility of
those lines and boundaries that structure social space. More than that,
monumental space, by being impressive and attractive, warrants, and sta-
bilizes the structure of social space.

To this theory of social space, Lefebvre adds a historical account.
In it he describes how towns and cities, from the high Middle Ages into
modernity, gradually allowed monumental space to be dominated less by
ecclesiastical and more by political and, most recently, by economic edifices. Market places were shifted from outside to inside towns and cities,
and economic transactions became defining and not simply expedient
parts of urban life. This drift of towns and cities toward the prominence
and even dominance of commercial interests went unabated, and continues in the present day.[4]

Lefebvre's analysis and historical sketch point out that while economic edifices have grown to dominate urban landscapes, the church
has, along with political monuments, a long and important role to play
in cities. That role is to be part of monumental space and to stand as a
visible sign of the largely invisible beliefs and directives that contribute
to the construction of social space. True, churches are often smaller than,
and even squeezed between, the monuments of business and of political
power. But the church and the city are closely bound, and cities devoid of
churches are anomalies. While churches may not always make good use
of their long-standing and legitimate place in cities, their presence is by
no means an imposition or irrelevancy. Their role, among other things, is
to call attention to those attitudes and beliefs that underlie and influence
the structures and behaviors of urban life and to question, augment, or
affirm them in light of their own understandings of what makes for the
city's peace.

III

This affirmation of the traditional and normative place of churches in the
city is now met, from the side of urban theories, by more positive secular
assessments of the city, assessments that indicate those points to which an

4. Lefebvre, *The Production of Space*.

understanding of the legitimate place of the church in the city can attach. Beginning with Jane Jacobs' paradigm-altering book of 1961, *The Death and Life of Great American Cities*, theories and critiques of urban spaces have been more complicated and positive than attitudes that dominated the culture from the Romantics to the present day. The principal mark of these differing and more positive assessments of urban space is that they move not from the top downwards in their views of the city but from the ground upwards. That is, they give more attention to particular communities within cities, especially of people who live not only in proximity to but also take an interest in one another. This gives rise to a view of the city as a federation of communities and interests rather than as a single thing.

This move in the reappraisal of urban life is supported by an increased interest among cultural critics and theorists as well as the general public in ethnicity. Italian, Jewish, Greek and other ethnic urban groups are part of the main current of cultural interest. A related interest is in popular culture. The distinction between high and low culture has broken down, and popular forms of expression are widely associated with the city. Indeed, some theorists, such as Sharon Zukin, argue that universities, as they turn more into training places for professional and other skills, have been replaced by cities as sites of cultural production.[5]

It is not surprising that much of the more positive understanding of cities and their potential is offered by feminist geographers. There can be no doubt that cities have given more opportunities to women than have small towns and rural locations. In addition to women, minorities have found opportunities to develop their own identities and to enhance their social and economic status in the cities. African Americans, gay and lesbian people, and other marginalized people have found room in the city to develop common cultures and social and economic structures. Indeed, negative attitudes toward the city under-value the actual and potential changes being exerted on the development of urban societies by women and traditionally oppressed peoples. This, along with the rapid increase of immigrant populations, makes cities the bellwethers of the increasingly pluralistic nature of national identities.

Finally, assessments of the city have shifted because these perspectives, interests, and demographics attach to a differing way of understanding the relation between culture and social/economic power.

5. Zukin, *The Cultures of Cities*.

Since much of urban geography is influenced by Marxist analyses, the kinds of cultural shifts and influences that we have been looking at have tended to be seen as overshadowed by political and economic power. However, it is now thought by many theorists that culture is not simply the effluent of social/political conditions but that it can itself alter those conditions. The cultures of cities have effects. More largely, it can now be seen that an altered evaluation of cities can itself effect changes in the way that cities are treated and developed. It would be a mistake to become, in reaction to a history of negative views of the city, overly optimistic about the prospects of changed attitudes toward the city and of their positive effects on city life. Many problems continue to face cities and confront those who are trying to develop them more positively and to enhance the lives of urban people. It is also clear, however, that we are in a state of transition regarding cities, and churches can and should enter the newly developing conversations.

IV

It was in the spirit of the 1960s and, perhaps, of the changing attitudes toward the city that followed Jane Jacobs' work that Harvey Cox wrote his influential *The Secular City* (1965). In it he celebrated the new freedom and the challenges offered by urban space and the social changes that cities would be able to effect. While too optimistic in his view of the city and too uncritical in his association of freedom and change with Christianity, his book continues to be a rare, positive assessment of the city by a Christian theologian. Reading it again, in the light of the reappraisals of and new approaches toward urban sites, Cox's book, however, does not look quite so unrealistic and uncritical as it once did.[6]

My approach differs from Cox's. As a Reformed Christian, I take reading Scripture as a definitive, central act. However, the Reformed have also made much of the medieval trope of reading nature as a second scripture, and that second scripture became, not long after Calvin, required reading if one is to know the full story of who God is and what the Christian life is all about. That second scripture shifted, in the modern period, from nature to history, and Reformed theologians also read history as a kind of second scripture. But in the postmodern period, another shift has occurred, from an historical to a spatial emphasis. We have come

6. Cox, *The Secular City*.

to read places as texts, and an increasingly significant place/text to read
is, as it is sometimes called, the urban landscape. I think that Christian
people, therefore, should read cities as another kind of second scripture.[7]

One of the first things that reading the city as scripture would teach
the church is that the city brings the needs of people, material and spiritual, to the church. The church does not have to go out to find those needs.
This is a gift of the city to the church, and the church should be thankful
for, rather than annoyed by, the gift. The second thing that can be read
is that the church in the city is free, when compared to its suburban and
small town counterparts. Gibson Winter, in his book of 1961, pointed
to what, in his title, he called *The Suburban Captivity of the Churches*.
Suburban churches are determined by the wealth and interests that drive
them out of the cities and into the protective and relatively homogeneous
environments of the suburbs. Churches in small towns are also captives,
usually of the homogeneity and inertia of such locations. But churches in
the city, in comparison, have a freedom to respond faithfully to challenges
and opportunities that churches in other locations can hardly dream of.
Of course, there are retarding and distorting interests in urban churches
as well, but urban churches are in a position to benefit from the cultural
movements characteristic of many urban environments. This means,
among other things, recognizing marginalized people and bringing them
within its circumference or allowing various groups and individuals access to the church's meeting rooms and other facilities.

I shall end with an example of what I have in mind by the church
reading urban spaces as scripture. Recently a new cathedral was built in
Los Angeles, The Cathedral of Our Lady of the Angels, the first cathedral
of the twenty-first century. It was a controversial project both because it
cost so much and because its design was provocative rather than reas-
suring. But its construction was defended, one of the reasons being that
the people of Los Angeles, particularly poor people, needed and deserved
something striking and beautiful to look at. In addition, while its design
is not traditionally churchly but angular and intrusive, it should be remembered that not all cathedrals look like Chartres. Some, for example,
are fortress-like. This one makes a statement, although it is not repetitive
of statements made by most other cathedrals.

7. For a more detailed account of what it means to read something as scripture, see
my '*Take, Read.*'

What impresses me about this cathedral is not only its physical presence but also its life. It is a refuge for poor and homeless people, and it has an active ministry in response to their presence. In other words, it receives the needs of people, physical and spiritual, brought to the church without the church having to go out to find them. It has become a positive and active location, with its own meaning, complementing but also in counterpoint with other structures and institutions of the city.

It also has aesthetic power. Within it, for example, are the remarkable, large tapestries done for the cathedral by John Nava. Over the baptistry is his rendering of the baptism of Christ, and, perhaps as importantly, on the wall behind the altar is his rendering of the new Jerusalem, which is a street map of Los Angeles with imposed figures. Between these two works and along the walls of the church's nave are the tapestries that form the Communion of the Saints. Nava took as his models of the saints people living near the cathedral, people of various ethnic and racial identities, women, and young people. Included among the named saints are anonymous saints, ordinary people in very ordinary dress.

Nava's tapestries of the saints find their living counterpart in the use made by the cathedral of the many languages resident in its location. Indeed, the mass of consecration for the cathedral was celebrated in many languages. Here again is a gift that the city makes to the church. The promise and hope of differing kinds of people, many traditionally at odds, gathered into celebration together is realized, however temporarily, by the linguistic polyphony of the mass. This partial but unmistakable realization of the coming together of peoples is made possible by the city. The city did the gathering, and its gathering was a gift from the city to the church.

What the cathedral is doing makes so much sense because, as is well known, the best thing one can do in response to a victim is to listen. The city has been a victim, and this church is listening to it, reading it. The city needs to be listened to or read. The principal task of Christian thought in the twenty-first century, in my opinion, then, is to read the city and to discern what the city is inviting and enabling the church to become.

Bibliography

Cox, Harvey. *The Secular City: Secularization and Urbanization in Theological Perspective.* New York: Macmillan, 1965.

Eliade, Mircea. *The Sacred and the Profane*. Translated by Willard R. Trask. New York: Harcourt, Brace, and World, 1959.

Kort, Wesley A. *Place and Space in Modern Fiction*. Gainesville, FL: University Press of Florida, 2004.

————. *'Take, Read:' Scripture, Textuality and Cultural Practice*. University Park, PA: Pennsylvania State University Press, 1996.

Lefebvre, Henri. *The Production of Space*. Translated by Donald Nicholson-Smith. Oxford: Blackwell, 1991.

Ward, Graham. *Cities of God*. New York: Routledge, 2000.

Zukin, Sharon. *The Cultures of Cities*. Oxford, Mass: Blackwell, 1995.

PART 5

Approaches to English Literature and Film

21

Reflections on Literary Theory and Criticism

SUSAN FELCH

EARLY IN 2005, STANLEY Fish, a long-standing member of the North American academic literary establishment, roused his slumbering colleagues with a column in the *Chronicle of Higher Education* entitled, "One University, Under God?" The title was provocative; the question mark rhetorical. For Fish suggested that the old boundaries separating the educational and religious enterprises had already crumbled and that universities needed "to take religion seriously. . . not as a phenomenon to be analyzed at arm's length, but as a candidate for the truth."[1] He concluded with these words: "When Jacques Derrida died I was called by a reporter who wanted to know what would succeed high theory and the triumvirate of race, gender, and class as the center of intellectual energy in the academy. I answered like a shot: religion."

Not all of Fish's colleagues agreed with him, of course, and the *Chronicle* printed a number of rebuttals throughout the year, but subsequent events supported Fish's claim. At the close of 2005, over two dozen sessions were devoted to topics on religion and literature at the Modern Language Association (MLA) convention and many other papers presented there invoked religious themes and issues. In a special session on "The Role of the Intellectual in the Twenty-First Century," Ng`ug`i wa Thiong'o, the Kenyan novelist, reflected that the 2005 Presidential Forum

1. Fish, "One University, Under God?," 1.

had been dominated by two concerns: the crossing of language and cultural boundaries and the keen interest in religion and the divine.

Twenty-five years ago, participants at the MLA would have been pressed to find serious discussions of religion outside of panels organized by the Division on Literature and Religion or by the Conference on Christianity and Literature. And scholars who themselves professed Christianity often felt battered on the one side by poststructuralist claims that language could reveal neither God nor the world around us and on the other side by cultural studies that saw religion, and particularly Christianity, as an alien and oppressive force.

Of course, the renewed interest in religion, spirituality, and the divine does not automatically translate into an openness for Christian thought in the fields of language and literature. And there is a particular challenge for those who wish to enter the current dialogue as Christian scholars, for Christian thought occupies the unusual position of being both familiar and exotic.

As a *paterfamilias*, Christianity looms over Western literature, casting the shadow of its grand narrative and multiple allusions across poems, stories, essays, and criticism. More distressingly, that shadow has, at times, darkened both creativity and the lives of real people. Contemporary scholars do well to remember and repent of such failings without, however, conceding that Christianity's pock-marked history is responsible for all the ills of the world. Were Christianity to be banned tomorrow, violence would not cease. In the field of literature, for instance, psychoanalytic disparagement of female experiences, Marxist complicity in acts of terror and genocide, and poststructuralist paralysis in the face of ethical dilemmas—to mention only three prominent theories—share responsibility for causing suffering both mental and physical. Yet none of these theories can, or should, be reduced to their worst manifestations. In other words, Christianity is not alone in having a checkered past. Yet it is a *checkered* past, colored by songs of freedom as well as edicts of oppression, the lyrics of Phillis Wheatley as well as the novels of Joseph Conrad, and responsible proponents of Christian thought will survey both the light and the shadows.

The general historical and cultural illiteracy rampant today, however, means that fewer people understand the complexities of Christian teaching or the varieties of Christian practice. Consequently, despite its putative familiarity, actual encounters with Christianity on the page or in person often exude an unfamiliar or exotic aura. If one, for instance, knows little of the Christian liturgy, John Donne's "Good Friday, 1613. Riding Westward" loses much of its poetic power. Nor is the problem confined to older or western literature; as the weight of Christianity shifts to the south and to the east, younger writers from around the world draw on its tropes and language for their own literary works. In this situation, Christian scholars can serve the academy as guides through an unfamiliar landscape.

As Wendell Berry once noted, a writer who is a farmer learns to speak with an exact, particular language and, in addition, will "be apt actually to know some actual country people, and this is a significant advantage. Reading some fiction . . . one cannot avoid the impression that the writers don't know any country people and are afraid of them. They fill the blank, not with anybody they have imagined, but with the rhetorically conjured stereotype of the hick or hillbilly or redneck . . . This does harm. If you wish to steal farm products or coal or timber from a rural region, you will find it much less troubling to do so if you can believe that the people are too stupid and violent to desire the things you wish to steal from them."[2] Similarly, scholars who are themselves professed Christians have not only learned to speak a particular language but also to live in community with particular people. Because they experience Christianity in its everyday guise, they are in a unique position to help the academy avoid foolish errors and stereotypes about religion and religious people and thus to encourage better and stronger readings of all literatures that are marked by religious concerns. Christian scholars, like Berry's farmer-writer, can undo the harm perpetuated by rhetorically conjured stereotypes.

The current interest in all things religious, then, offers two challenges. The first is to strengthen a religiously-inflected critical sensibility within the particular tradition of Christianity; the second is to develop more vigorous theoretical paradigms.

Scholars of Christian thought should be alert to opportunities that raise the awareness of Christian resonance in texts and of Christian concerns among authors. One need not profess Christianity, of course, to be attentive to religious themes but sympathy with such matters is essential. A critic who understands that religious commitment is implicated in social, cultural, political, and psychological matters, but cannot be reduced to

2. Berry, "Imagination in Place," 49.

them, exercises a judicious religious sensibility. The best of such criticism, as in Barbara Lewalski's *Protestant Poetics and the Seventeenth-Century Religious Lyric*, illuminates structures of thought as well as particular literary works.[3] In contrast to some earlier forms of criticism that hunted down sources and allusions or rewrote literary works as implicit theology, a religiously-inflected sensibility weighs the delicate register of belief and unbelief. Not every man with his arms outstretched is a Christ-figure. Nor is every non-believer an anonymous Christian.

A religiously-inflected critical sensibility also raises awareness of the stance critics and readers take toward Christianity. In a theoretical climate where disinterest is itself suspect, admitting one's own religious commitments can lead to greater interpretive clarity, fueled by an empathetic charity based on this critical principle: we know best what we love well.

All these efforts—attention to religious resonance in texts, awareness of authorial commitments, recognition of readerly predispositions—require an appreciation of the generative aesthetic effect of religious belief, even when that belief is no longer operative. In this critical endeavor, the scholar of Christian thought may find allies among those who are pursuing turns to ethics, to retro-formalism, and to authorial intentionality—all issues that have recently moved from the margins to the center of the academic study of language and literature.

In addition to criticism, which talks about specific works of literature and their authors, contexts, genres, and readers, scholars of Christian thought also face the challenge of engaging in the paradigmatic task of theory-formation. Although Christian scholars have either loosely used or more formally joined themselves with various critical schools—new criticism, archetypal criticisms, new historicism, structuralism and post-structuralism, psychoanalysis, feminism, to name just a few—the more challenging proposition is to create theories that, to quote Stanley Fish, "take religion seriously . . . not as a phenomenon to be analyzed at arm's length, but as a candidate for the truth."

Efforts in this direction have been mixed. Some classical formulations retain their interpretive power: one need only think of Augustine's nuanced understanding of the varied relations between words and things, *verba* and *res,* or Sir Philip Sidney's Horatian depiction of literature that

---

3. Lewalski, *Protestant Poetics and the Seventeenth-Century Religious Lyric.*

delights, teaches, and moves to action. Attempts in the twentieth century to limn a theology of reading or to build an archetypal carapace that might contain and explain literary plots, characters, and genres, however, have been less successful, and none has markedly influenced the academy at large. The challenge here is to articulate a theory that is both generous and generative, one that is inflected by religious sensibilities and that opens up a literary work to interpretations that are, at the very least, interesting. Simply put, a reader who looks through any pair of theoretical glasses should see more rather than less, and, at best, should experience an "aha" moment of insight and delight.

Christian scholars might here take their cue from the ancient ecumenical creeds. The first statement of the Apostles' Creed, "I believe in God the father almighty, maker of heaven and earth," opens up many possibilities for thinking about language and literature. What does the claim "I believe" say about the discursive and rhetorical powers of language? In what ways do presuppositional propositional statements—such as "I believe in God the father almighty"—direct theoretical work? Or to put it another way, what is the effect of methodological theism, a critical method that begins with the fact of God rather than the fact of his absence or disappearance? Or to put it in the words of Ng`ug`i wa Thiong'o', what does it mean that "God is the first intellectual"? What are the implications of a God who, in Christian theology, is neither male nor female but is incarnated in a first-century masculine body who calls upon the "father"? What does it mean to read and write from a place that is named "creation" rather than "cosmos"?

As these questions suggest, creeds are generative; their stark statements bubble with inferences. But like all deep wells, indeed like all fertile wombs, they are productive because they are particular; they have boundaries. Because creeds are formed out of controversy, they know how to say "no" as well as "yes." Certain views of language or literature may not be compatible with saying "I believe" or "God" or "maker" or "heaven and earth." For instance, the Russian thinker Mikhail Bakhtin refused abstracted notions of language that isolated it both from transcendent penetration and from a robust sense of reference to the physical world, arguing instead that form and meaning *must* be given from the outside, across boundaries, and accepted as a gift: "A lived experience is a relationship *to* meaning and *to* an object, and beyond this relationship it does not exist for itself," he said, adding that "Aesthetic culture is a culture of boundaries and hence presupposes that life is enveloped by a warm atmosphere of deepest trust." He concluded with this statement: "Revelation characterizes the natural world just as much as natural laws do."[4] This deeply personalist and referential notion of language and literature was motivated by Bakhtin's own sense of, and commitment to, Christian thought.

We might call this way of thinking and acting *transmodern*, a word that retains the intellectual rigor of modern scholarship while reinstating an appreciation for earlier traditions (*trans* or across historical periods) as well as an openness to *trans*cendence.[5] In a discipline newly alert to religion and its potential, the prospects for reinvigorated, transmodern Christian thought in the field of literary criticism and theory are bright indeed.

Bibliography

Bakhtin, Mikhail. "Author and Hero in Aesthetic Activity." In *Art and Answerability: Early Philosophical Essays by M. M. Bakhtin*, edited by Michael Holquist and Vadim Liapunov. Austin: University of Texas Press, 1990.

Berry, Wendell. "Imagination in Place." In *The Way of Ignorance and Other Essays*. New York: Shoemaker and Hoard, 2005.

Felch, Susan M. and Paul J. Contino, ed. *Bakhtin and Religion: A Feeling for Faith*. Evanston, IL: Northwestern University Press, 2001.

Fish, Stanley. "One University, Under God?" *The Chronicle of Higher Education* (7 January 2005).

Lewalski, Barbara. *Protestant Poetics and the Seventeenth-Century Religious Lyric*. Princeton: Princeton University Press, 1979.

Vitz, Paul C. "The Future of the University: From Postmodern to Transmodern." In *Rethinking the Future of the University*, edited by David Lyle Jeffrey and Dominic Manganiello, *The Mentor Series*. Ottawa: University of Ottawa Press, 1998.

4. Bakhtin, "Author and Hero in Aesthetic Activity," 115, 203; Felch and Contino, ed., *Bakhtin and Religion*, 219.

5. Vitz, "The Future of the University," 113–14.

22

A Time of Promise and Responsibility

Teaching English Literature in the Christian Academy

ARLETTE ZINCK

The days are coming, declares the Sovereign Lord, when I will send a famine through the land—not a famine of food or a thirst for water, but a famine of hearing the words of the Lord. Amos 8:11

WORD HUNGER. I ENCOUNTERED it in a class on Milton and the Seventeenth Century. The prophet Amos describes a hunger for the Word of God, for words alive with power to transform a life, words big enough to allow room for questions and doubts but also sufficient to convey shape, to provide parameters, to create a solid base from which to launch action. It was not until I met one particular class, a group of students from a variety of backgrounds who were attending a large secular university, that I came to appreciate more fully what word hunger might look like in an academic context, and what its implications might be for work in my discipline.

Word Hunger, as I am defining it here, is the desire that asserts itself when all foundations have been shattered, all confidences melted down by skepticism, all strategies for change or recovery demolished. It often emerges out of the ashes of grand narratives and hubristic confidences that provided false certainty, but in all cases it is accompanied by the awareness that the literary work, be it sacred or secular—the text—has lost its capacity to speak to us, or, that we have lost the ability to hear what the text has to say. For those who make a living in university lecture halls, particularly those who proclaim a Christian worldview, the question is this: how do we teach literature in the age of theory and interdisciplinarity so the text regains its power to move us? How do we inspire a praxis deeply informed by theoretical and interdisciplinary awareness rather than a theoretical analysis that leads to paralysis?

According to several scholars who work outside of the literary discipline, it is precisely the text's ability to move its readers, the narrative's power to grant access to an imagined event or circumstance, that makes the study of narrative so important and powerful. In her account of the history of human rights, for example, historian Lynn Hunt argues that the epistolary novels of the eighteenth century actually helped to create the cultural context in which the development of human rights could take place in the West. Her historical analysis links Samuel Richardson's *Pamela* and Rousseau's *Julie* to the American Declaration of Independence and the French Declaration of the Rights of Man and Citizen and proposes that these novels helped to create the context out of which the self-evident claims of key human rights documents could be asserted. Hunt argues that these novels helped to create the context for culture-wide empathetic connections with the "other."[1]

Martha Nussbaum, professor of law and ethics at the University of Chicago, also argues for the unique contribution that the study of literature can make in preparing people for civic engagement. Nussbaum uses Dickens' novel *Hard Times* to critique the utilitarian-economic mindset that she sees at work in many aspects of world economic policy analysis.[2] She argues that novels like *Hard Times* are invaluable learning tools for helping us to see the pitfalls and limitations of many of our policy assumptions. Nussbaum's decision to use the novel to point out the inadequacies of one line of political and economic thought fascinates me. She is a philosopher who has served on international committees charged to devise economic indices. She could choose any number of approaches to her topic, but she, like Dickens, believes that telling a story is the best way to let us see and feel the full implications of an abstract theory. If the worldview held by utilitarian economists is to determine our common

1. Hunt, *Inventing Human Rights,* 38–69.
2. Nussbaum, "Literary Imagination," 877–910.

good, if it is to be taken as a norm that we will be asked to live by, then it is important for us to understand what abiding by that norm on a consistent basis might look like. Dickens' novel does exactly this.

Narratives, Nussbaum reminds us, help us to understand what each of us holds to be true and good and worth framing a life around. They can connect us with our own deepest values and help us to notice when our actions are inconsistent with them. It is exactly the sort of work that is necessary for making good policy decisions in the real world and exactly the sort of work that imaginative fiction, narratives of all varieties, has the potential to do very well.

The first time I stepped in front of that class on Milton and the Seventeenth Century I felt the surge of my own enthusiasm as I announced that we would be spending our year with passionate idealists who wanted to change the world. Our evenings, I said, would be spent reading some of the most stimulating and controversial ideas about who we are, who God is, and why either of those ideas matters. Our days, I promised, would be filled with conversation about these readings, opportunities to debate the issues and to learn more about these authors and the circumstances in which they wrote. We would do these things not only so that we could understand them—the ideas and the texts—but also so that we might understand ourselves. It had never occurred to me that many who sat in that staid auditorium were there against their wills. I have always counted it a great blessing that I was so blissfully unaware of how much inherent disinterest in the stated topic of study these individuals claim to have had in this early moment of our acquaintance. Before long, however, the conversations began and the confessions came forth.

"What is Truth? said jesting Pilate, and would not stay for an answer."[3] In reading seventeenth-century writers, in this case Francis Bacon, these students expected to find the oppressive dictums of an all too certain autocrat. What they found instead was a fertile thinker whose affirmation of independent thought and whose desire to see the proof of any assertion tried out upon the pulse of the individual seemed to them disarmingly sane. These students were in their final year; they had spent the previous three years being initiated into the practice of deconstructing meaning. They had learned to unmask the language of power and repression. They had honed their skill in the hermeneutic of suspicion to such a fine edge

---

3. Bacon, *"On Truth,"* 61.

that it shredded virtually anything they allowed it to touch. Their training in literary theory and interdisciplinary awareness, while equipping them superbly to ask important questions of the text, had also gone the extra step of replacing the primary works. As a result, these students had a lot in common with Bacon's depiction of Pilate, jesting as he asks "What is Truth" and never "staying for an answer." In rendering the primary texts subservient to the theories used to read them, the texts themselves had been stripped of their power and insight. These students found they were hungry for another way of reading, hungry for another story. Then they met Milton.

In *Paradise Lost* they found an opinion, if not several, on just about every major issue they had ever confronted or thought about. They observed as Milton mapped his own inquiries. They watched him build his "great argument" with its compelling portrait of Satan and its complex portrait of the Godhead. They listened as his narrator's voice gave its imperial judgements. They noted with interest how all of Milton's speculations work into and around Scripture. The story told in *Genesis* remains at the core of the poem. The vast range of ideas that Milton explores starts from this narrative and circles back to it.

The debates that ensued in that classroom were intense and the students' literary training equipped them well. They asked questions of the text, author, and of themselves as readers. They discovered not one *Paradise Lost*, but many *Paradise Losts*, and considered the plurality of texts each reader might engender. Sexist assumptions were named and theological contradictions were pointed out. There was much deliberation, little universal agreement. Throughout, however, our classroom approach modeled Milton's own: the text remained at the center of the discussions and the theories came and went once their insights were gleaned. In the end nearly all agreed that the process of watching Milton wrestle with words had been transformative for them. One student announced that Milton had shown her a God she could love. Another averred that Milton's Satan was a compelling portrait of the divine in the post-holocaust era. They saw in *Paradise Lost*, no matter which *Paradise Lost* they saw, a way to forge action out of critical paralysis. In Milton's writing they encountered his deliberate decision to understand his life and his world in the context of a story big enough to shape that life. In the midst of the contradictions and the unknowns, Milton—perhaps the greatest mind in his generation—surrenders to the shape of his chosen story, becomes "lowly wise" and as his word hunger is sated, he finds his poetic voice.

There have been many Milton classes since that first one, but the pattern that emerged in that particular classroom has held over the intervening years. As I understand it, the literary discipline has moved from one end of a continuum and is now on its way back toward the center. Training in literary theory and interdisciplinarity has shaken up the structures of thought and belief that had once tended toward unwarranted certainties and the reduction of possibilities. But in the academy's wholesale embrace of theory and interdisciplinarity, the literature that the theory and other disciplinary perspectives are intended to elucidate has often been displaced. Efforts to see a work from a multiple of disciplinary positions has sometimes left both students and faculty cross-eyed and blind to important elements in the primary object itself. Curricular programs that should develop the particular gifts of literary scholars are sometimes truncated by competing desires to build methodological competencies in a variety of disciplines. Familiarity with constituent elements, ability to analyze different genres and modes of literary expression, and a deep acquaintance with the literary tradition and history out of which any given work emerges, get watered down or lost. Worse yet, the deep pleasure that comes with immersion in narrative is often sacrificed. As a result many readers have found themselves untouched by the reading experience. They are beyond words, beyond confidence, and beyond action. Recently, however, an opportunity for a new approach to literary studies has been created.

It has been fashionable for the last decade to describe the literary discipline as being "post" theory. Titles like *Life After Theory*[4] and *Challenging Theory*[5] suggest a general readiness to re-evaluate critical procedures. Terry Eagleton, for example, decries many of the uses to which theory has been put in his book *After Theory*. With his characteristic clarity, Eagleton reminds his readers that theory is intended to help us figure out what is actually going on.[6] In his reminder there is an implied corollary statement: a right assessment of what is going on is necessary if one intends to take action. As Mark Edmundson observes in his book

---

4. Payne and Schad, *Life After Theory*.

5. Burgass, *Challenging Theory*.

6. Eagleton, *After Theory*, 4–21.

entitled *Why Read?*, readers are now eager for a mode of encountering literature that will allow them to forge action out of their newly won intellectual freedom. Edmundson, who describes himself as an atheist, a secular humanist by profession, argues that it is the job of professors of English Literature to teach stories that help students determine how to live and to ask questions that allow them to figure out how they "imagine God"[7] and why their answer to that question should matter to them.

To the extent that training in literary theory and interdisciplinarity has taught us to be more open, humble, inclined to listen, it is a process for which we should be grateful. These intellectual trends and literary practices have levelled the field of inquiry by challenging the notion that any one of us can read without bias; all are acknowledged to have worldview assumptions and encouraged to declare to one another what these are. They have also poked holes in the myth of self-contained disciplinary silos that can function without reference to other fields of inquiry. To the extent that these theoretical and interdisciplinary practices have replaced literature rather than enhanced the study of it, however, they have also left us word hungry.

Throughout this age of theory and interdisciplinarity it has been the particular challenge of Christian scholars to justify the centrality of the word, to make room for the narrative at the core of the critical debate. The process of its formal justification within the academy has only just begun. Contributions to literary theory by professing Christians like Alan Jacobs and Valentine Cunningham chart out a path for future critical inquiry. Deborah Bowen's edited collection of essays on Christian approaches to postmodernity is similarly inspiring.[8] Significantly, emergent Christian literary theorists do not generally devise a ramified substitution for secular theories. Instead, they attempt to define a spirit, a mode of inquiry that arises out of the very best that our Christian convictions allow us to offer the world: our inclination toward charity, our willingness to recognize and listen to the other. In *A Theology of Reading: The Hermeneutics of Love*, Alan Jacobs calls for a just and charitable reading practice. Jacobs advocates a loving discernment that will allow us to pay our "debt of loving and constant attentiveness" to all books and enable us to determine

---

7. Edmundson, *Why Read?*, 23.
8. Bowen, *The Strategic Smorgasbord*.

which among these books should be read as "friends, foes or neighbours."[9] In *Reading Beyond Theory* Valentine Cunningham makes an eloquent plea for a tactile literary theory, a theory that is designed to "touch" the narrative, to listen attentively and compassionately to the "other" voice.[10]

But let me be clear. This is not a call to eliminate either theory or interdisciplinarity in the literary classroom. Far from it. Students, and if my experience is representative, especially students at confessionally Christian institutions of higher learning, need to be granted the freedom to explore all manner of narrative, encouraged to understand the integrality of all knowledge, and to understand all types of theory. They need to see modeled in teaching and research a distinctly Christian approach to literary analysis, one where foundational faith assumptions are interrogated, and where a willingness to listen and understand (however provisional that understanding may be) is as evident as book learning and scholarly expertise. Most especially, these students need to see how others satisfy word hunger. They deserve to know how to read so that narrative still has the potential to be pleasurable, move people, ignite compassion and empathy, and mobilize readers for action in the midst of all uncertainties and limitations.[11] The experience must be offered as gift, not as dictum; as individual testimony, not universal imperative.

In the years since teaching that first class in a large secular university, I have taught Milton and the Seventeenth Century to many groups of students at The King's University College, a much smaller and decidedly Christian institution. I have often discovered that Milton is, at least at the outset, a far less powerful voice in that setting. In a world where the Christian story is assumed, Milton's ability to provoke liberating insights is sometimes muted by the students' own certainties. In this setting I have watched with some disappointment as students hear an unfamiliar position on a familiar theological question and tune out. They have it right; Milton has it wrong. In other moments I have struggled to stimulate student interest when the poem and its assumptions sound all too familiar. As their eyes glaze, their thoughts appear like ribbons of text across their foreheads: "move along; nothing new here." Their fragile attention is lost. I have also

9. Jacobs, *A Theology,* 67

10. Cunningham, *Reading Beyond,* 140–64.

11. Alan Jacobs has tackled directly the task of restoring pleasure to reading in his latest book. Among others things, he advocates reading on a "Whim." See *The Pleasures of Reading in an Age of Distraction.*

watched in some amazement, however, as the almost audible mental "click" that my first students experienced with *Paradise Lost* happens when these Christian students encounter a Marxist, Feminist or Eco-critical perspective on Milton. Suddenly they are no longer threatened or bored. The experience of watching and listening as gifted critical thinkers either agree or disagree with Milton sharpens their own desire to think more deeply about where and why they too agree or disagree. All that once was old for these students is now new again, and they are engaged.

In the Christian academy it may be that some readers will have to find their way back to texts written with express reference to a Christian tradition and worldview, to reignite hunger for it, through a disciplined investigation of literary theories and interdisciplinary perspectives. If literary practices within the secular academy have left many with word hunger, reticence to engage with these same practices in the Christian academy has, in some instances, led to forms of intellectual bloat where false certainties fill the mind and curb the appetite for the thinking and growing that is required of Christian disciples.

Although *Paradise Lost* is still at the center of my class on Milton and the Seventeenth Century, students are prodded to consider a variety of theoretical approaches and they are asked to evaluate what they might otherwise dismiss as "unthinkable" heretical thoughts. Students are encouraged to use both theory and methodological tools from other disciplines to garner new insights and to look for a "just" or "charitable" reading of the text. In seeking to see the complexity in a given issue they stretch beyond limitations to dismantle some uniquely Christian idols. When students are encouraged to seek "what so ever things are true," they follow what is best in the Christian tradition and set themselves apart in a Christ-ordained experience of freedom to, as Milton so eloquently advocates, "see and know and yet," where appropriate, "abstain."[12] In allowing the narrative to keep its rightful place at the center of inquiries, and in the insistence that students learn the terminology, practices, and history of English literary studies, the integrity of the discipline is maintained and students are set free to access the power of the narrative. As they do so, they experience the story's unique capacity to allow readers to imagine beyond the limits of direct experience and to build the insight necessary for compassion and empathy.

12. Milton, *Areopagitica*, 1006.

Changes apparent within the classroom during this last number of years speak of both promise and responsibility. The academy is hungry for a new way to read. Diverse worldviews expressed in critical theory and fresh insights garnered from interdisciplinary thinking have enriched both the secular and the Christian classroom, and while these gains should not be lost, narratives need to return to their central place. These last years have taught me that my job as both a Christian researcher and teacher is to make room for the story, for the word that nourishes my own word hunger, and to allow students space in which to do the same. My job is to model self-challenging reading practices that are theoretically informed and interdisciplinary in scope. These practices must also accommodate the complexity and uncertainty of our lives, but still allow an orientation point and an honest place from which to proceed. The study of English literature matters because we continue to find in it a pattern by which we might, "with some regard to what is just and right, . . . lead [our] lives."[13]

Bibliography

Bacon, Francis. "On Truth." In *The Essays*, edited by John Pitcher. Harmondsworth, England: Penguin, 1985.

Bowen, Deborah. Editor. *The Strategic Smorgasbord of Postmodernity: Literature and the Christian Critic*. Newcastle: Cambridge Scholars, 2007.

Burgass, Catherine, *Challenging Theory: Discipline after Deconstruction*. Aldershot, England: Ashgate, 1999.

Cunningham, Valentine. *Reading Beyond Theory*. Oxford: Blackwell, 2002.

Eagleton, Terry. *After Theory*. New York: Basic, 2003.

Edmundson, Mark. *Why Read?* New York: Bloomsbury, 2004.

Hunt, Lynn. *Inventing Human Rights*. New York: W.W. Norton & co., 2007.

Jacobs, Alan. *A Theology of Reading: The Hermeneutics of Love*. Boulder, CO: Westview, 2001.

———. *The Pleasures of Reading in an Age of Distraction*. New York: Oxford University Press, 2011.

Milton, John. *Areopagitica* in *The Riverside Milton*. Edited by Roy Flannagan. Boston: Houghton Mifflin, 1998.

———. *Paradise Lost*, in *The Riverside Milton*. Edited by Roy Flannagan. Boston: Houghton Mifflin, 1998.

Nussbaum, Martha C. "The Literary Imagination in Public Life." *New Literary History*, 1991: 877–910.

Payne, Michael and John Schad. *Life After Theory*. London: Continuum, 2003.

13. Milton, *Paradise Lost*, 689.

23

Thomas Merton

Retrospect and Prospect

BONNIE THURSTON

T HE PAST OFTEN SETS the agenda for the future, both for societies and individuals. To give but one example: the American monk of the twentieth century, Thomas Merton, is an icon of his time in history and prophetic in addressing the "agenda for the future." Primary challenges facing Christian thinkers today, ecumenism and inter-religious dialogue, issues of social justice, and spiritualities (the multiplicity of "ways to the center") were key concerns of this monastic theologian.[1]

In retrospect, Merton's life, its rootlessness, privilege and conversion, is an apt metaphor for his century. Born in France on January 31, 1915 to an American mother and father from New Zealand, Merton moved to Douglaston, New York in 1916 because of World War I. His only sibling, John Paul, was born there in 1918. After their mother died in 1921, Merton was taken by his artist father to Bermuda (1922), New York (1923), France (1925–1927), and finally enrolled in school in England in 1928. In 1931 his father died. After graduating from Oakham School, Merton went to Clare College, Cambridge in 1933 to study languages. The year was a disaster, and he was called "home" to New York in 1934 where, in 1935, he enrolled in Columbia University from which he earned a B.A. (1938) and M.A. in English (1939). Merton's rootlessness mirrors

---

1. For another analysis of Merton's significance see Reiser, "Thomas Merton," 3–13.

conditions during and between the two Great Wars. He was a man without a country and a man without a family. Merton's grandparents died in the early 1940s, and, having gone to Canada to enlist in the air force before America entered World War II, Merton's brother was shot down in 1943 and died at sea. Like many in the twentieth century, Merton was a man in search of roots, grounding, and a sense of belonging.

He was also a man of privilege. One might ask, "What is privileged about being orphaned at fifteen?" Emotionally, very little. However, Merton's father and maternal grandparents left him materially provided for. He was not rich, but he wanted for little. He had a varied but excellent education at the Lycee in France, Ripley Court and Oakham Schools in England, and at Cambridge and Columbia, venerable universities. Merton grew up on two continents and had both leisure and money to travel extensively in Europe in the 1930s where he saw the rise of National Socialism (about which he wrote a novel, *My Argument with the Gestapo*) and in Cuba in 1940.

Furthermore, from the time he was a small child Merton was exposed to the arts. His father was a successful painter and musician, and his mother was a gifted woman who encouraged him to write and draw. Merton's childhood was shaped by artistic sensibilities and he was introduced to a level of culture of which most Americans are still ignorant. In his wildly popular 1948 autobiography, *The Seven Storey Mountain*, Merton says of himself: "I was the product of my times, my society and my class."[2] And he was encouraged to articulate what he experienced and, as an adult, was not only a writer but a calligrapher, artist, and photographer.

Merton said of his youthful life: "I became the complete twentieth-century man. I . . . belonged to the world in which I lived. I became a true citizen of my own disgusting century: the century of poison gas and atomic bombs. A man living on the doorsill of the Apocalypse, a man with veins full of poison, living in death." (SSM 109) He was, in short, a man ready for conversion. The Greek word for conversion, *metanoia*, literally means "change direction" or "turn around." This is precisely what Merton did in the late 1930s and early 1940s. Indeed, "turning" became his vocation as a monk committed to *conversatio morum*, conversion of life, which Merton called "the essential monastic vow."[3]

---

2. Merton, *The Seven Storey Mountain*, 166. Hereafter in the text as SSM.

3. Merton, *The Monastic Journey*, 107.

The Seven Storey Mountain details Merton's conversion, which culminated at Corpus Christi Church, New York City on November 16, 1938 with his baptism as a Roman Catholic Christian. Between 1938 and his entrance as a postulant at the Abbey of Our Lady of Gethsemani in Kentucky on December 13, 1941, Merton taught English at the university level, applied to and was turned down by the Franciscan order, and seriously considered long-term work at Friendship House in New York. When he joined the Cistercian Order of the Strict Observance (he made solemn vows in 1947 and was priested in 1949) his journey was from privilege to poverty, from rootlessness to stability. As "reformed Benedictines," Cistercians take vows of poverty, chastity, obedience, *and* stability. I agree with Lawrence S. Cunningham and John Eudes Bamberger, O.S.C.O. that the key to Merton's thought is his monastic context and conviction. Both suggest he was, first and foremost, a monastic theologian and, as Bamberger says, "a prophet of monastic renewal."[4] The voluminous journals of the monastic years (six and a half long volumes in the Harper-Collins editions)[5] make clear that Merton thought himself a man literally saved by Christ—from the world and from himself. Now in a new century, and from the outside, I think that he was saved by Christ from the world *for* the world.

Merton's legacy, the reason his life is prospect as well as retrospect, is both literary and intellectual. Between 1941 and his death by accidental electrocution in 1968, he wrote some seventy books. Since his death, his journals, letters, and collected essays have been published.[6] Notwithstanding the variety of forms in which he wrote, the sheer volume is staggering. Merton wrote novels (only one of which apparently survives), poetry (the collected edition is over a thousand pages), plays (verse dramas like those of T.S. Eliot and Christopher Fry), literary criticism, autobiography in several forms (*an* autobiography, journals, letters), social analysis and criticism, monastic history and theology, and

4. See Bamberger, *Thomas Merton* and Cunningham, *Thomas Merton and the Monastic Vision.*

5. For helpful reviews of the journals see Carr, "Prose into Prayer," 570–73 and Kramer, "'Crisis and Mystery,'" 77–97. An extremely good selection from the journals has been edited by Br. Patrick Hart (for many years Merton's secretary at Gethsemani) and Jonathan Montaldo, *The Intimate Merton.*

6. Christine Bochen's selection, *Thomas Merton: Essential Writings* is a particularly good introduction to the breadth of Merton's writing.

spiritual and devotional works.[7] In my opinion Merton's *New Seeds of Contemplation* is to the twentieth century what *The Cloud of Unknowing* or the *Showings* of Julian of Norwich were to the fourteenth. The point is that Merton's is one of the most documented lives in twentieth century America and for that reason alone is noteworthy. Canadian writer Patricia A. Burton has compiled a Merton time line detailing what he wrote day by day from 1931 to 1968.[8] After twenty years his papers were made public and *everything* was "revealed."

A temptation in surveying autobiographical writing is to focus on the sensational and salacious. Some who have written about Merton have succumbed. I suggest that Merton's intellectual legacy marks him as a seminal thinker in what, in my analysis, are the three most important religious issues of the last half of the twentieth century, issues that chart the course for our own century: ecumenism and inter-religious dialogue, social justice, and spiritualities (the challenge of a variety of religious practices).[9]

Merton's life is a study in ecumenism and religious dialogue. He journeyed from "religionlessness" to Roman Catholic exclusivism to openness not only to the other historic Christian traditions (especially Orthodoxy) but to other religions. Etymologically "ecumenism" means "within the household" (from the root, *oikos*, house); that is, within Christianity. From callow judgments about other denominations in *The Seven Storey Mountain*, Merton embraced the wisdom of a variety of Christian traditions. Before the Second Vatican Council, he hosted dialogues with professors and students from the Baptist seminary in Louisville, the Christian Church (Disciple of Christ) seminary in Lexington, and others. He read widely in Orthodox theology with which he had a special affinity. Now Christians of many confessions are drawn to his spiritual writings.

By the late 1950s Merton's theological interests had broadened to include other religions, particularly Buddhism and Islam. He is a pioneer of Buddhist-Christian dialogue and his books *Mystics and Zen Masters* and *Zen and the Birds of Appetite* (fruit of conversation with D.T. Suzuki) are classics. Merton is well known in Buddhist-Christian circles and prepared

7. For more on Merton's literary legacy see Thurston, "The Man of Letters," 284–87.

8. Burton, *Merton Vade Mecum.*

9. Bochen uses similar categories to introduce Merton's thought: Contemplation (what I call "spiritualities"), Compassion (social justice), and Call to Unity (what I call ecumenism and cross religious dialogue). See note 6.

an interesting edition of Chuang Tzu.[10] Less commonly known is that he had an equally important dialogue with Islam[11] and significant contact with Jewish scholars.[12] Long before recent unhappy events, Merton read widely in Islamic tradition and corresponded with leading scholars and practitioners. In the current climate in which Islam is demonized and "other" is seen as not simply different but "evil," Merton's Islamic-Christian dialogue (especially as represented in his letters to Abdul Aziz[13]) may be his most important dialogical contribution.

The late 1950s and 1960s were times of incredible social unrest in America. Civil Rights, the Viet Nam War, nuclear proliferation, President Lyndon Johnson's "war on poverty," were played out in the public media, media with which Merton had scant direct contact but often excoriated for mindlessness and consumerism. In correspondence with often-controversial figures of the time (Dorothy Day, James Forest, the Berrigans, Martin Luther King, Jr., for example), Merton's contribution was to articulate a profound vision of what the Kingdom of God might look like. His consistent motivation for social action was rooted firmly in the Gospels and the life of prayer. In addition to letters and journal entries, his thought on racism appears in Part Three of *Faith and Violence* and in Part One of *Seeds of Destruction*. Merton was such an outspoken voice on issues of war and peace that in April, 1962 the Abbot General of the Order (Gabriel Sortais) formally requested he no longer write on the subject, especially on nuclear weapons. The book which lead to his silencing, *Peace in the Post-Christian Era*, was privately circulated at the time and only in 2004 published in its entirety.[14] Other essays on the subject occur in *Faith and Violence* and *Seeds of Destruction*.

As does his work in religious dialogue, Merton's writing on war and peace has an eerily contemporary ring. "Blessed Are the Meek" in *Faith and Violence* outlines seven conditions "for relative honesty in the practice of Christian non-violence" which are as fresh now as in 1967.[15] Similarly "The Root of War is Fear" in *New Seeds of Contemplation* observes: "hatred

---

10. Merton, *The Way of Chuang Tzu*.

11. For more see Baker and Henry (eds.), *Thomas Merton and Sufism*.

12. For more see Bruteau (ed.), *Thomas Merton and Judaism*.

13. In Shannon (ed.), *The Hidden Ground of Love*, 43–67.

14. Merton, *Peace in the Post-Christian Era*.

15. Merton, *Faith and Violence*.

of ourselves which is too deep and too powerful to be consciously faced
... makes us see our own evil in others and unable to see it in ourselves."[16]
Merton foresaw not only the disintegrations and dangers of Western society, but the necessity for Christians to address those issues precisely *from*
their conviction as Christians, always "speaking the truth in love."

Merton is perhaps most well known as a spiritual writer; he was
not a systematician, a fact sometimes overlooked by his critics. Certainly
Merton's devotion to Christ, and the life of prayer that sprung from it,
were wellsprings of his creativity and energy. His writing provided an oa-
sis for the spiritually thirsty post-war and subsequent generations.

Three concepts seem to me fundamental to Merton's spiritual the-
ology. The first is his carefully conceived understanding of the human
person. His theology of prayer assumes that we are both a True and a
False self. The True self is the person as he/she was created by and exists in
God. It is toward that True self the Christian must grow. Second, Merton's
writing about contemplative prayer is fundamental to his thought. The
"Centering Prayer" movement (represented in America by Fr. Thomas
Keating, O.S.C.O. and the late Fr. Basil Pennington, O.S.C.O.), which
has popularized the tradition of Christian mystical prayer, is indebted to
Merton's writing on prayer which was, itself, influenced by his studies
of prayer in other religions. Perhaps more than any other contemporary figure, Merton revitalized the ancient, contemplative traditions of
Christian prayer and reminded us that language does not set the limits of
our knowledge.

Finally, Merton's spiritual writing presumes the centrality and reality of Immanuel, "God with us." For Merton God isn't "out there" some-
where but immanent, resident in creation, our inner lives, our struggles.
In "making the transcendent God immanent," Merton goes a long way
toward shattering dualism in Christian thought and practice. He gives
glimpses of the practical meaning of the Incarnation by insisting that we
find God, not by withdrawing from life, but by *living* our lives. He writes
in *Thoughts in Solitude*: "If we want to be spiritual, then, let us first of all
live our lives. Let us not fear the responsibilities and the inevitable dis-
tractions of the work appointed for us by the will of God. Let us embrace

---

16. Merton, *New Seeds of Contemplation*, 112. Hereafter in the text NSC.

reality and thus find ourselves immersed in the life-giving will and wisdom of God which surrounds us everywhere."[17]

Merton articulated a besetting sin of our age: few of us live genuinely authentic, *individuated* lives. Many have "bought" the cultural myths, accepted an unexamined conformity, and, unaware, become the herd. Relatedly, Merton reminds us that there *is* no monolithic Christian spirituality; we are enriched by many *spiritualities*, many ways of expressing faith in and allegiance to Jesus Christ. Some of us will express this conventionally; others will be "on the edges," but we are both "in the house." As we Christian scholars face the challenges and uncertainties of a new century, certainly this is a helpful reminder. We make our most potent contribution to the coming of God's Reign and to the human family, not by shrill denunciation of others, but by prayerfully looking for commonalities and allowing our discourse about our inevitable differences to arise from what we share. As Merton noted, the one "who lives in division is living in death" (NSC 48). But when we reach the "perfection of love . . . each one of us will find himself in all the others and God will be the life and reality of all. *Omnia in omnibus Deus*" (NSC 70).

Bibliography

Baker, Rob and Gray Henry, eds. *Thomas Merton and Sufism: The Untold Story*. Louisville: Fons Vitae, 1999.

Bamberger, John Eudes O.C.S.O. *Thomas Merton: Prophet of Renewal*. Kalamazoo, MI: Cistercian Publications, 2005.

Bochen, Christine ed. *Thomas Merton: Essential Writings*. Maryknoll, NY: Orbis, 2000.

Bruteau, Beatrice, ed. *Thomas Merton and Judaism*. Louisville: Fons Vitae, 2003.

Burton, Patricia A. *Merton Vade Mecum: A Quick-Reference Bibliographic Handbook*. Louisville: Thomas Merton Center Publications, 1999. Reprint, 2001.

————. *More Than Silence: A Bibliography of Thomas Merton*. Lanham: Scarecrow, 2008.

Carr, Anne. "Prose into Prayer: Merton in His Journals." *Christian Century* (May 22–29, 1996) 570–73.

Cunningham, Lawrence S. *Thomas Merton and the Monastic Vision*. Grand Rapids: Eerdmans, 1999.

Hart, Br. Patrick and Jonathan Montaldo, ed. *The Intimate Merton: His Life from His Journals*. San Francisco: HarperSanFrancisco, 1999.

Kramer, Victor A. "'Crisis and Mystery': The Changing Quality of Thomas Merton's Later Journals." In *The Vision of Thomas Merton*, ed. Patrick O'Connell, 77–97. Notre Dame: Ave Maria, 2003.

Merton, Thomas. *Faith and Violence*. Notre Dame: University of Notre Dame Press, 1968.

17. Merton, *Thoughts in Solitude*, 46–47.

————. *The Monastic Journey*, ed. Br. Patrick Hart. Kansas City: Sheed Andrews and McMeel, Inc., 1977. Reprint, Collegeville, MN: Liturgical Press, 1992 and 2002.

————. *New Seeds of Contemplation*. New York: New Directions, 1961. Reprint, 1972.

————. *Peace in the Post-Christian Era*, ed. Patricia A. Burton. Maryknoll, New York: Orbis, 2004.

————. *The Seven Storey Mountain*. New York: Image, 1970.

————. *Thoughts in Solitude*. New York: Farrar, Straus, Giroux, 1956. Reprinted, 1958 and 1977.

————. *The Way of Chuang Tzu*. New York: New Directions, 1965.

Reiser, William S.J. "Thomas Merton: A Parable for Our Time." *Merton Seasonal* 29/2 (Summer, 2004) 3–13.

Shannon, William, ed. *The Hidden Ground of Love*. New York: Farrar, Straus, Giroux, 1985.

Thurston, Bonnie. "The Man of Letters." *America* 159/11 (October 22, 1988) 284–87.

24

Thomas Merton's Divinations for a Twenty-First Century Christian Reader

LYNN R. SZABO

"From now on, everybody stands on [their] own feet."
—*The Asian Journal of Thomas Merton*[1]

IN THE POST-MODERN CONTEXTS of the late twentieth century, a host of literary critics came to accept, almost as *de rigueur,* hermeneutics for reading literature which are best engaged by strategies of irony and infinite deferrals of meaning. The powerful influences of deconstructionist philosophers of language such as Jacques Derrida, Michel Foucault, and Ferdinand de Saussure have been embraced in English Studies with an enthusiasm that has nearly totalized the discipline in the larger, secular academy. The instabilities of fragmentation and subjectivity have been seized as the conditions of language, producing a critical discourse that has fundamentally departed from the previous privileging and authorizing of texts as autonomous literary artifacts. One of the preponderant outcomes of this shift has been the replacement of literary studies with cultural studies in university English departments; therein, literature becomes a site for social and philosophical inquiry, often enmeshing literary scholars in the eruption of "culture wars" as they attempt to relocate their discipline amidst the clashes of competing Marxist, feminist, poststructuralist, and psychoanalytic hegemonies.

1. Stone et al, *The Asian Journal of Thomas Merton.*

Just as for Christian scholars in other disciplines, such tensions have been compounded by the simultaneous marginalization of Christianity in the secular academy and by cultural influences that have seemingly deposed the relevance of any form of institutionalized religion. In such a context, Christian scholarship in literature is intensely interrogated by deconstructionist suspicions about language and meaning, about any willingness to assign authority to literary texts, sacred or otherwise. In this frame of reference, the approaches of earlier criticisms are perceived as naïve, provoking amusement, if not castigation. Texts are now designated as constructs around and through which readers are forever destined to negotiate interpretations that resist closure and cohering meanings. Surrounded by this uncertain climate, some scholars have clung to their old paradigms hoping the sea storms of postmodernism would pass, leaving in their wake a known and calmer sea. Others, not wanting to be left behind, have leapt aboard the ships headed on uncharted and sometimes futile journeys into the ingenious extremes of theories not yet ready to be tested for seaworthiness and integrity.

For my own scholarly pursuits, the writings of Thomas Merton, Catholic monk and renowned American writer, have provided a fertile category of engagement that counters either of these extremes. At its foundations is his profound and prophetic capacity to embrace and espouse the fundamental unity in all things while refusing panacean responses to the apparent dissolution of that unity. One can imagine that were he alive today, his prophetic insights would continue to engender divinations that lend themselves to the rediscovery of unifying principles in the cosmos. Merton's ontology is his apprehension of the "hidden Wholeness . . . [the] mysterious Unity and Integrity . . . *Natura naturans*"[2] of all things, embedded in the acknowledgment that it is in the identity and power of God that all things are imagined and incarnated; that it is God's desire for humanity to recover its lost and paradisial Wisdom.

One of the compelling attractions for Merton's readers is his relentless search for the ground of his authenticity and significance. Additionally, Merton's place as a marginal person appeals to many readers who seek relief from technological displacement, as well as from the estrangements and dissonances of the forces of globalization and their overwhelming personal and social complexities. For such an audience, Merton offers

2. Merton, "Hagia Sophia," 65–71.

encounters with the human longing for contemplative space and time in which to reflect on and imagine other modes of and epistemological approaches to Being. His seemingly transparent narrative voice enhances the reader's entrance into Merton's persistently recorded pathways to self-knowledge, both before and during his monastic life at the Abbey of Gethsemani near Louisville, Kentucky. His more than seventy books of essays, poetry, journals, and letters continue to be published and republished to a ready readership of spiritual seekers and religious and literary scholars. The number of publications related to Merton studies is growing almost exponentially, making his presence known in wider circles than ever before; as an example, his works are now translated into dozens of languages, including most recently Polish and Russian.

His writings depict his early life as an embrace of the modernist's brave existential despair—a resonant and prevailing paradigm for the study and creation of twentieth-century cultural and literary texts. The personal tragedies of having lost his entire family of origin by the time he was twenty-eight are central to his search for a spiritual home, recorded in his compelling autobiography, *The Seven Storey Mountain*.[3] Albeit earnestly triumphalist in its early rendering of Merton's monastic Catholicism, this story remains a *piece de resistance* for readers searching for their sense of spiritual place amidst the personal and religious chaos that the twentieth century has produced. His response to this most human of conditions is mirrored in his journals,[4] which record the profound tensions caused by the extremities of his intellectual genius and his monastic pursuits of poverty, obedience, and stability of place.

The loss of his mother when he was six, in particular, retains its unimaginable impact throughout his life, grounding his psychology and theology of the feminine, portrayed in his many dreamscapes and in his powerful prose-poem, "Hagia Sophia." Its scope engages significant new thought, particularly for many Protestant readers, on the feminine aspects of God derived from the figure of Wisdom in the Hebrew Proverbs. Its beautiful liturgy invites Christian readers to an essential encounter with feminist theologies, perhaps quite unexpected from a celibate monk—the sort of iconoclasm that the seasoned reader of Merton comes to anticipate and expect from his wide-ranging "uncaged mind."

---

3. Merton, *The Seven Storey Mountain*.
4. Hart and Montaldo, ed., *The Intimate Merton*.

Another significant and reaffirming aspect of Merton's writings is the centrality of literary and religious texts as influences on his conversion. Following from his studies of Étienne Gilson's *The Spirit of Medieval Philosophy*, Augustine, Thomas à Kempis, and, in particular, G.M. Hopkins, Merton acts with astonishing directness in pursuing his conversion to Christianity, much to the chagrin of his friends and peers. He continuously endorses belief in the incarnational powers of language and literature and their transcendent possibilities, both in his personal experience and in his legacy of lifelong engagement with the *literati* of his times.

The "Cold War Letters," containing Merton's exchanges with Boris Pasternak,[5] and his intense correspondence with Rosemary Radford Ruether[6] regarding feminism and social issues are only two of many such engagements. To these and many other encounters with the ideas of his literary and religious contemporaries, Merton responds with a series of essays and reviews on social and cultural issues, many of which are focused on marginalized and oppressed peoples caught in the violence of the decline of modern western culture.[7]

Further ensuing from Merton's spiritual and cultural vantage point is his willingness to move beyond rational and empirical analysis in face of his mystical experience. In this he heralds his validation of a kind of knowledge that transcends deduction and discursive reasoning and lies outside realms confined by the discourse of scientism, while retaining its powers to interrogate post-Enlightenment, even post-Christian contexts. In so doing, Merton conjures a prophetic voice. At the core of his later mysticism one recognizes his early endorsements of intuition, the ephiphanous, and the apophatic as the pathways of his search for truth and authenticity. In the contemplative ethos of the Cistercian Abbey, the continuing evolution of Merton's poetics parallels his journey with and through silence in his life and in his art—his search for "place" and "voice," grounded in, but not defined by, the monastery. As Alan Altany has observed, "Merton believed mystical experience directed him towards silence, but the poetic vision compelled him to speak."[8]

5. *Witness to Freedom*, edited by Shannon.

6. *At Home in the World*, edited by Tardiff.

7. As examples, see Merton, *Disputed Questions* and Merton, *Raids on the Unspeakable*.

8. Altany, "Thomas Merton's Poetic Incarnation of Emptiness," 110–30.

Against all expectation and in spite of the persistent efforts of the hierarchy of the Roman Church, he emerged in the sixties as one of the most prominent and effective social critics of the political and racial policies of America. This divine irony is not lost on the profound conflict Merton experienced between a calling to solitude and the expression of his relentless social conscience. In the decade prior to his death, Merton reaches far into and beyond his own monastic spirituality to deepen his explorations of and his commitment to oneness with humanity and God. He critiques cherished prejudices and the icons of the material culture of American life, passionately focusing on the debasement of language as a corollary of the decline of Western culture and inviting his readers into the poetics of his ever-widening apprehensions of the wholeness of all Being, which he claims as the "Hidden Ground of Love."[9]

The central concern of Merton's last years was self-transcendence. At the time of his unfortunate death by accidental electrocution in Thailand in 1968, his monastic life had led him abroad for the first time in twenty-six years. His understanding of and experience with Eastern mysticism had been profound, documented in scholarly and personal commentary on the Taoist philosophy of Chuang Tzu.[10] That Merton became a spiritual and literary master is not surprising, given his genius and relentless passion for knowledge and wisdom, grounded in the Christological imperatives at the core of his interior geography. His spiritual explorations moved between his own lived experience and his scholarly examinations of the mysticism of many traditions; in this, he did not abandon his search for oneness with Christ, yet he captured the respect of those engaging the highest levels of inter-religious dialogue.

Merton's embrace of mystery, silence, and solitude is a fecund hermeneutical space from which I have come to re-envision my own approaches to literature and spirituality. In this paradigm, language and narrative arise from silent places that hold the secrets of the *imago Dei*—the indestructible presence of God in the world—and unleash His creativity and incarnational powers in all Being. This mystery arouses in me a compassion for the often-silenced beauty and brokenness of human story and an enduring hope for reconciliation and redemption for the world it portrays; it is at the core of my scholarly pursuits.

9. *The Hidden Ground of Love*, edited by Shannon.
10. Merton, *The Way of Chuang Tzu*.

As a Christian scholar mentored by Merton's literary writings on spirituality, in particular his poetry, I have been given opportunities to engage in meaningful and satisfying dialogue with others whose interests go beyond monastic Catholicism and conservative Protestant theology. I have also discovered that Merton has created spaces for Christian dialogue in the pluralistic culture of Canada where one often finds profound interest in religious writings, from Charles Taylor to Salmon Rushdie, with the acknowledgement of one voice often permitting the recognition of another. The honor of participating in inter-religious and interdisciplinary dialogue with respected scholars from traditions other than my own enriches and pleasures my studies immeasurably.

Promisingly for literary studies as a whole, more recent shifts in literary criticism are turning towards an ethics of reading and scholarship that seeks to encourage alliances amongst critics who can find mutually fertile grounds for engagement of texts and theories. Such an agenda currently seems to be spawning new collectives of scholars, programs, and disciplines related to literature. It has the markings of interdisciplinarity not before seen in its crossing of boundaries—cultural, religious, spiritual, and historical. It is also giving rise to new genres of literature in which previously narrowed fields of interpretation and production are amalgamating: for example, life writing is now one of the most prolific literatures, providing creative cultural and spiritual engagement for readers, writers, and theorists in their attempts to re-imagine and identify authentic human experience.

At the same time, the arrival of this new century presents literary studies with complex and immense issues: the value of literary texts in a technological world; the attendant decline in literacy in face of purely pragmatic readerships; the devaluation of studies in the humanities with their requisite needs for contemplation and reflection in a world constantly at war; the competing ideologies, political and religious, at play in the negotiation of ethics and art; the pressures of defining one's own subjectivity in relation to one's discipline—at the heart of practicing and creating good scholarship.

As always, the most respected of Christian literary scholars will need to demonstrate an agility of mind and heart that allows them to acknowledge and own the failures of Christianity that are so elaborately depicted in the post-colonial literature of the last century. With humility and tenacity, they will be required to address the study of new cultural theories whose agenda clearly marginalizes Christian scholarship and refuses Christianity's historical and religious value, culturally and politically. Such scholars will be neither reactionary nor revolutionary in their response, realizing that integrity in scholarship and demeanor transcends apologetics and polemics.

In sum, the Christian literary scholar today faces organic and dynamic challenges that may seem overwhelming in their complexities and influences. To serve the discipline, to demonstrate courage and indefatigable creativity, and to commit oneself to openness of mind and heart, call for a life of faith and scholarship that is fed by one's embrace of and by Christ, the Incarnated God who is all and is in all; grounded in the knowledge that one only "sees through a glass darkly" into the mysteries of human life and art.

Bibliography

Altany, Alan. "Thomas Merton's Poetic Incarnation of Emptiness." *The Merton Annual* 10 (1988) 110–30.

Hart, Patrick and Jonathan Montaldo, ed. *The Intimate Merton*. New York: Harper SanFrancisco, 1999.

Merton, Thomas. *The Asian Journal of Thomas Merton*. Edited by Naomi Burton Stone et al. New York: New Directions, 1973.

———. *At Home in the World: The Letters of Thomas Merton and Rosemary Radford Ruether*. Edited by Mary Tardiff. Maryknoll, NY: Orbis, 1995.

———. *Disputed Questions*. New York: Farrar, Straus, and Cudahy, 1960.

———. "Hagia Sophia." In *In The Dark Before Dawn: New Selected Poems of Thomas Merton*, edited by Lynn R. Szabo, 65–71. New York: New Directions, 2005.

———. *The Hidden Ground of Love: The Letters of Thomas Merton on Religious Experience and Social Concerns*. Edited by William Shannon. New York: Farrar, Straus, Giroux, 1985.

———. *Raids on the Unspeakable*. New York: New Directions, 1966.

———. *The Seven Storey Mountain*. Fiftieth Anniversary Edition. New York: Harcourt Brace, 1998.

———. *The Way of Chuang Tzu*. New York: New Directions, 1965.

———. *Witness to Freedom: The Letters of Thomas Merton in Times of Crisis*. Edited by William Shannon. New York: Farrar, Straus, Giroux, 1994.

Stone, Naomi Burton, Patrick Hart, and James Laughlin, ed. *The Asian Journal of Thomas Merton*. New York: New Directions, 1973.

Szabo, Lynn R., ed. *In The Dark Before Dawn: New Selected Poems of Thomas Merton*. New York: New Directions, 2005.

25

Christianity and the Cinema

An Inter-religious Conversation

ANNE MOORE

T HE DIALOGUE BETWEEN CHRISTIANITY and the cinema is filled with
paradoxes. On the one hand, Christianity at times has opposed
the subject content of specific films or the depiction of the faithful by
the film industry. The creation in 1929 of the "Catholic Movie Code"
is a case in point. This code formed the basis for the American "Hays
Office Code" that governed the content of movies into the 1960s. The
code censored nudity and explicit sexuality and it positively reinforced
the family and social values of the church.[1] Another example is the various Christian demonstrations against the showing of Martin Scorsese's
The Last Temptation of Christ (1988). The film's depiction of a sexually
aware Jesus, who expressed guilt over his sins and doubt over his mission, was too fallible and human for many Christian believers. Finally,
Hollywood is even seen as battling against Christian values, as suggested
in Michael Medved's *Hollywood vs. America: Popular Culture and the War
on Traditional Values*. On the other hand, since the 1990s there has been
a proliferation of books promoting the use of various films as discussion
points or illustrations of Christian morals, theology, and values, and film
clips are increasingly used to reinforce or demonstrate points in Christian

---

1. Lyden, *Film as Religion*, 129.

sermons.[2] The conversation between Christianity and the cinema has been formulated along an assumed dichotomy between religion and the secular world; however, in recent analyses, this dichotomy has been challenged by a more complex view of the intersection of Christian spirituality and film.

The dichotomy of Christianity and cinema finds its roots in H. Richard Niebuhr's book *Christ and Culture*. Niebuhr proposed five categories for Christian engagement with secular culture. These are: 1) Christ rejecting culture; 2) the Christ of culture; 3) Christ above culture; 4) Christ and culture in paradox, and 5) Christ transforming culture.[3] The first category results in the separation of the Christian believer or community from the wider society. This separation is evident in the acceptance of only films made by Christians for Christians such as the *Left Behind Series* (2000, 2002, 2004), or *The JESUS Film* (1979) sponsored and distributed by Campus Crusade. The only films watched are Christian films, or films that contain approved Christian content, and films associated with the wider secular culture are rejected. The second category, the Christ of culture, represents the other extreme in which the larger culture is adopted and classified as Christian. Cecil B. DeMille's *The King of Kings* (1927) and many of the biblical epics of the 1950s and 60s such as *Ben-Hur* (1959), *The Robe* (1953), *King of Kings* (1961), and *The Greatest Story Ever Told* (1965) fit this classification. They blended a specific understanding of Protestant Christianity with democratic values, producing cinema that advocated a form of American piety.[4] Christ above culture reaffirms the positive value of culture; however, culture is incom-

2. The dialogue between Christianity and the cinema began in the 1970s with the publication of two books: Cooper and Carl Skrade, ed., *Celluloid and Symbols* and Wall, *Church and Cinema*. It continues with books such as: Johnston, *Reel Spirituality*; Anker, *Catching Light*, and Barsotti and Johnston, *Finding God in the Movies*. Most of the dialogue has been dominated by either examinations of Jesus and Christ figures in film, such as: Hurley, "Cinematic Transfigurations of Jesus," 61–78; Malone, *Movie Christs and Antichrists*; Kinnard and Davis, *Divine Images*; Tatum, *Jesus at the Movies*; Baugh, *Imaging the Divine*, and Walsh, *Reading the Gospels in the Dark*. Or, scholars have focused on the use of scriptural text, symbol, motif, or narrative within film, such as: Jewett, *Saint Paul at the Movies*; Jewett, *Saint Paul Returns to the Movies*, and Aichele and Walsh, eds. *Screening Scripture*.

3. Lyden, in *Film as Religion*, analyzes how Niebuhr's typology has influenced the scholarly discussion and examination of religion and film (11–35).

4. Walsh, in *Reading the Gospels in the Dark*, briefly discusses these films as "cultural and ideological products" (1–20).

plete and finds its fulfilment when it is augmented with Christian spirituality. This seems to be the view adopted in a number of books on film and
faith. In Roy M. Anker's *Catching Light: Looking for God in the Movies*,
the Incarnation is a major theme within *Superman* (1978) and *The Deer
Hunter* (1978) is a parable about redemption. There exists already within
film a synthesis of Christianity and culture that requires elaboration or
illumination through Christian theology. The fourth category is Christ
and culture in paradox. This view advocates the existence of two parallel
life styles centred on one's private life as a Christian and one's public life
as a member of society. In other words, one may appreciate films like the
North Country (2005) that advocate the equal treatment of women in the
work place; yet, one may not find any overt Christian themes to apply to
one's private spiritual journey. The final category is Christ transforming
culture, in which Christianity is actively engaged in converting the larger
culture to Christian values. Mel Gibson's *The Passion of Christ* illustrates
one attempt to present a specific form of Christian theology and worldview to a wider audience in the hope of educating and perhaps transforming the wider culture.[5]

Niebuhr's view assumes the popular cultural notion that a dichotomy exists between religion and secularism; however, this dichotomy may
not be appropriate in the case of film. Many film directors credit their
film-making with religious or spiritual meaning. The most eloquent and
frequently quoted is Andrey Tarkovsky. In his book *Sculpturing in Time:
Reflection on the Cinema*, Tarkovsky makes the following comments
about filmmaking: "Modern Mass culture, aimed at the 'consumer' . . .
is crippling people's souls, setting up barriers between man and the crucial questions of his existence, his consciousness of himself as a spiritual
being" (42). In contrast, Tarkovsky thinks film should serve a specific
function: "The allotted function of art is not, as is often assumed, to put
across ideas, to propagate thoughts, to serve as example. The aim of art is
to prepare for death, to plough and harrow his soul, rendering it capable
of turning to the good" (43). Further, this function of film does not take
the form of platitudes or sweet moral stories. "Art only has the capacity, through shock and catharsis, to make the human soul receptive to
good. It is ridiculous to imagine that people can be taught to be good; any

---

5. Mel Gibson may not have intended the film as a 'transforming' vehicle; however,
numerous Evangelical communities have used the film within the context of mission
work. King, "Truth at Last," 151–62.

more than they can learn to be faithful wives by following the 'positive' example of Pushkin's Tatiana Larina. Art can only give food—a jolt—the occasion—for psychical experience" (50). In other words, for Tarkovsky film imitates religion by focusing the audiences' concerns on issues of morality and mortality; it addresses questions about the significance of human existence.

Numerous scholars in the area of religion and film have made similar observations. Margaret R. Miles in her book, *Seeing and Believing: Religion and Values in the Movies*, notes "that films contain images and characters that enable us to discuss the perennial religious question, 'How should we live?'" (182) In other words, films are addressing the same question that has been part of the spiritual search for thousands of years. Clive Marsh, in his recent work *Cinema & Sentiment: Film's Challenge to Theology*, compares film-watching with worship and concludes that film-watching may be regarded as a spiritual discipline that offers reflection on the human condition and/or a transcendent experience. Further, he advocates a constructive dialogue between Christianity and film that he thinks will revitalize Christian worship and may, through the teaching of critical theology, enhance film-watching. This constructive dialogue though requires an educational program in which theologians and religious studies scholars learn more about film and film critics and academics in film studies become more versed in theology and religion.

John C. Lyden provides one of the more extensive examinations of the intersection of religion and film. In *Film as Religion: Myth, Morals, Rituals*, he first discusses the limitations of various definitions of religion such as Paul Tillich's theological definition based on "a concern with ultimate reality," or psychosocial explanations that view religion as a human or social product. He advocates the definition provided by anthropologist Clifford Geertz. Geertz thought that religions provide a means for dealing with the ups and downs of human existence such as suffering, injustice, chaos, and evil. With this definition, Lyden views film or film-going as a religion because various movies attempt to address issues such as suffering, injustice, chaos, and evil. Drawing upon the work of John B. Cobb, Mark S. Heim, and Raimundo Panikkar in their discussions of Christianity and Pluralism, Lyden suggests a type of inter-religious dialogue should take place between religious studies and film. In this dialogue "we are willing to acknowledge the possibility that our view is not the only one, and that none of us is likely to be exactly right about everything, we can hold our own views even as we have a dialogue with others and learn from them in the process" (Lyden 125). The first stage of this dialogue is fully to understand the religious function of film. In other words, one of the major shifts in the last few years has been the rejection of film as solely a secular medium; the cinema may be religious.[6] This shift in perspective suggests the conversation between Christianity and film should no longer assume a dichotomy between the secular and religious, and, as proposed by Lyden, it might become an inter-religious dialogue.

Viewing film as "religious," or equating film-watching with religious worship, raises issues about the place, purpose, and practice of Christianity and religion within twenty-first century North America. The challenge to Christianity is not to discover or find the Christian themes or images within film that may be used to strengthen the faith of the believer or illustrate doctrine to the congregation. The task is to discover why and how film has assumed a "religious" status in our society and what this suggests about the search for meaning in the contemporary situation. Do films address specific issues related to the search for a meaningful human existence that are not a major part of the church conversation? The cult status of *Fight Club* (1999) is due, in part, to the film's resonant chord with young adults who find themselves conflicted in a world that advocates consumerism and sensual experience. The protagonist adopts a form of violence as a direct consequence of the violence inflicted upon his sense of self-identity by systematic cultural systems beyond his control. In an analysis of recent films, particularly those within the science fiction genre such as *Blade Runner*, this theme of the individual as a victim of cultural systems returns.

The presence of this theme of the individual as a victim raises the issue of whether individuals are attending the cinema as part of their spiritual search to find a meaningful answer to life within a North American society dominated by massive social systems. The presence of this theme also raises the issue of whether this is an issue currently addressed within Christian congregations. Do movies use different narratives, stories, or ideas that resonate with the contemporary viewer? *The Matrix* (1999) and *Lord of the Rings* (2002, 2003, 2004) embrace ancient and Eastern mythologies, and often introduce audiences to biblical symbols and narratives. The cinema's continuous use of mythology and the appeal of these

---

6. This is not to suggest that all films perform a religious function; there are films that are intended for entertainment, information, propaganda, etc.

cinematic myths for audiences suggests that storytelling and myths still resonate with contemporary society. The continuing attraction of these myths raises the issue of whether Christianity needs to place its myths and stories in the foreground. Does the cinema, with its visuals and sound effects, restore a sensory experience traditionally associated with religious rituals? Mel Gibson's *The Passion of the Christ* (2003) may be seen as a cinematic revision of the Fifteen Stations of the Cross. The director used the visual heritage of centuries of Christian iconography.[7] He combined the images with music and sound and brought them to life in a cathedral-like structure during the sacred season of Lent. The power of Gibson's film may be in its adoption and adaptation of elements of religious rituals; Gibson may have produced the first highly effective cinematic ritual. If so, what does this film suggest about how Christianity might construct its worship and rituals?

The conversation between Christianity and the cinema is beginning to acknowledge some of the complexity that is reflective of both entities, a complexity that is part of any inter-religious dialogue. This dialogue needs to take the differences between Christianity and the cinema seriously. Discussion of films cannot be reduced to the idea that all film reflects or confirms Christian ideas and concepts; every film hero is not a Christ figure. The conversation should not return to the dichotomy of Christianity and secularism. This does not preclude a Christian from making a judgment about a film; however, as Lyden suggests, one should not be dogmatic about these judgments and one must be open to seeing films as expressions of alternatives within the search for religious meaning. Christianity has much to learn from the cinema as together they engage with the search for meaningful human existence.

Bibliography

Aichele, George and Richard Walsh, eds. *Screening Scripture: Intertextual Connections Between Scripture and Film.* Harrisburg, PA: Trinity Press International, 2002.

Anker, Roy M. *Catching Light: Looking for God in the Movies.* Grand Rapids: Eerdmans, 2004.

Apostolos-Cappadona, Diane. "On Seeing *The Passion.*" In *Re-viewing the Passion: Mel Gibson's Film and its Critics,* edited by S. Brent Plate, 97–108. New York: MacMillan, 2004.

7. Apostolos-Cappadona, "On Seeing *The Passion,*" 97–108; Morgan, "Catholic Visual Piety and *The Passion of the Christ,*" 85–96.

Barsotti, Catherine M. and Robert K. Johnston. *Finding God in the Movies: 33 Films of Reel Faith*. Grand Rapids: Baker, 2004.

Baugh, Lloyd. *Imaging the Divine: Jesus and Christ-Figures in Film*. Kansas City: Sheed & Ward, 1997.

Cooper, John and Carl Skrade, ed. *Celluloid and Symbols*. Philadelphia: Fortress, 1970.

Hurley, Neil P. "Cinematic Transfigurations of Jesus." In *Religion and Film*, edited by John R. May and Michael Bird, 61–78. Knoxville: University of Tennessee Press, 1981.

Jewett, Robert. *Saint Paul at the Movies: The Apostle's Dialogue with American Culture*. Louisville: Westminster John Knox, 1993.

———. *Saint Paul Returns to the Movies: Triumph Over Shame*. Grand Rapids: Eerdmans, 1999.

Johnston, Robert K. *Reel Spirituality: Theology and Film in Dialogue*. Grand Rapids: Baker, 2000.

King, Neal. "Truth at Last: Evangelical Communities Embrace *The Passion of the Christ*." In *Re-viewing the Passion: Mel Gibson's Film and its Critics*, edited by S. Brent Plate, 151–62. New York: Palgrave MacMillan, 2004.

Kinnard, Roy and Tim Davis. *Divine Images: A History of Jesus on the Screen*. New York: Citadel, 1992.

Lyden, John C. *Film as Religion: Myths, Morals, and Rituals*. New York: New York University Press, 2003.

Malone, Peter. *Movie Christs and Antichrists*. New York: Crossroad, 1990.

Morgan, David. "Catholic Visual Piety and *The Passion of the Christ*." In *Re-viewing the Passion: Mel Gibson's Film and its Critics*, edited by S. Brent Plate, 85–96. New York: MacMillan, 2004.

Tatum, W. Barnes. *Jesus at the Movies: A Guide to the First Hundred Years*. Santa Rosa, CA: Polebridge, 1997.

Wall, James. *Church and Cinema*. Grand Rapids: Eerdmans, 1971.

Walsh, Richard. *Reading the Gospels in the Dark: Portrayals of Jesus in Film*. Harrisburg, PA: Trinity Press International, 2003.

Index of Proper Names